How to Do *Everything* with Your

Blac

CW00632090

M

Curt Simmons

Osborne/**McGraw-Hill**

New York Chicago San Francisco Lisbon
London Madrid Mexico City Milan New Delhi
San Juan Seoul Singapore Sydney Toronto

Osborne/**McGraw-Hill**
2600 Tenth Street
Berkeley, California 94710
U.S.A.

To arrange bulk purchase discounts for sales promotions, premiums, or fund-raisers, please contact Osborne/**McGraw-Hill** at the above address. For information on translations or book distributors outside the U.S.A., please see the International Contact Information page immediately following the index of this book.

How to Do Everything with Your BlackBerry

1234567890 CUS CUS 01987654321

ISBN 0-07-219393-X

Publisher	Brandon A. Nordin
Vice President &	
Associate Publisher	Scott Rogers
Acquisitions Editor	Margie McAneny
Project Editor	Madhu Prasher
Acquisitions Coordinator	Emma Acker
Technical Editor	Chris Ridabock
Copy Editors	Ami Knox
Proofreader	Pamela Vevea
Indexer	Claire Splan
Series Design	Mickey Galicia

This book was composed with Corel VENTURA™ Publisher.

Contents at a Glance

Contents

About the Author

Curt Simmons is a technology author and trainer whose focus is Windows operating systems and Internet technologies. He has written almost twenty computing books on a variety of topics, from high-level networking titles to operating system guides. Curt is also the author of *How to Do Everything with Windows Me* and *How to Do Everything with Windows XP*, both published by Osborne/McGraw-Hill. Curt enjoys working with new operating systems and wireless gadgets, and when he is not training or writing books, he spends his time with his wife and children. Visit Curt on the Internet at http://curtsimmons.hypermart.net, or send him an e-mail at curt_simmons@hotmail.com.

About the Technical Editor

Chris Ridabock Jr. has worked with numerous technologies and has used the BlackBerry and its predecessors for over five years. For the past three years Chris headed up a specialized property services group for Internet- and technology-sector companies and is currently the president and CEO of CanXCentral Inc., a technology services firm based in Toronto, Canada.

Acknowledgments

I would like to thank everyone at Osborne/McGraw-Hill for taking this title on and working with me to iron out the details. I would especially like to thank Roger Stewart for giving me the green light and a very special thank you to Margie McAneny who was so interested in the topic and so great to work with—thanks for being a great acquisitions editor, Margie! Also, I owe a big debt of gratitude to Lindsay Brown at Broduer Worldwide, who provided us with BlackBerry units for testing, graphics for the book, and just about anything else we asked for—thanks, Lindsay, you helped us make this book great. Next, thanks to Chris Ridabock Jr. for a thorough technical review and content comments—thanks for your help, Chris. Also, thanks to Madhu Prasher, Emma Acker, and Ami Knox for keeping things moving in the right direction and for the careful attention to details. Finally, thanks to my agent, Margot, for helping me find a home for this title, and to my wife and kids who always support me.

Introduction

Imagine a world where information is always at your fingertips. Your e-mail follows you wherever you go instead of being stuck inside of a PC. You send e-mail at will, check out Web sites on the Internet, send a page, consult a calendar, and are notified of upcoming events. What if all of this could be done by a single device that easily fits in your pocket or purse and is your constant electronic companion?

If all of this sounds like something from a science fiction movie, it isn't. Research In Motion (RIM), a small company, sought to make this dream a reality a few years ago—and they have succeeded with the RIM BlackBerry. Early on, RIM thought that wireless e-mail would be the killer application for the corporate user, and they were right. The BlackBerry, designed for both corporate and Internet users, is the hot device in wireless connectivity. Using an always on, push model of wireless communication, your e-mail arrives on your BlackBerry device automatically and with no effort from you. Messages that you send are sent right away—no waiting for you to connect. Combine this with a number of personal management applications; a slim, sleek design; and a miniature keyboard and trackwheel that work like a computer keyboard and mouse, and you get the BlackBerry.

The product of choice for mobile professionals and the new product of choice for individuals and small businesses, the BlackBerry is a true communications device and personal information manager. It is designed to be your right-hand assistant in all that you do, and it lives up to this expectation.

If I seem a little head-over-heels about the BlackBerry, that is because I am! As a technology author, I come into contact with a lot of software and supposedly cool electronic gadgets. Frankly, I ignore a lot of them, but the BlackBerry instantly became a helpful tool to me, and I liked it so much that I wrote this book.

Speaking of this book, *How to Do Everything with Your BlackBerry* is designed to be your one-stop solution to help you use your BlackBerry. This book helps you get started in Chapter 1 and takes you step-by-step through the use and management of your BlackBerry. This book will help you learn what you need to know quickly and easily, and often in a step-by-step format.

This book starts you out at ground zero. Part 1, "What Is the BlackBerry?," you learn all about the BlackBerry unit—how it can help you in your business and in your life—and the features the BlackBerry brings to the table. If you are reading through this book in an effort to decide if the BlackBerry is right for you, then Part 1 is just what you need.

Part 2, "Get to Know the BlackBerry," describes how to maneuver using the BlackBerry keyboard and trackwheel. Next, you get a detailed look at the BlackBerry software and configuration options. You see how to make the BlackBerry work in a way that is just right for you. Finally, you learn all about the BlackBerry desktop software that is used to synchronize the BlackBerry with your PC—how to install it and how to use all of its features.

Part 3, "Communicate with the BlackBerry," covers all you need to know about wireless e-mail. You see how to connect your BlackBerry to the network, send and receive e-mail, manage e-mail messages, and even create e-mail rules. You also learn how to use the address book and how to make the best use of its features. Finally, you learn about Internet connectivity and paging in this part.

Part 4, "Personal Management Tools," discusses the additional applications included on your BlackBerry. I demonstrate how to configure and use the BlackBerry calendar, tasks, alarms, and MemoPad. In this part, you'll find plenty of step-by-step instructions and examples to help you along the way.

In Part 5, "Appendixes," you learn about various third-party solutions designed to work with the BlackBerry and the options that are available to you. I cover additional applications and games you can download and use on your BlackBerry. You also get a chance to surf BlackBerry.net and check out some important troubleshooting problems and solutions.

Finally, the book wraps up with several appendixes that show you keyboard shortcuts and provide a number of additional features and advice.

I've written this book in an easy-to-read format. You can read the entire book cover to cover, or you can skip around and find the specific information you need—the choice is yours. To help you along the way, this book includes the following features:

- ■ **"How to" sidebars**   These boxed sidebars tell you how to do something, usually in a step-by-step format. Be sure to check them out—they are full of helpful information.

■ **"Did You Know" sidebars**   These sidebars contain ancillary information you might find useful and even entertaining. I've put great stuff in these sidebars, but they are interesting asides rather than important information, and you can skip over them if you like.

■ **Note**   These icons provide you with helpful information. You should always read every note you see.

■ **Tip**   These icons provide you with a friendly piece of advice or a little extra information that might make your work the BlackBerry easier. Be sure to read them!

■ **Shortcut**   These icons show you a quick-and-easy way to do some task. Take note of these and you can make your work with the BlackBerry much faster!

Well, that's about it. Are you ready join the wireless world of the BlackBerry? Then it's time to get started. Before you do, though, I would love to hear from you. Visit me on the Internet at http://curtsimmons.hypermart.net or send me e-mail at curt_simmons@hotmail.com.

Part 1

What Is the BlackBerry?

Chapter 1

The BlackBerry... and You!

How to…

■ Use the BlackBerry to organize your business

■ Use the BlackBerry to manage your personal schedule

Welcome to *How to Do Everything with Your BlackBerry*. If you are reading this book, you have most likely entered, or are considering entering, the wireless e-mail and Internet realm made possible by the BlackBerry. Developed by Research In Motion (RIM), the BlackBerry has quickly become the wireless communication device of choice among mobile professionals, and it is quickly spreading to the general population as more and more people join the world of wireless e-mail and wireless Internet. Perhaps you have had the BlackBerry for some time and you want to hone your usage skills—this book is just for you! Or maybe you have had the BlackBerry thrust on you at your job, and as you stare at the little handheld, you're not quite sure what to make of it. This book is for you too, but this chapter especially. In this introductory chapter, you'll take an initial look at the BlackBerry and how it can help you in your business and your life. So, are you ready to enter the world of the BlackBerry? If your answer is yes, then this book is the guide that will take you every step of the way!

Business in the 21st Century

In the not-so-distant past, business professionals typically stayed in one place. They arrived at work each day to a busy desk and tended to stay at that desk until quitting time. Business was conducted via postal mail, or what has been lovingly called "snail mail," and over the telephone. In a typical day, only a few people ever traveled to other locations or businesses, and the concept of being mobile didn't mean a whole lot.

That business landscape began to slowly change in the mid–1980s when the Internet became a public reality. At first considered an anomaly, the Internet soon became the buzzword and the buzz technology of the 1990s. E-business rose and fell, and the Internet was and continues to be a shaky ride. However, one simple fact remains: The Internet and e-mail have changed the way we do business. Snail mail isn't fast enough, and no one wants to wade through a library looking for information. The Internet provides e-mail and instant information at our fingertips. In fact, e-mail has become so common that most professionals spend at least one hour a day reading and sending e-mail—and many spend much more time than this.

1

The changing face of business has also caused us to become more mobile. Companies today are more likely to work with clients in other cities, states, and countries and more likely to try joint ventures with other companies. In turn, business professionals are on the move. Once tied to a desk five days a week, business people now travel and move around a lot.

However, mobile professionals face many challenges. Access to e-mail and information is not easy. The solution for the mobile professional for the past several years has been the laptop. You probably know the drill—you take your laptop wherever you go, then you find a phone port, dial an access number to your company servers, and try to manage your e-mail while connected to a remote server. Sure, it works, but the question asked time and time again is, does it work well?

The answer is not really. Remote access connectivity poses a number of problems for Information Technology teams and well as users, such as

- **Access**   The wired connection via a laptop requires a connection to a phone jack. Although available in many public places, such as airports, you cannot read or send mail unless you are connected to the wired world. This, in turn, causes you to be tied to cables. You can't do anything without a connection, and you can't connect without wires and ports. You can connect at office buildings, airports, and hotels; but if you are in transit, such as an hour-long cab ride, you are out of luck.

- **Inconvenience**   Have you ever run through an airport with a laptop? How about a laptop, your overnight bag, and your briefcase? The simple fact is laptops are bulky and often unnecessary. If you are a mobile professional, how many trips have you taken where the main reason for carrying your laptop was e-mail?

- **Expense**   Let's face it, laptops are expensive. Sure, you can do a lot of stuff with them, after all, laptops today are full blown computers. However, in many circumstances, professionals use their laptops mainly for e-mail when they are on the road. This equipment is too big of an investment to be used only as an e-mail device. Additionally, your network must maintain modems and remote access software as well as access numbers. Remote access can be a nightmare to manage from the IT administrator's point of view as well as rather costly.

- **No real-time access**   The laptop requires you to take an active part in checking your e-mail. The laptop doesn't do anything on its own—connectivity and mail retrieval are all up to you. Unless your laptop is

The Growth of E-mail and Internet Usage

You hear so much about e-mail and the Internet that it seems as though it has been around forever. True, e-mail and the Internet have become an integrated part of our lives, but e-mail and the Internet are still new. First developed in the 1960s, the Internet did not become a public entity until the early 1990s. At that time, e-mail and Internet traffic were left to the computer-savvy people who are always on the hunt for the latest development. That small beginning has caused an e-mail and Internet avalanche. There are millions upon millions of e-mail and Internet users today, and recent reports estimate that hundreds of millions of e-mail messages are sent every day. E-mail and the Internet are here to stay, and it looks like there is no end to its growth.

outfitted with a wireless modem, you are basically in a dead zone, cut off from the wired world and from the information that you need.

Now, don't misunderstand, laptops are great machines and I own one myself, but the laptop as a remote access solution has its problems and difficulties. In a nutshell, business has become mobile—and the information of the business world needs to be just as mobile.

Life in the 21st Century

If business in the 21st century has become more mobile, life certainly follows the same pattern. Quick—how much time do you spend in your car or on mass transit every day? How many hours are you away from home each day? How often do you travel to another city? If you are like most of us, you are on the move. In fact, we are the most mobile society that has ever existed.

Mobility, in and of itself, is no problem. The problem is that many people use the Internet and e-mail on a regular basis, even when they are away from work. You may send and receive multiple e-mails every day, shop on the Internet, manage your money and stocks, get travel information and movie reviews—you name it. The problem is that access to the Internet has been a wired event; you must sit in front of a computer or carry a laptop with you, and in the end, the laptop is still a wired solution, just one that you can carry around from wired location to location.

Consider this scenario: I take a cab to meet some friends on the other side of the city. The ride is 45 minutes long. I need to answer some e-mail and place an order on the Internet for a book I have been wanting, but instead, all I can do is sit in the cab and stare out the window. The end result is simply this: Like business, if life is mobile, then e-mail and Internet access must be mobile if it is to become a truly integrated part of your life.

Enter the BlackBerry

The BlackBerry was designed for people like you and me, and people like you and me designed it. Research In Motion saw a real need in the business community for wireless e-mail connectivity—and not just static wireless connectivity, but e-mail that arrives to you effortlessly and is sent automatically, e-mail that is always with you. Past solutions, such as the laptop, didn't really respond to the need of the mobile user. We need e-mail all of the time, we need it effortlessly, and we need it without dragging a computer around with us.

RIM developed the BlackBerry with these goals in mind. Available in the 950 pager-size model and the 957 PDA sized model, shown in Figure 1-1, the BlackBerry is your total wireless e-mail solution as well as total Internet access solution, should you choose to add the latter service. You can completely manage

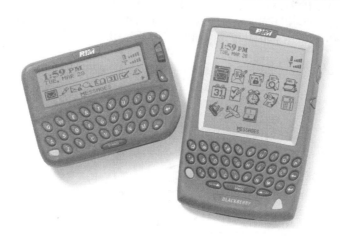

FIGURE 1-1   The BlackBerry 950 and 957 models

your corporate e-mail from the BlackBerry just as if you were sitting at a desktop computer. In short, the BlackBerry is the wave of the future—total wireless connectivity that is easy, reliable, and always on.

As you can see, the BlackBerry units are small, contain a QWERTY keyboard that you can operate with your thumbs, and feature an easy to view, icon-based home screen, as shown more closely in Figure 1-2. You can learn all about the icons and getting around the BlackBerry in Chapter 3.

The BlackBerry's main feature is wireless e-mail. After all, the BlackBerry server software allows you to get your corporate e-mail on your BlackBerry—no checking, no authentication, it happens automatically. You can use your e-mail just as if you were sitting at a PC. But the BlackBerry is more than an e-mail gadget. The BlackBerry also provides the most popular PDA features found today. For example, you can manage your calendar, create tasks lists, write memos, use a calculator, manage your address book, and use many additional add-on features and applications. The BlackBerry ships to you with a cradle that connects to your PC so you can synchronize your calendar, address book and other personal information management software with a desktop application, such as Lotus Notes or Microsoft Outlook. It's quick, easy, and painless.

The BlackBerry and Your Business

The BlackBerry is designed to be a total wireless business solution. As you are reading this chapter, you're probably wondering how the BlackBerry can really help you—especially if you are thinking about getting a BlackBerry or if one has been thrust upon you by your company. The BlackBerry is like any software

The BlackBerry interface

1

device—the more you become familiar with it, the more helpful it will be to you. As a starting point, though, the following sections highlight the immediate benefits you will see using the BlackBerry at your business.

Stay Connected

The first and obvious consideration is access to corporate e-mail. The BlackBerry is designed to work with the Microsoft Exchange and Lotus Domino environments. IT managers install and configure the BlackBerry server software on the Exchange or Lotus servers, and at this point you can access your e-mail using the BlackBerry. The BlackBerry uses a "push" model for e-mail delivery. This means that you do not connect with the BlackBerry and "pull" your e-mail from the server. The BlackBerry is always connected, and e-mail arrives on your BlackBerry unit automatically. You can reply to messages or compose new messages, and send them immediately. The key point is that e-mail is instantly and always available to you. You don't have to wait on important messages or wonder what messages are waiting for you on a server. Messages arrive to you with no work on your part.

 *BlackBerry connectivity is available in most major cities. In less populated areas, you will most likely lose connectivity.*

Manage Information

As I mentioned, the BlackBerry contains personal information management applications that are designed to synchronize with your desktop application, such as Outlook or Notes. This feature enables you to update your address book, calendar, and other related applications through your BlackBerry. For example, let's say you attend a conference and you make 20 contacts. In the past, you would have to write those contacts on paper and enter them into Outlook or Notes upon your return to the office. If you use a laptop, you may have attempted to keep the laptop with you to enter information each time you met someone—a solution that is not very practical.

With the BlackBerry, you can easily carry the unit wherever you go, enter information quickly and easily, then synchronize that information with your desktop application. Returning to the conference example, if you meet 20 people, you simply enter their contact information into your BlackBerry, and then synchronize the address book with your desktop application. It's a real snap to use. The key here is that information can be entered into the BlackBerry easily and anywhere, and then that information can be transferred over to a desktop application. The

FIGURE 1-3   The 957 BlackBerry is easy to carry everywhere

larger BlackBerry model is no bigger than your hand (as you can see in Figure 1-3), so you can carry it wherever you go and enter information at any time.

NOTE   *Even when you are not connected to the network, such as when you travel on an airplane or when you are out of a network coverage area, you can still compose e-mail. The e-mail will be held in your Outbox until you are reconnected to the network, then they will be sent.*

In terms of electronic calendars, the BlackBerry can perform over-the-air calendar synchronization in Exchange and Domino environments. Let's say you make some changes to your calendar, and you have several assistants who manage your schedule. Using your BlackBerry, the information does not have to synchronize manually with your desktop application—this can be performed wirelessly and without help from you. The reverse is also true. Let's say an assistant makes several calendar changes while you are away. In the past, you would not know what changes had occurred to the calendar unless the assistant called you or sent you e-mail about those changes. With the over-the-air calendar synchronization, you can receive calendar updates wirelessly. This way, you are always informed about changes.

You can learn all about these information management applications and synchronization with desktop applications in Chapters 5, 8, 10, 11, and 12.

Save Time

The old saying "Time is money" is certainly true. In our fast paced, technology-driven world, there are often more things to do on any given day than you can reasonably manage. Believe me, I know the time-crunch factor just as well as you do. This is one reason the BlackBerry is so handy—it saves time. It helps you complete tasks throughout the day so you can avoid being slammed by an avalanche of e-mail those times you can connect. If you can manage tasks throughout the day, you get more done and end up with more rest and relaxation time, which is great news for us all.

Gather Information

Using an add-on Internet service, such as Go America, or an add-on paging service, the BlackBerry can act like a Web browser or even a pager. You can use the Go America software and access hundreds of wireless Internet sites. Shop, gather

Did you know?

Your Time...Your Life

The wireless communication features of the BlackBerry are great, but one of the best side effects of wireless connectivity is that you will have more time for yourself. When you are traveling, you are faced with limited opportunities to connect and respond to e-mail. If you receive a lot of e-mail (like many of us do), unanswered e-mail messages can quickly pile up, and the amount of time required to catch up can be overwhelming. The BlackBerry helps eliminate this problem because new mail arrives to you with no delay. This feature allows you to respond to mail and send e-mail throughout the day instead of having to work an hour or two on e-mail correspondence in your hotel room. The end result—more time for your own enjoyment, which is always great news.

information, check financial records, or do research. The wireless Internet functions a lot like the wired version—only without as many graphics and in smaller text. Do you need a pager? The BlackBerry is all you need. You can use the BlackBerry to send and receive numeric and text-based pages—it's a single device with many functions.

> **TIP** *You can learn more about Internet access and paging via the Blackberry in Chapter 9.*

The BlackBerry and You

So, you can see that the BlackBerry is great for business, but what about the individual user or the small business user who does not have corporate e-mail? The BlackBerry was developed with the corporate user in mind, but it is becoming increasingly popular among individuals and small business users. The BlackBerry

Did you know?

BlackBerry on the Fly, BlackBerry on the Sly

Without saying, the key feature of the BlackBerry is wireless e-mail. After all, communications and information are at your fingertips when you travel with the BlackBerry. If you talk to professionals who use the BlackBerry on a daily basis, you'll hear the same story: "I save two to three hours of time per day because e-mail is always with me—no catching up on e-mail when I return to the office." With the BlackBerry, you are always connected so your e-mail is always "on the fly"—no waiting for connectivity, and no waiting until you get back to your desk.

In the same manner, the BlackBerry can be a great way to get information quickly and secretly. For example, I know a business person who uses the e-mail solution to connect with his lawyer during business meetings. If he needs advice, he just e-mails his lawyer and waits for a response—without the other party even knowing what is going on! Because the BlackBerry is always on, always connected, other people are always at your fingertips via e-mail.

Internet Edition provides you with access to standard Internet Service Provider (ISP) mail and even Web mail, such as Yahoo Mail and Hotmail.

In fact, the BlackBerry is currently being cobranded with a number of other products, including Compaq PCs and even an AOL unit. The BlackBerry is currently exploding on the home and small office user scene rapidly. So, if you use the BlackBerry for your work or just for Internet e-mail access, how can it help you? The following key points are important to consider.

Information Management

You can use the BlackBerry's standard applications to manage your personal information, just like you would with your business information. The BlackBerry will keep track of this information for you and help you manage the schedules and tasks of your daily life.

Are you worried about missing an appointment? Not a problem, you can enter the appointment on the BlackBerry calendar and the BlackBerry will alert you at a preset time before the appointment. Need to jot down some information quickly and easily? Again, not a problem—MemoPad lets you enter any information you might want to keep and saves the information as a file.

TIP   *The BlackBerry can synchronize with any number of desktop personal information managers, even Outlook Express. You can create information on the BlackBerry and move that data to your desktop PC quickly and easily.*

Internet Access and More

If your BlackBerry has an Internet service provider (ISP) account, such as with Go America or PocketGenie (see Chapters 9 and 13), you can surf the Internet and gather the information you need while you are on the move. You can even download additional BlackBerry games and applications and install them on the unit using your desktop PC. See Chapter 14 to learn more about additional software and games.

Let the BlackBerry Take Care of You

As I mentioned, you can use the BlackBerry to notify you when an appointment is coming up or when you receive new e-mail. The BlackBerry can turn itself on and off each day as you prescribe—and you can even use it as an alarm clock! The BlackBerry is your total mobile solution, one that can be used in many different ways. After all, that is the focus of this book!

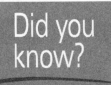

Did you know?

The BlackBerry Doesn't Forget

One of the great things about the BlackBerry is that the device can help you remember things. That's right, the BlackBerry isn't just a static device into which you enter information—the BlackBerry can help keep you on track. Let's say you have a 1 P.M. appointment. How about a 30-minute warning at 12:30 P.M.? Using the BlackBerry calendar, you can have the BlackBerry warn you when important, time-sensitive items are coming up. Does this sound helpful? There's much more, and you can learn about it all in this book!

Chapter 2

Explore the BlackBerry's Features

How to...

- Use the BlackBerry for your work and life
- Explore the BlackBerry's features
- Understand BlackBerry applications

The BlackBerry is designed to give you everything you need for wireless communications along with common PDA-type tasks. With the BlackBerry, you can easily communicate via e-mail, no matter where you are, and you can perform other typical tasks, such as creating address book entries, while you are on the move. The result? The BlackBerry keeps you connected to the network when you are not at your desk, and it helps you save time by allowing you to complete your work anywhere. Add in a web browser, and your BlackBerry becomes a complete Internet solution. E-mail your colleagues while you are in a cab and even place an order over the Internet for Mom's birthday present—it's that simple.

If you have just purchased your BlackBerry, or just received your unit as a part of a corporate rollout, then this chapter is written especially for you. In this chapter, you will explore the primary features of the BlackBerry. You can think of this chapter as your crash course for the BlackBerry. You'll find a number of cross-references to other chapters here so you can quickly locate related information you need. Are you ready? Then let's explore the BlackBerry!

The BlackBerry Handheld and Pager Models

If you purchased your BlackBerry, one of your first decisions was choosing the model that was right for you. If you received your BlackBerry through a corporate rollout, you may not have had that opportunity. The good news is that regardless of what model you have, you can essentially do the same thing on each one, and this book explores each model and notes any differences throughout. The BlackBerry is available in either the 957 handheld model or the 950 pager model. You can read a quick explanation of each in the following two sections.

BlackBerry 957 Handheld

The BlackBerry 957 handheld looks like a typical personal digital assistant (PDA) that easily fits into the palm of your hand. The 957 gives you a larger screen that makes viewing text and related information much easier. As you can see in Figure 2-1, the screen takes up most of the unit and the keyboard fits neatly under the screen. This model typically ships with a nice leather case with a clip attachment so you can wear the BlackBerry in your shirt pocket or pants pocket, or you can clip it inside your purse or briefcase.

BlackBerry 950 Pager

The BlackBerry 950 model, shown in Figure 2-2, is about the size of a typical pager. It is important to note here that the name "950 pager" simply refers to the BlackBerry's size, not its capabilities. You can essentially do everything with the 950 model that you can with the 957 model—it's just smaller and easier to carry. However, the 950 has a much smaller screen. The 950 model ships with a pager-type belt clip. It is designed to be worn like a pager so that you easily access your information.

FIGURE 2-1   BlackBerry 957

FIGURE 2-2   BlackBerry 950

Features of Both Models

If you have not yet purchased your BlackBerry, you may wonder which unit is best for you. That is difficult to say, because they both provide the same functionality. Since that is the case, it really comes down to a matter of choice. The 957 has a much larger screen, which I prefer. However, if portability is a key issue for you, then the 950 model is easier to carry because it looks and feels more like a pager, whereas the 957 looks and feels more like a PDA. However, you can clip both of them to your belt and travel, and many custom cases designed for the Palm V also fit the BlackBerry. So, it's really all about preferences.

As I said, the good news is that the 950 and 957 models provide the same basic functionality, both in terms of hardware design and software. In terms of the interface and physical aspects of the unit itself, you'll find the following features:

■ **Tough design**   The BlackBerry is sleek, yet very durable and tough. The unit is made to travel with you, and RIM knows that it will be dropped, sat on, crammed into briefcases and purses, and just about anything else that goes along with the perils of travel. Although the BlackBerry is not indestructible (especially the screen), it is a tough little machine that is designed to be your travel companion.

■ **QWERTY keyboard**   The BlackBerry contains a QWERTY keyboard, which is a miniature, full-featured keyboard that you use with your thumbs. Although thumb typing takes a little getting used to, it is much easier than using a stylus and having to learn stylus symbols, as is typically the case with other PDAs. (If you have ever tried to use a stylus while in a cab ride, you know what I mean.) Almost everything you can do on the BlackBerry can be done via the keyboard, and there are even many keyboard shortcuts available for the BlackBerry (which are given throughout this book where appropriate, and compiled in Appendix A).

■ **Trackwheel**   The BlackBerry works more like a PC—it features a keyboard to enter information into the unit and a trackwheel that works a lot like a computer mouse. The trackwheel is simply a round wheel that you roll to scroll through the cursor selections on your screen. When you've highlighted, or selected, an item that you want to open, you click the trackwheel much in the same way you would click a computer mouse. This keyboard/trackwheel design makes the BlackBerry very easy to use and very familiar the first time you pick it up.

TIP   *You will get into the specifics of using the keyboard and the trackwheel in Chapter 3.*

■ **LCD screen**   Although the 957 model has a larger screen than the 950 model, they both have an easy-to-read, clear, adjustable LCD screen. A backlighting feature is even available when you are in low-light situations and you can't see the screen well (although backlighting does drain the battery more quickly).

■ **Icon-based interface**   The BlackBerry provides you with a Home screen, shown in Figure 2-3, which is essentially an icon-based interface. You can scroll to and click the icon to open the associated program. You can also easily maneuver through programs using menus, much like you would do on a desktop computer. These features make moving around the BlackBerry intuitive and easy.

TIP   *You can learn more about these features and the basics of how to use them in Chapter 3.*

FIGURE 2-3 Icon-based interface

PC Synchronization

The BlackBerry is not an island. Information that is contained on the BlackBerry needs to be accessible in other ways, and RIM is certainly aware of this fact. Because information may need to be transferred and managed, your BlackBerry unit ships with the Desktop Manager, which is a PC/Macintosh software application that enables your BlackBerry to connect with the PC. Using a cradle connection, the

Did you know?

BlackBerry and Cobranded Products

The BlackBerry 957 and 950 are the only two BlackBerry units that are produced in terms of actual models. There are also 857 and 850 models, which are identical to the 957 and 950 models but specifically designed for certain networks. You'll also find a few cobranded products. For example, there is an AOL BlackBerry, a Yahoo BlackBerry, and a few others as well. These cobranded products appear out of joint ventures between these companies and RIM, but the actual units are the same. Regardless of what BlackBerry you use, the information you find in this book will apply to your model and unit style. Check with your network provider to find out about additional BlackBerry software that might be available to you.

BlackBerry can synchronize with personal information management (PIM) software, such as Lotus Notes, Microsoft Outlook, GroupWise, and others. For example, let's say you make 15 new contacts at a convention. You add those contacts to your BlackBerry's address book. When you return to the office, you can easily synchronize the BlackBerry with your desktop PIM so that those contacts are transferred.

The Desktop Manager gives you a simple and familiar window-and-icon interface, as you can see in Figure 2-4, and it contains the following features:

- **Application Loader**   You can remove existing applications from your BlackBerry and add new ones using the Application Loader software. This feature of the Desktop Manager makes application installation or removal a real snap.

- **Backup and Restore**   You can back up the information on your BlackBerry to a file on your PC. In the event that your BlackBerry is damaged or stolen, your data can be easily recovered and replaced on the BlackBerry using the Restore feature.

- **Intellisync**   The Intellisync software enables you to synchronize the BlackBerry with a desktop PIM. You set up the software and choose the type of PIM you are using, and the BlackBerry will handle the synchronization tasks. You can even configure Desktop Manager to synchronize automatically at desired intervals.

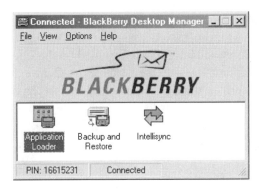

FIGURE 2-4   Desktop Manager

 *See Chapter 5 to learn all about Desktop Manager installation, configuration, and usage.*

Wireless Connectivity

The main purpose of the BlackBerry is wireless connectivity. After all, without wireless connectivity, the BlackBerry wouldn't be very useful. The BlackBerry works differently than other PDAs and even the typical PC. Most PDAs that have wireless capabilities must open a connection to the network. In fact, you must open this connection, and then check your e-mail. Remote PCs are the same way—you typically have to dial an access number, check your mail, and so on.

The BlackBerry does not function this way. If your BlackBerry is turned on and you are in the network coverage area, your BlackBerry is connected to the network. In fact, it stays connected all of the time. You don't ever have to physically connect to the network unless you turn off the radio modem and need to turn it on later (see Chapter 3). As such, the BlackBerry and back-end servers use a push model of e-mail delivery. This means e-mail is directly sent from the server and to the BlackBerry without your having to check for mail. If you are not connected to the network, the mail is held on the server until you are connected, and then it is pushed to you. This "always on, always connected" feature takes you out of the loop; you don't have to check your e-mail—it just arrives to you directly.

The BlackBerry basically provides two different wireless solutions, or *editions*, of the BlackBerry, as described in the following sections.

Enterprise Edition

The Enterprise Edition of the BlackBerry is designed to work in corporate environments that use Microsoft Exchange or Lotus Domino as their e-mail server. RIM provides BlackBerry software that is installed on the Exchange or Domino servers so that they will function with the BlackBerry. Corporate users automatically receive their corporate e-mail through the BlackBerry and can easily stay connected to the corporate e-mail system, regardless of where they are.

Internet Edition

The BlackBerry Internet Edition is designed for Internet connectivity. With the Internet Edition, your unit connects to the wireless Internet in order to retrieve your mail from your Internet service provider. Using third-party web browsing tools (see Chapters 9 and 13), you can access news and related information on the

How Is Push E-Mail Different?

If you are curious about how e-mail works, you should know that the subject is fraught with technical terms and gory details. I don't mind telling you, however, that push technology is primarily not used with other types of e-mail systems and clients. For example, consider the home PC. Typically, you dial a connection, and then use a program, such as Outlook, Netscape, or Eudora, to check for mail. These programs query your mail server and then download the mail from the server. This method of delivery is called *pull transmission*—the client application is "pulling" data from the server.

With the BlackBerry, the server knows if your unit is connected to the wireless network and takes a more proactive role in the e-mail process. If you are connected, the data is pushed from the server to your BlackBerry. Because the BlackBerry uses a push model instead of a pull model, there is nothing for you to do except read and respond to your mail. The BlackBerry keeps you on track with your job and your mail in that you don't have to deal with network connectivity and constantly checking for mail. That's great news for busy people— you can rest assured that your mail will always arrive in a timely and automatic manner. You can even set alerts so that you know when e-mail arrives. See Chapters 6 and 7 to learn more about e-mail, and see Chapter 4 to learn how to configure alerts.

Internet as well as browse wireless web sites. You can even access Internet mail sites, such as Hotmail and Yahoo.

NOTE   *You can also browse the Internet and use web browsers on the Enterprise Edition as well. The difference between the two is mail connectivity.*

E-mail

Wireless connectivity isn't much help without applications that can make use of this type of connectivity—namely e-mail. The BlackBerry provides you with e-mail software that is available right from the Home screen. These tools work together to give you a full-featured e-mail client right on your BlackBerry. You can send, receive, and manage e-mail using these tools and even synchronize your

What about Security?

If you work in a corporate environment where security is of high importance, it may seem that the BlackBerry would be a security weakness. After all, in order to receive mail, the mail has to leave your company's network and be transferred to the wireless network, and then transferred to your BlackBerry. Not so. The BlackBerry Enterprise Edition uses industry-standard encryption technology so that your e-mail is always encrypted during transit to and from your BlackBerry. So, the BlackBerry is up-to-speed with corporate security standards and is a safe device for you to manage your confidential e-mail.

BlackBerry with your desktop PIM, such as Lotus Notes, Microsoft Outlook, and a number of others.

In order to help you manage e-mail and use e-mail simply and easily, the BlackBerry provides you with four different e-mail interfaces:

- **Messages** The Messages folder contains all messages that have been sent and received, as shown in Figure 2-5. Various icons are used to indicate the status of messages. Through the screen menu you can mark messages, delete them, create new ones, or move messages to the Saved Messages folder.

- **Compose** This folder option opens your address book (explained in the next section), from which you can choose who you want to send an e-mail to. You can send mail to multiple recipients, copy recipients, and even blind copy recipients, just like you would in a typical e-mail client program.

- **Saved Messages** All sent and received messages are held in the Messages folder until you choose to either delete them or save them. Saved messages are stored in the Saved Messages folder so you can easily refer to them time and time again.

- **Search Messages** The Search Messages option enables you to quickly search through the messages on your BlackBerry and find e-mail by name and subject.

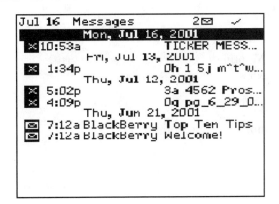

FIGURE 2-5   Messages folder

TIP *You can learn all about the BlackBerry's e-mail features and how to use them in Chapters 6 and 7.*

Address Book

Remembering the e-mail addresses of all the people you know is certainly no fun, so the BlackBerry includes a storage location, the address book, where you can enter all kinds of contact information about people. The BlackBerry's address book works just like the address book for a desktop PIM. You can store names, phone numbers, e-mail addresses, physical addresses, company information—you name it, you can store it. You can then easily access the address book to recall this information and send e-mail to contacts within your address book. You can even include an address book entry as an attachment to an e-mail message. See Chapter 8 to learn all about the BlackBerry's address book.

Calendar

Electronic calendars have become very popular within corporations and even for individuals. Corporate calendars keep you on track with deadlines, appointments, meetings, and basically anything else, and other people can even manage them as you designate. The BlackBerry calendar can be synchronized with your desktop calendar so that information you enter on the BlackBerry or the desktop PIM can be synchronized. The calendar provides a number of important features, such as the following:

- Day, Week, Month, or Agenda views so you can easily manage your schedule (as shown in Figure 2-6)

- Easy appointment creation and management

- Alerts to remind you of appointments

- Easy desktop synchronization

- For Microsoft Exchange environments, over-the-air calendar synchronizing

TIP   *You can learn all about the BlackBerry calendar by reading Chapter 10.*

Tasks and Alarms

The BlackBerry enables you to keep track of various tasks through the Tasks application. Synchronizable with your desktop PIM, the Tasks application enables you to create new tasks and set priorities and a variety of status indicators for tasks as needed. You can then track tasks and manage them. This feature is very helpful if you have a number of different items that must be completed by a certain date or time.

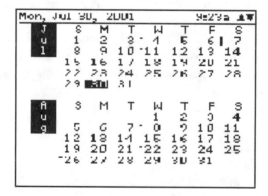

FIGURE 2-6   Calendar Month view

Did you know?

What Is Over-the-Air Calendar Synching?

Let's say you are in New York for a week-long conference. Your home office is in Philadelphia. On Monday, your secretary makes a number of changes to your calendar at the home office. Since you are in New York, your BlackBerry calendar would not show those changes. So, your secretary would have to call or e-mail you with the changes and you would have to manually enter them. This is a real pain and a big waste of time.

Now, with over-the-air calendar synching, your BlackBerry calendar can synchronize with your PIM calendar via the wireless network. The end result is that changes made on either the BlackBerry end or the PIM can be automatically synchronized with no additional effort from you. Changes are automatic, and you can remain focused on your real work tasks without having to worry about data entry for your BlackBerry.

The BlackBerry can also keep you on track and act as your alarm clock. That may seem trivial, but remember that the BlackBerry is designed to be your wireless companion. It can travel with you, get your e-mail, help you manage your schedule, and even wake you up in the morning. Using a number of configuration options you can learn about in Chapter 4, you can even program the BlackBerry to automatically turn itself on and off at certain times of the day. See Chapter 11 to learn more about tasks and alarms.

MemoPad

MemoPad is a simple application that enables you to create memos, documents, or basically anything else. Information entered in MemoPad is savable with a typical filename. You can even transfer these text-based documents to your desktop PIM, and then cut the text and paste it into a desired word processing format. Again, this application saves you time because you can complete work while you are in transit instead of waiting until you get to the office.

MemoPad in the Real World

The BlackBerry is obviously not the device you want to use if you are writing the Great American Novel—after all, it was not designed for this purpose. However, the great thing about MemoPad is you can write whatever you need to write—notes, thoughts, formal letters, and even longer documents—and then transfer those documents to your desktop PIM and convert them to another format. I have even used MemoPad to write portions of book chapters while I am in transit. I next transfer the MemoPad documents to Microsoft Outlook, which sees them as notes, and then cut and paste the information into Word. Sure, it's not a great device for writing long documents as a practice, but it does enable you to get a lot of work done while you are on the move—time that would have been wasted. By saving that wasted time, you can spend your own time doing what you want to do instead of having to catch up in the evening because you were traveling all day.

Calculator

The BlackBerry includes a calculator, shown in Figure 2-7, that functions the same as a typical desktop calculator. Using the QWERTY keyboard, you'll find the calculator easy to use and helpful in a number of obvious cases.

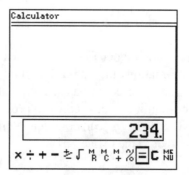

FIGURE 2-7   Calculator

Options

The BlackBerry contains a number of helpful options that you can configure. These options determine how your BlackBerry operates and behaves. You can learn all about these in Chapter 4, but here's a quick list of the items you'll find:

- ■ **Auto On/Off**   Have your BlackBerry turn itself on and off when you want.

- ■ **AutoText**   Let the BlackBerry help you type by automatically generating common text for you.

- ■ **Date/Time**   Keep your date and time configured.

- ■ **Notify**   Configure alerts here. You can even configure special alerts for priority messages.

- ■ **Screen/Keyboard**   Configure screen font, brightness, and even keyboard behavior.

Third-Party Solutions

The BlackBerry contains a number of third-party solutions that extend its functionality and usefulness. There are several corporate solutions available as well as Internet solutions. For example, you can browse the wireless Internet using a browser from GoAmerica or PocketGenie. With these wireless add-on solutions, the power of the Internet becomes truly mobile, traveling with you everywhere.

There are also a number information management solutions available that are primarily deployed in the corporate environment. Chapter 13 explores these options.

Applications and Games

The BlackBerry ships to you with a standard set of applications, which I've described in the previous sections. However, third-party companies and individuals have developed a number of additional applications and games that you can purchase and install on your BlackBerry. Most of these items are available for a nominal fee and several of them are actually free. For example, Attachmate is a simple utility that enables you to attach calendar data and even information from MemoPad to your e-mail. Are you bored? How about a quick game of Solitaire or RIM Chicken?

These are just a few of the options that are available to you, and you can learn more about them in Chapter 14 and see my Top Ten picks in Appendix B.

Are You Ready?

As you can see, the BlackBerry has a number of great possibilities—software and wireless connectivity that can help you with your business and save you time. Are you ready to experience all the BlackBerry has to offer? Then let's get started! In the rest of this book, I show you how to do everything with your BlackBerry, from basic configuration to solving problems. Remember, this book is a reference book—you can read everything in order or skip around if you like. The more you read, the more you learn, and the more you use the BlackBerry, the more you will discover about the power and freedom of wireless connectivity!

Part 2

Get to Know the BlackBerry

Chapter 3

Get to Know the BlackBerry Interface

How to...

- ■ Use BlackBerry controls
- ■ Manage the BlackBerry keyboard
- ■ Check out the BlackBerry interface
- ■ Start your BlackBerry for the first time

As you have learned in previous chapters, the BlackBerry is an easy-to-use personal communicator that is ready to go to work right out of the box. If you're like me, you tend to be a little impatient with any new device. After all, I don't want to spend half an hour reading about the device first—I want to use it right away! That's fine, and although using the BlackBerry is rather straightforward, there are a number of options and keyboard controls you'll need to become familiar with in order to make the best use of your BlackBerry. In this chapter, you'll get an in-depth look at the BlackBerry interface. You'll learn the different button controls, keyboard strokes and options, and I will show you how to start the BlackBerry for the first time. So if you've just received your BlackBerry and are getting ready to use it for the first time, this chapter is just for you.

The BlackBerry...A First Look

Both the BlackBerry hand-held (957) and BlackBerry pager (950) models provide you with essentially the same standard interface and controls, with some variations. I'll point out the controls for each model in the following two sections.

Getting to Know the Hand-Held Model

Using just a few buttons and controls, you can do practically everything with your 957 hand-held BlackBerry. Figure 3-1 shows the basic controls for the hand-held BlackBerry model.

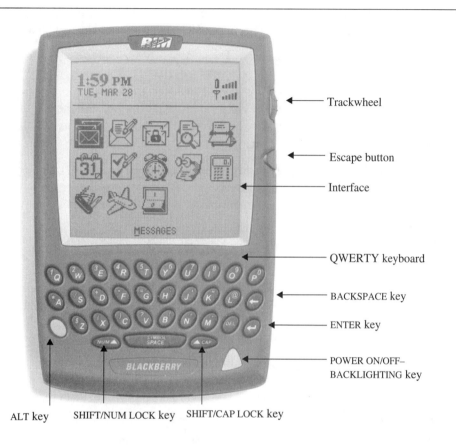

- Trackwheel
- Escape button
- Interface
- QWERTY keyboard
- BACKSPACE key
- ENTER key
- POWER ON/OFF–
  BACKLIGHTING key

ALT key   SHIFT/NUM LOCK key   SHIFT/CAP LOCK key

FIGURE 3-1   Hand-held BlackBerry controls

The following list explains these control features:

- **Trackwheel**   The BlackBerry trackwheel functions a lot like a mouse does for a desktop computer. You turn the trackwheel to scroll through icon lists or through options on any page that you see. As you scroll, icons are highlighted as you move over them. When you land on something you want, you can press down (click) the trackwheel to open the item. For example, I use the trackwheel to scroll through my Home icon list to highlight the calculator icon, and then I open the calculator by clicking the trackwheel when the icon is selected. Once I have the calculator open, I can maneuver through the available functions by using the trackwheel's scroll-and-click features. The trackwheel is your main tool for moving around the BlackBerry interface. You will use it to navigate as well as to make selections all of the time.

- **Escape**   The Escape button works just like the Back button on a Web browser. Wherever you are in the BlackBerry interface, the Escape button takes you to the previous screen. Continuing with the calculator example, if I use the trackwheel to scroll and click open the calculator, I can simply press the Escape button to return to the Home screen.

- **Interface**   The LCD display provides the device interface where you will interact with the BlackBerry. The BlackBerry software gives you an easy-to-use, icon- and menu-based interface so you can maneuver around easily.

- **QWERTY keyboard**   The QWERTY keyboard is a miniature keyboard that provides you with the same standard functionality as any computer keyboard. You use your thumbs to type with the BlackBerry QWERTY keyboard, and most people agree that the QWERTY keyboard is much easier to use than a stylus, which is the input device commonly employed with other PDAs.

- **BACKSPACE**   The BACKSPACE key is considered a part of the keyboard and works like the BACKSPACE key on a computer. If you are typing letters or numbers and you make a mistake, just press the BACKSPACE key to delete the character that you just typed.

- **ENTER**   The ENTER key is another primary control feature, along with the trackwheel and the Escape button, that you will use frequently. ENTER allows you to issue a command to the BlackBerry, and in many cases it does the same thing as a trackwheel click. For example, I can use the trackwheel to scroll and click 2+2 on the calculator, and then either click the trackwheel once more or press ENTER to get the result.

TIP   *On the BlackBerry handheld, the BACKSPACE and ENTER keys look similar and are close to each other. You can expect to make a few keystroke mistakes as you are learning to use the BlackBerry. Don't let these mistakes frustrate you—you'll be a pro in no time.*

- **POWER ON/OFF and BACKLIGHTING**   On the hand-held model, use this silver key to turn the power on and off and to use backlighting. To turn on the unit, just press and release this key. To turn off the unit, press and hold down the key for a couple of seconds. To turn on backlighting, which lights up your screen so you can see the interface while in bright light, just quickly press this key.

TIP *Pressing and holding down the* POWER ON/OFF *key turns the unit off, and quickly pressing and releasing the key turns on backlighting. In order to conserve battery power, backlighting will only remain on when you are using the unit. Once twenty seconds of inactivity passes, backlighting will turn itself off.*

- **SHIFT/CAP LOCK**   This works like the SHIFT key and the CAP LOCK key on a typical keyboard. By pressing SHIFT and a key, you enter the capitalized version of the letter you typed. To use CAP LOCK, press the ALT key and the SHIFT key at the same time to activate CAP LOCK. Press ALT-SHIFT again to turn off CAP LOCK.

- **SHIFT/NUM LOCK**   The SHIFT portion of this key works in the same manner as SHIFT/CAP LOCK, but pressing ALT-SHIFT here changes the function to NUM LOCK. This feature is helpful if you are using the calculator or sending an e-mail containing a bunch of numbers. Once you enable NUM LOCK, press ALT-SHIFT to turn off this function when you're done.

NOTE *When using CAP LOCK, a small arrow appears in the upper right-hand corner of the screen, as shown in Figure 3-2. When NUM LOCK is on, an "N" appears in the upper right-hand corner of the screen.*

- ALT   The ALT key gives you access to a number of controls when using the keyboard, such as CAP LOCK or NUM LOCK.

TIP *Note that the ALT key is colored orange, which correlates to the orange characters and symbols above each keyboard letter. Press ALT plus the desired key to enter the orange character. Also note that an "A" icon appears in the upper right-hand corner of your interface screen when you are using the ALT key.*

FIGURE 3-2   CAP LOCK is turned on

Getting to Know the Pager Model

The BlackBerry 950 gives you a pager-size unit with basically the same interface
as the 957 hand-held unit. However, there are some fundamental differences.
Figure 3-3 shows the basic controls for the pager model.

Notice in Figure 3-3 that the controls used on the pager model are essentially
the same. You still have a clickable trackwheel, Escape button, and ENTER key,
as well as the ALT and SHIFT/CAP LOCK keys. However, the 950 has the following
keyboard management differences:

- To turn on backlighting, press the ALT key three times in a row. Remember
  that backlighting will remain on as long as you are using your BlackBerry,
  but will be automatically turned off after ten seconds of inactivity on the 950.

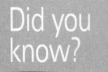

Turn Off the BlackBerry

Some BlackBerry users choose to turn their units off at the end of every day.
Many users, however, prefer to keep the BlackBerry turned on at all times.
As long as you keep an eye on available battery power, you can leave your
BlackBerry on all the time, ensuring that e-mail messages always arrive to
you immediately. In fact, you can even use the BlackBerry as an alarm clock!

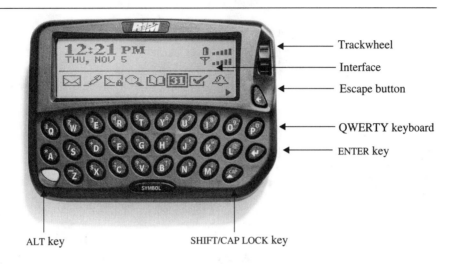

Trackwheel

Interface

Escape button

QWERTY keyboard

ENTER key

ALT key

SHIFT/CAP LOCK key

FIGURE 3-3   Pager BlackBerry controls

■ In order to turn on NUM LOCK, press ALT-SHIFT. An "N" will appear in the upper right-hand corner to indicate the NUM LOCK function is on.

Other than these keyboard issues, the 950 and 957 models are controlled in the same manner, with the trackwheel, Escape button, and ENTER keys being the main items that enable you to maneuver throughout the BlackBerry interface. The keyboard on the 957 model is slightly larger than the 950 model, making it a little easier to use, but overall the two units are very similar.

Getting to Know the BlackBerry Interface

The LCD screen displays the BlackBerry interface, which is primarily made up of icons and menus. This easy to navigate "operating system" allows you to access all of the tools and features that the BlackBerry has to offer.

When you first power up the BlackBerry, the Home screen appears, and this is your primary area for accessing all of BlackBerry's features and functions. The Home screen gives you the date and time as well as a number of icons that you can select in order to access BlackBerry's different features. You can see the 957 Home screen in Figure 3-4 and the 950 Home screen in Figure 3-5.

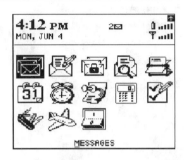

FIGURE 3-4   BlackBerry 957 Home Screen

Home Icons

As you can see, the primary differences between the 957 and 950 interfaces are the number of icons displayed and the appearance of some of those icons. Aside from these differences, the interfaces for the two units look the same. Figure 3-6 shows you the Home screen with the different interface areas highlighted.

FIGURE 3-5   BlackBerry 950 Home Screen

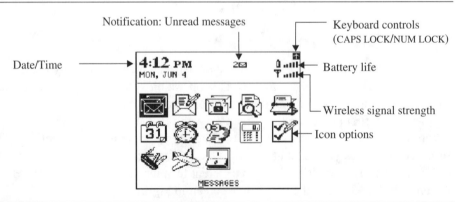

FIGURE 3-6   BlackBerry Interface Components

As I noted, the only differences between the 950 and 957 interfaces are the number of icons displayed on the opening Home screen and the appearance of some icons. You have, however, the exact same options available on each model. Table 3-1 shows you the icons for the 957 model and gives an explanation of what each represents.

Icon	Name	Description
	Messages	Scroll to and click this icon to open your messaging inbox. You can read all mail that you have received and even old mail that you have kept.
	Compose Message	Scroll to and click this icon to enter and send a new mail message.
	Saved Messages	This icon lets you save messages that are in your inbox for later review so that they appear in the Saved Messages folder.
	Search Messages	Use this handy search feature to locate a particular message.
	Address Book	Access the address book through this icon to enter contact information for an individual and examine current address book entries.
	Calendar	Use the BlackBerry calendar feature to keep track of all your appointments.
	Alarm	Set a variety of alarms through this icon.
	MemoPad	Scroll to and click this icon to enter and save memos.
	Calculator	Scroll to and click this icon to use the BlackBerry calculator.
	Tasks	Scroll to and click this icon to enter and manage tasks.
	Options	Use the Options feature to manage all kinds of system settings, which I'll explain in more detail in Chapter 4.
	Wireless	This option turns BlackBerry's wireless communications on or off.
	Power Off	This option turns the BlackBerry off.
	Others	Depending on your BlackBerry's configuration, you may see additional icons, such as a Web browser, on the Home screen.

TABLE 3-1   Icons on the 957 Home Screen

Table 3-2 shows the features on the BlackBerry 950 pager model. You'll notice that you have same features as the 957 model, but the icons are slightly different.

Icon	Name	Description
	Messages	Scroll to and click this icon to open your messaging inbox. You can read all mail that you have received and even old mail that you have kept.
	Compose Message	Scroll to and click this icon to enter and send a new mail message.
	Saved Messages	This icon lets you save messages that are in your inbox for later review so that they appear in the Saved Messages folder.
	Search Messages	Use this handy search feature to locate a particular message.
	Address Book	Access the address book through this icon to enter contact information for an individual and examine current address book entries.
	Calendar	Use the BlackBerry calendar feature to keep track of all your appointments.
	Tasks	Scroll to and click this icon to enter and manage tasks.
	Alarm	Set a variety of alarms through this icon.
	Calculator	Scroll to and click this icon to use the BlackBerry calculator.
	MemoPad	Scroll to and click this icon to enter and save memos.
	Options	Use the Options feature to manage all kinds of system settings.
	Wireless	This option turns BlackBerry's wireless communications on or off.
	Power Off	This option turns the BlackBerry off.
	Others	Depending on your BlackBerry's configuration, you may see additional icons, such as a Web browser, on the Home screen.

TABLE 3-2   Icons on the 950 Home Screen

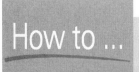 **Access BlackBerry Icons**

To access the BlackBerry icons, maneuver through the Home screen and open icons using the BlackBerry's trackwheel. Just follow these steps:

1. Scroll through your icon list using the trackwheel. Icons will be highlighted as they are selected with the trackwheel.

2. To open a program, just scroll to its icon and highlight it, and then click the trackwheel.

3. The program you selected opens. As this point, you can use the program and click the trackwheel to get menu options.

4. When you want to return to the Home screen, just press the Escape button. If you have waded through several screens in the program, you may have to click the Escape button several times, or just click the trackwheel to access the menu and then select the Close option.

Home Status Icons

As I noted earlier, the Home screen also gives you a number of other status icons, such as those indicating wireless connectivity and battery power. However, there are additional icons that may appear in the top-right portion of the Home screen, depending on activity. Table 3-3 gives you an illustration of these icons and what they mean.

 BlackBerry also gives you messaging status icons as well. You can learn about these in Chapter 9.

Keyboard Shortcuts

Just like your desktop computer, the BlackBerry gives you several helpful keyboard shortcuts so you can easily access icon items on the Home screen without using the trackwheel. The keyboard shortcuts are the same for both

Icon	Description
	Battery power indicator
	Wireless connectivity indicator
	Charging indicator
	Data is being sent
	Data is being received
A	ALT key mode is activated
↑	SHIFT key mode is activated
N	NUM LOCK mode is activated
✉	Unread messages are waiting

TABLE 3-3   Home Screen Status Icons

the hand-held and pager-size models, but if you are using the pager-size model, you must press the SHIFT key before issuing the command. Table 3-4 lists the keyboard shortcut commands available to you.

TIP   *This table is also located on the inside back cover of this book for quick reference. In addition, when you scroll over an item, the BlackBerry will give you the shortcut for that item by displaying the appropriate key underlined. For example, you access the calculator by pressing the U key (or pressing SHIFT-U on the 950 model). If you scroll over the Calculator icon, the unit will display "CALCULATOR" at the bottom of the Home screen. The underlined U tells you that the letter U is the hot key.*

To Open This...	Press This Key
Messages	M
Compose	C
Saved Messages	V
Search Messages	S
Address Books	A
Calendar	L
Alarm	R
Calculator	U
MemoPad	P
Tasks	T
Options	O
Lock	K (this option only appears if you enabled password protection)

TABLE 3-4   BlackBerry 957 Keyboard Shortcuts

TIP

Remember, if you are using a BlackBerry 950 pager model, you must press the SHIFT *key when issuing these commands. For example,* SHIFT-O *opens Options.*

Turning on Your BlackBerry for the First Time

When you first receive your BlackBerry, you'll need to charge the battery, or in the case of the pager-size model, you'll need to physically install a battery. If you received your BlackBerry in a corporate setting, the unit may already be charged and ready for your use. However, you should familiarize yourself with these tasks since you will need to do them on your own from time to time.

The 950 and 957 models function a little differently when it comes to battery power, so I'll cover the battery issues and startup functions for each unit separately. If you are just now opening the box to your new BlackBerry, make sure you read the section appropriate for your unit before beginning.

BlackBerry Handheld

The BlackBerry 957 hand-held model has an internal lithium battery that is designed to last for one week or longer on a full charge. Your unit includes a cradle, which not only connects to a PC for synchronization, but also is used to charge the BlackBerry's internal battery. The cradle has an AC adapter port so you can connect the included AC adapter to the cradle and charge the BlackBerry's battery. You'll use the cradle again and again to recharge the battery. See "Charge the Hand-Held BlackBerry" to learn how to connect the BlackBerry to the cradle for charging.

TIP *When you first charge the BlackBerry, a full charge will require about three hours. In the future, you can maintain the charge by simply charging the unit for about 15 to 20 minutes each day. In other words, the battery does not need to be completely discharged before recharging. If the battery is completely discharged, you should once again allow it to charge for about three hours. Whenever the unit is connected to the cradle, the battery charges itself.*

Once the BlackBerry has been fully charged, you are ready to begin using it. Simply remove the BlackBerry from the cradle, and then press the POWER ON/OFF

 **Charge the Hand-Held BlackBerry**

To charge the BlackBerry, just follow these steps:

1. Locate the cradle and AC adapter that shipped with your BlackBerry unit. Insert the AC adapter into the back of the cradle's serial port connection, as shown in Figure 3-7, and then plug the AC adapter into any typical outlet.

2. Insert the BlackBerry into the cradle, as shown in Figure 3-8.

3. The message "Initializing" appears on the BlackBerry. In a moment, you will see the Home screen. You should allow the BlackBerry to charge for about three hours before initial use.

FIGURE 3-7   Plug the AC adapter into the cradle's serial port

FIGURE 3-8   Insert the unit into the cradle

(silver) key. The BlackBerry turns on, and you can now begin using the trackwheel to maneuver around your Home screen. It is possible that wireless connectivity may not be turned on by default when you start the unit for the first time. If it is not, the wireless icon on the Home screen will appear as a communications tower, as shown in Figure 3-9, instead of an airplane. When you use the trackwheel to scroll to the icon, the message on the Home screen will say "Turn wireless on." To turn on the wireless feature, just click the icon with your trackwheel. To learn more about BlackBerry's wireless features, see Part 4 of this book.

BlackBerry Pager

The BlackBerry 950 pager model does not use a cradle for charging, but rather a standard AA battery. Depending on your amount of usage, a single AA alkaline battery will last you for several weeks. The 950 model also contains an internal lithium battery, but this battery is charged by the AA alkaline battery that you insert into the unit.

TIP   *Save your money! You do not need to use Ultra or lithium AA batteries with the BlackBerry because the BlackBerry does not pull large amounts of power at one time. You will see the same results using a less expensive (but high-quality) alkaline battery.*

Did you know?

Battery Indicator

You can keep track of the BlackBerry's battery power by checking out the battery power status icon that appears on the BlackBerry's Home screen. If the battery power becomes too low, the signal strength bars that appear on the Home screen will be replaced with the word "BAT." At this time, all wireless functionality will cease to work on your BlackBerry until you charge the battery. The easiest way to avoid "low battery syndrome" is to simply charge the battery for about half an hour at the end of every day. This will ensure that your BlackBerry is always functioning when you need it and that your e-mail is always available to you.

FIGURE 3-9   Turn on wireless capabilities

As with the 957 model, you may need to turn on wireless connectivity. Just use the trackwheel and scroll through the Home screen to locate and highlight the wireless tower icon, and then click the trackwheel to turn on wireless connectivity.

When the battery power becomes low, the battery status indicator bars on the Home screen will become reduced, and are replaced with the message "BAT" when the battery is very low. At this time, wireless connectivity will cease to function until you change the battery. Simply remove the old AA battery and

Did you know?

Wireless Connectivity

If the BlackBerry is a wireless communication device, then why does the BlackBerry give you the option to turn on or off the wireless feature? The answer is simple: The BlackBerry gives you the option to turn on or off wireless connectivity because if you travel with your BlackBerry, you may need to enter areas where wireless communications are prohibited—specifically, aboard airplanes. You can turn off BlackBerry's wireless transmitter while you are on an airplane; however, you can still compose e-mail messages—they are simply held on the unit until you reactivate wireless connectivity. In short, the BlackBerry is designed to go with you everywhere—even to places where wireless communication is not allowed.

replace it with a new one. You will not lose any data on your BlackBerry when you perform this action because the internal lithium cell continues to operate.

If the BlackBerry Will Not Turn On...

In most cases, there are two reasons that the BlackBerry will not turn on. Either the battery power is too low (or nonexistent), or there has been some lockup with the BlackBerry operating system. First, check out the battery. For the 957 model, try completely recharging the battery for three hours. For the 950 model, ensure that the AA alkaline battery is inserted correctly and is a good cell. Allow the AA battery to recharge the internal BlackBerry lithium cell for six to eight hours.

If none of these solutions work, you may have an operating system lockup, in which case the unit needs to be reset. A reset button is located on the back of both the 950 and 957 models. The button is inside of a tiny hole (it is the only hole on the back cover that is not a screw hole). To reset the BlackBerry, gently insert the end of a paperclip into the hole to press the reset button. This should restore the

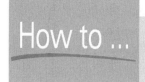

How to ... Install the Battery and Turn on the 950 Unit

To install the battery and turn on the 950 unit for the first time, just follow these steps:

1. On the back of the 950 unit, slide the lock switch to the unlocked position, and then use your thumb to slide off the battery cover. Be careful not to break the lock!

2. Insert a single AA alkaline battery, as shown in Figure 3-10. Do not press on the LCD screen when you are inserting the battery, as pressure may damage the screen—hold onto the plastic edges of the unit when inserting a battery.

3. Replace the cover and slide the switch to the locked position.

4. To turn on the unit, simply click the trackwheel. The Home screen should now appear.

FIGURE 3-10   Insert a single AA alkaline battery

BlackBerry to normal operation. If the BlackBerry still does not work, it's time
to contact technical support, which may attempt a hard reset of the unit.

Conserve Battery Power

You can conserve battery power on both the 950 and 957 BlackBerry units by following just a few simple actions:

- Use backlighting only when necessary.

- Use the vibrate alarm instead of tone alarm when possible (tone requires more battery power).

- Avoid typing very long messages. Also, do not use the Reply with Text option unless necessary. The longer a message is, the more battery power it consumes. You do not need to become "word conscious" when using your BlackBerry, but do keep in mind that long messages require more battery power than short messages.

- Although the Reply with Text feature does consume more battery power, be sure you can live without it before deselecting it. In a reply string, the subject matter can quickly become confusing without the previous e-mail text. See Chapters 6 and 7 to learn more.

- Use the To and CC fields to send the same message to several people instead of sending the same message several times. This too consumes more battery power.

- If battery power is getting low and you cannot recharge or change the battery at the moment, turn off the wireless feature on the Home screen. You will not be able to send and receive e-mail, but this will conserve battery power until you can recharge the unit.

Chapter 4

Configure BlackBerry Options

How to...

- Access BlackBerry configuration options
- Examine available options
- Configure available options

When you first start the BlackBerry, it is configured for your use. In other words, you don't have do anything to use the BlackBerry—there are no setup procedures, no confusing menu screens, no tedious instructions just to get everything working. That's great news if you want to use your BlackBerry right away, but you'll also be happy to know that BlackBerry does not lock you into one basic configuration. You can change the BlackBerry's functionality for a number of different items if you so choose. In this chapter, you'll explore the BlackBerry configuration options that are available to you. Every option in this chapter is carefully explained, and you can expect to see a lot of step-by-step configuration examples so you can configure the BlackBerry to meet your specific needs. However, it is important to note that incorrectly specifying some of the settings available may cause you to lose wireless network connectivity. Make sure you read each section carefully before making any option changes on your BlackBerry.

Checking Out BlackBerry Options

Both the BlackBerry hand-held (957) and BlackBerry pager (950) models provide you with a standard set of configurable components so that you can make the BlackBerry work for you. Both the 957 and 950 models provide you with the same set of configuration options, with the exception of Storage Mode, which is only available on the 957 model. These configurable components, called *options*, are easily accessible from your BlackBerry Home screen. Just scroll to the Swiss army knife icon (957 model) or the wrench icon (950 model), or press O on the 957 keyboard or SHIFT-O on the 950 keyboard. The Options screen opens, listing several configurable items as shown in Figure 4-1.

The option items provided on this screen are

- **About** This option just tells you about the RIM BlackBerry's copyright information and the location of the BlackBerry Web site. There is nothing you can configure here.

- **Auto On/Off**   Your BlackBerry can automatically turn itself on or off using the settings you specify through this option.

- **AutoText**   BlackBerry attempts to recognize commonly misspelled words and correct them for you. AutoText is also used for typing shortcuts. You can configure the list using this option.

- **Date/Time**   Use this option to configure the date and time.

- **Message Services**   List any current message services through this option.

- **Network Settings**   Use this option to specify connectivity settings for your BlackBerry.

- **Notify**   Set notification alerts and options here.

- **Owner**   Use this option to specify owner information.

- **Screen/Keyboard**   Make font changes and keyboard behavior changes here.

- **Security**   Use this option to password-lock the BlackBerry when it is not in use.

- **Status**   This option displays a number of system components and their current status.

- **Storage Mode**   Available only on the 957 model, this option allows you to store your BlackBerry for an extended period of time while maintaining your settings and data.

FIGURE 4-1   BlackBerry Options screen

■ **Others**   Depending on your BlackBerry configuration, you may have other options as well, such as a Web browser, MobileClips, instant messaging software, and so on. Like the other options listed here, these items give you some setting options for the various applications you may have installed. Check your BlackBerry documentation for details on your specific configuration.

Through these options, you can configure the BlackBerry to meet your specific needs. The following sections explore each of these items and show you how to configure the options available. To open an item on the Options screen, just use the trackwheel to scroll to and highlight the item you want, and then click the trackwheel.

Auto On/Off

The BlackBerry has the capability to turn itself on and off at certain times during the weekdays and on weekends. This feature enables the BlackBerry to automatically

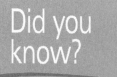

Configuration Tips

With any device, it may be tempting to try all kinds of settings and functions without considering your current needs. After all, curiosity dictates that you discover all the device can do. However, randomly making configuration changes can also cause you a lot of headaches, so before making changes to your BlackBerry options, keep the following tips in mind:

■ Each of the BlackBerry options are configured to a default setting. In many cases, the default setting is all you need. You do not need to make any changes to these options unless you have specific configuration needs.

■ Think carefully about your needs. Ideally, you only want your BlackBerry doing tasks that have specific meaning to you.

■ Try only one or two configuration changes at a time. It is easier to test a few changes than many changes at one time.

power down and conserve battery power during times when it is not in use. Using this feature, you can make sure the BlackBerry is on and active when you need it, but not using battery power when you don't. If you click the Auto On/Off entry on the Options screen, the Auto On/Off Times screen appears, as shown in Figure 4-2.

You'll notice that you have weekday on/off time fields and weekend on/off time fields. Also notice that for both weekday and weekend options, you can either enable or disable the feature (both are disabled by default). This is a good aspect of the feature, because you may want your BlackBerry to use Auto On/Off during the week but not on the weekends. In this case, you would configure the on/off values and enable the weekday option, but simply leave the weekend option disabled. Either way, you can configure the BlackBerry to meet both your weekday and weekend Auto On/Off needs.

TIP   *You cannot configure weekdays individually. You can only configure the BlackBerry for Auto On/Off with either weekday or weekend values.*

To configure the Auto On/Off feature, follow the steps in "Configure Auto On/Off."

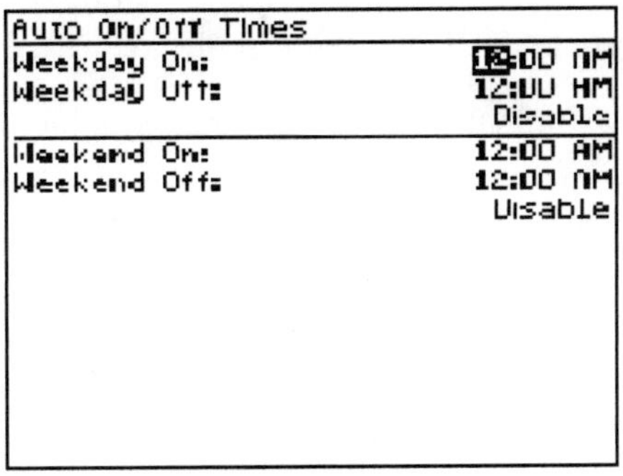

Auto On/Off Times
Weekday On: 12:00 AM
Weekday Off: 12:00 AM
                           Disable

Weekend On: 12:00 AM
Weekend Off: 12:00 AM
                           Disable

FIGURE 4-2   Auto On/Off Times screen

 **Configure Auto On/Off**

To configure Auto On/Off, just follow these steps:

1. In the Auto On/Off screen, use the trackwheel to select the hour you want to change.

2. Click the trackwheel. This will open the Auto On/Off menu, as shown in Figure 4-3.

3. Select Change Option on the menu by scrolling to it with the trackwheel, and then click.

4. A Change Option window opens. Roll the trackwheel to change the option and select the hour that you want. For example, in Figure 4-4, I want my BlackBerry to turn on at 5:45 A.M., so I select 5 for the hour in this window. Click the trackwheel when you're done.

5. Next, roll the trackwheel to select the next number that you want to change. For example, to set my BlackBerry's Auto On function for 5:45 A.M., after specifying the hour I would then scroll to the minutes to continue the configuration. For a shortcut, try entering the time using the keypad instead of the trackwheel.

6. Adjust the AM/PM setting if necessary by highlighting AM or PM on the Auto On/Off screen and repeating Steps 2 through 4.

7. Configure the Off value following the preceding steps.

8. On the Auto On/Off screen, scroll the trackwheel to select the Disable option, and then click the trackwheel to bring up the menu.

9. Select Change Option and choose Enable to enable Auto On/Off. When you're done, review the configuration and make sure it is accurate.

As you can see in Figure 4-5, I have configured my BlackBerry to automatically turn on at 5:45 A.M. and to automatically turn off at 10:00 P.M. The Auto On/Off configuration is disabled for weekends.

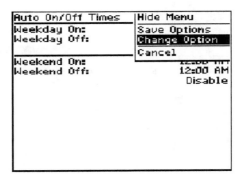

FIGURE 4-3   Auto On/Off Menu

AutoText

The BlackBerry's primary function is highly effective wireless messaging, so it's no surprise that the BlackBerry attempts to help you type e-mail messages. After all, the BlackBerry's QWERTY keyboard is easy to use, but it is not as easy as a standard computer keyboard. Because you are more likely to make typing and spelling mistakes, BlackBerry maintains a list of common mistakes that it can recognize and correct. For example, when you type "adn," the BlackBerry knows that you mean "and" and automatically corrects it for you. The default list also contains corrections for common spelling mistake, such as "believe" for "beleive."

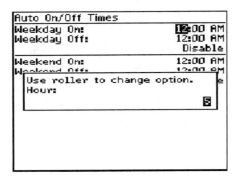

FIGURE 4-4   Roll the trackwheel and click the desired option

```
┌────────────────────────────────────┐
│ Auto On/Off Times                   │
│ Weekday On:              5:45 AM    │
│ Weekday Off:            10:00 PM    │
│                         ╔══════╗    │
│                         ║Enable║    │
│                         ╚══════╝    │
│ Weekend On:             12:00 AM    │
│ Weekend Off:            12:00 AM    │
│                         Disable     │
│                                     │
│                                     │
│                                     │
│                                     │
│                                     │
└────────────────────────────────────┘
```

FIGURE 4-5   Configured Auto On/Off

If you click the AutoText option with your trackwheel, you see of listing of the default entries, as shown in Figure 4-6.

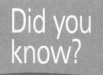

Letting the BlackBerry Sleep When You Sleep

Auto On/Off may not seem like a valuable feature at first glance, but it is always important to remember that the BlackBerry runs on battery power. The more you can conserve battery power, the better. Although it is fine to keep your BlackBerry turned on at all times, many users opt for a waking/ sleeping pattern that mimics their own routine. For example, I typically go to bed around 10:00 P.M. and get up around 6:00 A.M. Since I am not reading e-mail during the night, there is no reason for the BlackBerry to be receiving mail and running when I'm not. So I configure my BlackBerry to turn off at 10:00 P.M. and turn on at 5:45 A.M. This gives the BlackBerry 15 minutes to retrieve new messages while I am still asleep; when I wake up, my new mail is waiting for me. In fact, I even have a 6:00 A.M. alarm set on the BlackBerry so that it wakes me up each day. When I'm ready to go, the BlackBerry is awake and ready to go with me.

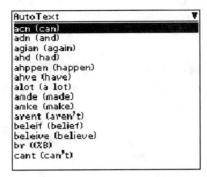

4

FIGURE 4-6   AutoText default entries

The default entry list contains many common spelling errors and their corrections (there are 99 default items). However, you can also make editorial changes to this list or create your own entries.

Select the desired entry, and then click the trackwheel. A menu appears through which you can delete the item or edit the item. If you click Delete, the item simply disappears. If you click Edit, a screen appears where you can change the entry for both the misspelled word and its correction, as shown in Figure 4-7. Simply use your trackwheel and keyboard to change the entry as desired, and then press Escape. You will be prompted to save your changes.

FIGURE 4-7   Edit a current AutoText entry

TIP *The default entries are common errors, so I recommend that you leave these intact, or make slight changes to them based on your own common mistakes.*

You can add new items to this list as well. For example, let's say you make a common keystroke error or spelling mistake. My hated word is "definitely." I seem to misspell that word more commonly than anything else, so on my BlackBerry, I add my common misspelling and enter the correction for it. To add a new entry, from the AutoText screen click the trackwheel to bring up menu options, and then click New Item. The screen shown in Figure 4-7 appears. Enter the mistake you want corrected in the When I type field and its correction in the Replace it with field, and then click the trackwheel and choose Save to save the item.

Aside from basic entries, you can also create macro entries. A macro uses a portion of the BlackBerry's operating system to complete certain fields in your e-mail. For example, let's say that you want to insert the current time into each

Did you know?   Other Helpful AutoText Uses

AutoText is used to correct common errors or misspellings; however, you can use AutoText for other purposes as well. For example, let's say you use your BlackBerry to e-mail other colleagues, and you notice that you type the phrase "consult the technical documentation" often. You could create an AutoText entry with an abbreviation for this phrase, as shown in Figure 4-8. Each time you type "const," the abbreviation is replaced by the phrase. Essentially, you can create your own shorthand whereby you type abbreviations for certain words or phrases. This feature can make e-mail messages quick and easy to compose. Just type the abbreviation and press the space key, and the BlackBerry will fill in the text for you. You can even use abbreviations to create full signatures and contact information to be added to the end of an e-mail. For example, I use "curtb," short for Curt's Business, which adds a signature using my name, phone number, e-mail address, and Web page. I also use a shortcut called "curth," short for Curt Home, which is just my name and home phone number signature for e-mails to friends. As you can see, AutoText opens a new world of easy typing, and basically anything goes!

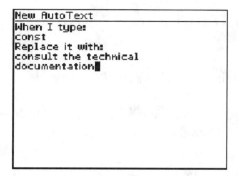

```
New AutoText
When I type:
const
Replace it with:
consult the technical
documentation█
```

FIGURE 4-8   Use AutoText with abbreviations

e-mail that you compose. Instead of getting the current time and manually typing it in, however, you want BlackBerry to handle it for you. No problem—you can simply create a macro entry that inserts the correct time when you enter a keyword, such as "time now" or "current time" or even an abbreviation, such as "ti." The following macros are available for you to use:

- Short date—Gives an abbreviated version of the month, such as Sept. 14, 2001.
- Long date—Gives the long version of the month, such as September 14, 2001.
- Short time—Gives a short version of the time, such as 7:25a
- Long time—Gives a long version of the time, such as 7:24 AM
- Owner name—Simply lists your name
- Owner info—Lists all info about you from the BlackBerry, such as your name, company name, phone number, etc.
- Backspace—Provides an automatic backspace
- Delete—Provides an automatic delete
- %—Figures a percentage

See "Create a Macro AutoText Entry" to learn how to set up a macro AutoText entry.

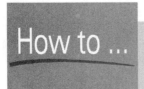

How to ... Create a Macro AutoText Entry

To create a macro AutoText entry, just follow these steps:

1. On the AutoText screen, click the trackwheel to access the menu for this screen. Scroll to and click New Item.

2. In the new item screen, enter the word(s) or abbreviation you want to use for the macro in the When I type field, and then scroll to the Replace it with field.

3. Click the trackwheel to access menu options, and then scroll to and click Insert Macro.

4. From the macro list that appears (see Figure 4-9), select the macro you want and then click the trackwheel.

5. The macro now appears in the Replace it with field. Click the trackwheel to access menu options, and then scroll to and click Save Item.

FIGURE 4-9   Select the desired macro

> NOTE   *The AutoText window also has an automatic search feature. When you open the AutoText window, just press the first letter of the item you are looking for on your keyboard, and the search feature will attempt to locate it. For example, if you press* T, *all AutoText entries beginning with "t" will be displayed.*

Date/Time

You can set the date and time on your BlackBerry so that your e-mail messages are correctly time stamped and all alarms or Auto On/Off functions occur at the proper time. You use the Date/Time function in the Options screen to set the date and time, but you can also do so by synchronizing the BlackBerry with your PC (assuming the date and time are correct on the PC). See Chapter 5 to learn more about synchronization.

To set the date and time, scroll to and click the Date/Time option. The Date/Time screen appears, as shown in Figure 4-10. Use the trackwheel to scroll to and click any item you want to change to bring up a menu with the Change Option function. Click Change Option, and then scroll to and click the desired entry. Configure each section of the Date/Time screen correctly, and then click the trackwheel and click Save Options from the menu that appears.

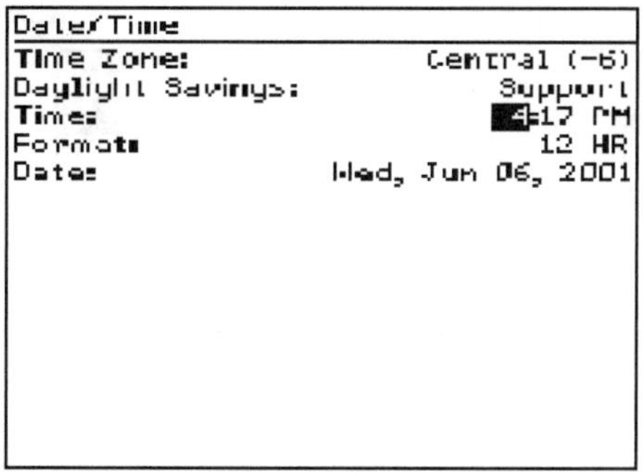

FIGURE 4-10   Date and time settings

Make sure that you choose to support daylight savings time if you are in an area that follows it. Also, when you change the date, notice that you cannot change the day of the week. BlackBerry will automatically correct this for you when you enter the right month, day, and year.

Message Services

Information in this area is used by BlackBerry to connect to your messaging service, such as Exchange, Domino, or an Internet account. There is nothing for you to configure on this screen, and doing so may prevent wireless connectivity. Do not change anything here.

Network Settings

The Network Settings screen contains three simple entries, which typically will not need any configuration from you, as you can see in Figure 4-11. The Roaming option either lists U.S or Canada, depending on your location. There is a service available that allows you to switch back and forth for U.S-Canada cross-border roaming. You can find out more about this service from your service provider.

The Radio option simply turns wireless communications on or off. This is the same thing as turning wireless communications on or off using the icon on your Home screen, which is much easier than accessing this Options screen should you need to turn off wireless communications (such as when traveling by airplane).

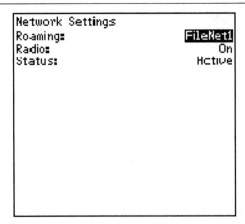

FIGURE 4-11 Network Settings screen

Last of all, the Status option is listed as either Active or Inactive. If you are a LAN user, this setting will be active when you receive the device. If you are an Internet user, activate your account on the Internet following your provider's setup instructions; you can then register and activate your account with the unit by clicking the trackwheel to access the menu and clicking Register Now. If you are an Internet user, you can learn more about account activation in Chapter 9.

Notify

The Notify feature allows your BlackBerry to tell you when new messages arrive on the unit, and several configuration options are available for changing the Notify feature to meet your specific needs. If you click Notify on the Options screen, you see several different setting options, as shown in Figure 4-12.

Use the trackwheel to scroll to the desired option, and then click the trackwheel to see the menu for the screen. On the menu, click Change Option to change the particular option that you selected. Use the trackwheel to scroll to and click the desired option. When you're done editing these settings, just click the trackwheel and click Save Options.

As you can see, there are several different setting configurations you can make:

■ **In Holster** This setting tells the BlackBerry how to notify you when the unit is in the holster. You have the options None, Tone, Vibrate, and Vibrate+Tone. The default setting is Vibrate+Tone, but you can change

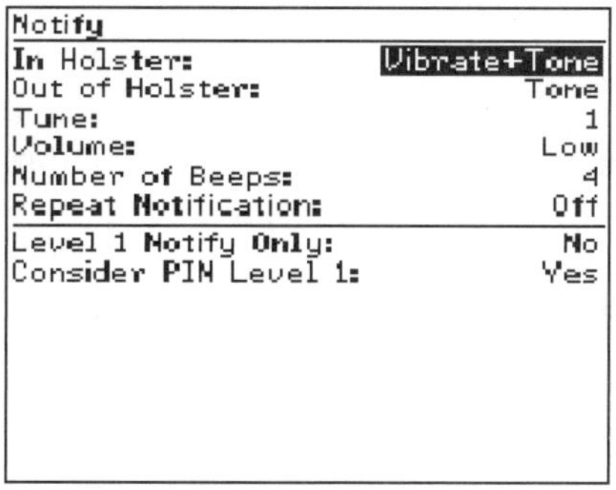

```
Notify
In Holster:            Vibrate+Tone
Out of Holster:                Tone
Tune:                             1
Volume:                         Low
Number of Beeps:                  4
Repeat Notification:            Off
Level 1 Notify Only:             No
Consider PIN Level 1:           Yes
```

FIGURE 4-12   Notify option settings

it to whatever you want. Do keep in mind that if you use the None setting, you will not be notified of new messages when the unit is in the holster.

- **Out of Holster** This setting tells the BlackBerry how to notify you when the unit is out of the holster. Again, you have the options None, Tone, Vibrate, and Vibrate+Tone. The default setting is Tone, but you can change it to whatever setting you want.

- **Tune** If you are using Tone notification for either the In Holster or Out of Holster setting, then you use this option to set the desired tune to be played. There are six different tunes (as well as an Off setting). If you click the trackwheel to bring up menu options for Tune and choose Change Option, you can scroll through each tone option and hear a portion of the tune. Of course, there is no right or wrong setting here, so just decide what Tune setting you like best (or the one that is least irritating).

- **Volume** Use this setting to adjust the notification volume. You have the options Low, Medium, High, and Escalating. Escalating starts out at a low level then gets louder each time it is played.

- **Number of Beeps** This setting is the number of times the tune that you selected is played before it stops. You can choose from 1 to 5, and the default setting is 1. If you are working in a noisy environment and there is a possibility of your not hearing the first beep, then you should set this number to more than 1 just to make sure you are notified when new messages arrive.

- **Repeat Notification** The Repeat Notification feature allows the BlackBerry to keep reminding you about new messages until you respond. This feature is good if the BlackBerry is on your desk and you step away for a few moments. You have a few different options, listed as follows, which you can see by selecting Repeat Notification, clicking the trackwheel, and choosing Change Option:

  - **Low** The BlackBerry will tone or vibrate every 15 minutes for 30 minutes. The LED will also flash.

  - **Medium** The BlackBerry will tone or vibrate every 10 minutes for an hour. The LED will also flash.

  - **High** The BlackBerry will tone or vibrate every 5 minutes for 2 hours. The LED will also flash.

- **LED Only**   The LED will flash for 15 minutes.

- **Off**   There will be no follow-up notification.

If your In Holster and Out of Holster settings are "None," then only the LED Repeat Notification option will work.

4

- **Level 1 Notify Only**   This option, which you simply turn on by selecting Yes on the menu that appears when you highlight this option and click the trackwheel, allows you to be notified only when Level 1 priority messages arrive. This way, you're not hearing a notification for every message, but only those that have high priority.

- **Consider PIN Level 1**   This setting, which is enabled to Yes by default, considers all PIN numbers to be Level 1 messages.

Did you know?

The Notification Who Cried Wolf

Do you remember the children's story about the little boy who was constantly alerting the people of his town to danger when no real danger existed? Eventually, a wolf came along and the boy cried for help, but no one paid him any attention because they were so used to hearing his false cries—and the wolf ate him. You're not likely to get eaten by a wolf when using your BlackBerry, but the Notify feature can get really annoying if you receive a lot of unimportant e-mail every day. If you are like me, you tend to get a number of messages that are important each day, and a bunch of messages that can wait until a later time or are not that important at all. If you are getting notified with each new message, you will tend to start ignoring the notification because it becomes more of a disruption than a help. This where the Level 1 priority setting comes into play. You can use this setting to alert you to important messages, but all others can be ignored until a more convenient time.

Owner

The Owner option simply provides a place for you to enter your name and any additional information that you want (or are required to enter). Typically, company names, departments, and phone numbers are listed in the information section on this screen, and RIM recommends that you place a phone number here so that you can be contacted in the event that you lose your BlackBerry.

Screen/Keyboard

The Screen/Keyboard option provides four different settings, as you can see in Figure 4-13, that affect the way your BlackBerry's screen looks and the way the keyboard operates.

You can change the four options by selecting the option, clicking the trackwheel, and selecting the Change Option menu item, just as you would with all other features on the Options screen. The following list explains the four options available:

- **Screen Contrast** The Screen Contrast setting is represented by a number, from 1 to 24, which determines the contrast of the black screen letters against the background. If you're having problems seeing the BlackBerry interface, you can use this option to change the contrast—a setting of 10 to 15 is typically right for most people. If you working in an environment with low light, use backlighting instead of adjusting the screen contrast.

- **Font Size** This setting affects the size of the letters and characters that you see on the BlackBerry. You have the options Large Font or Small Font, with the default being Large Font.

NOTE *If you're not sure which setting is right for you, change the Font Size option to Small Font. The screen will display the smaller font so you can see if you like the change before saving it.*

- **Key Tone** This setting causes the BlackBerry to make a small tone whenever the trackwheel, Escape button, or any keyboard key is pressed. In some cases, Key Tone, which is disabled by default, can be helpful when you want to know if buttons are pressed, but for the most part the Key Tone setting can get really annoying (unless you just like to hear little beeps over and over again). Also, Key Tone does tend to drain battery power, which is an ever important issue. If you think this setting may be helpful to you, try it out—you can always change it later if you want.

- **Key Rate**   This setting determines how fast the cursor moves when the Escape button or ENTER, BACKSPACE, or SPACE key is pressed on the BlackBerry. You have the options Off, Slow, or Fast, with the default setting being Slow. Keep in mind that Key Rate does not affect how fast you can type, only the cursor movement speed when using the four mentioned keys. It is also important to note that Key Rate controls the auto-capitalization feature, which lets you press and hold any key to produce the capitalized version of its letter. In order to use the auto-capitalization feature, you must have Key Rate enabled (either the Fast or Slow setting).

Security

The Security option enables you to password protect your BlackBerry. For example, let's say you step away from your desk for a few moments. Since you are leaving the BlackBerry unattended, someone else could access your private information. Using the Security feature, you can have the BlackBerry automatically lock itself after it has been idle for a certain period of time. This way, if you step away from the BlackBerry, it will automatically protect all information on your unit.

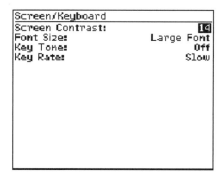

FIGURE 4-13   Screen/Keyboard options

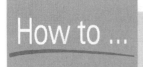
Use Password Protection

To set up password protection, follow these steps:

1. On the Options screen, scroll to and click Security.

2. Note the two options, Passwords and Security Timeout, as shown in Figure 4-14. Passwords is disabled by default. Click Disabled to access the menu for this screen, and then click Change Option.

3. Use the trackwheel to choose the Enable option. A New Password window appears, as shown in Figure 4-15.

4. Enter a desired password and click the trackwheel. You will be asked to confirm the password. Type the password again and click trackwheel.

5. Scroll to the Security Timeout value and click the trackwheel to see the menu for this option. Click Change Option and scroll to select a different timeout value (1 minute, 2 minutes, 5 minutes, 10 minutes, 20 minutes, and so on).

6. ISave your options. The unit is now password protected and will lock when the timeout value is reached.

You use this auto-lock feature by assigning a password to the BlackBerry. When the idle time expires, the BlackBerry locks itself, and you must enter the password to unlock the unit. To learn how to set up this feature, see "Use Password Protection."

When the security timeout occurs, the unit is locked and a blank Home screen appears that lists your name and any other information that you entered on the Owner screen, as shown in Figure 4-16. Press any key to get the password dialog box, and then enter your password to open the unit.

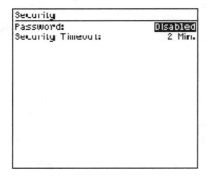

```
Security
Password:              Disabled
Security Timeout:       2 Min.
```

FIGURE 4-14   Security screen

TIP   *You can just enter the first letter of your password and the change over to the password dialog box will occur while you are typing. In other words, all you have to do is simply type your password to access the unit again.*

NOTE   *Once you set a password, you will need to reenter the password to access the Security options screen again. This prevents someone else from changing your password. You can then change the password by using the Change Password option on the menu or adjust the timeout value.*

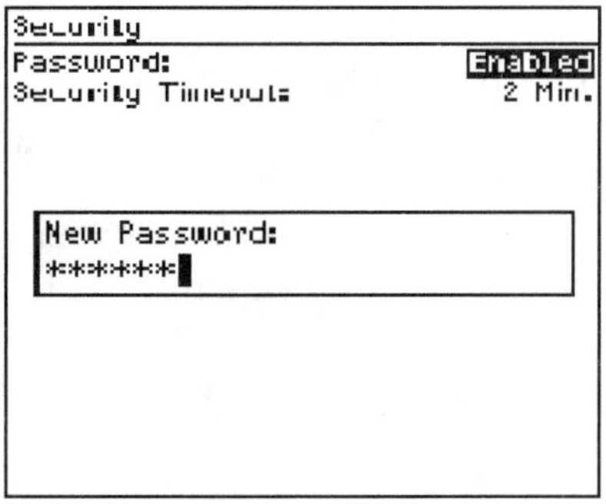

```
Security
Password:               Enabled
Security Timeout:        2 Min.


New Password:
*******
```

FIGURE 4-15   Enter password

4

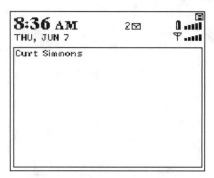

8:36 AM   2✉   0 ▮␣␣␣␣
THU, JUN 7   Ψ ␣␣␣␣

Curt Simmons

FIGURE 4-16   Locked BlackBerry

Once you have enabled password protection, you will see a Lock icon on your Home screen. This feature enables you to manually lock the BlackBerry instead of waiting for the timeout to occur. For example, if you are stepping away from your desk, you can lock the BlackBerry using the Lock icon so that is protected the moment you leave your desk.

By default, you can attempt to enter the password ten times to gain entry to the BlackBerry. After ten attempts, personal information may be erased and wireless communications are turned off. You will need to reload applications before the BlackBerry can be used again. This is a security feature of the BlackBerry, but also a reminder to you not to let anyone attempt to break your password—and not to forget it yourself!

Status

The Status option gives you a listing of a number of items on your BlackBerry and the current status of those items, as shown in Figure 4-17. This screen provides information only, as there is nothing you can configure here. However, this option is a great place to check on different components of your BlackBerry, especially if you believe there may be a problem with the unit. You'll find information about signal strength and battery life, free memory, the PIN and serial number of the BlackBerry, the software version, and related data.

4

Did you know?

Best Practices for Passwords

A common security problem in networking environments is passwords, and the BlackBerry is no exception. The problem isn't that passwords are not effective—the problem is that people tend to use passwords that can be guessed. If you need to secure your BlackBerry, keep the following password best practices in mind:

- Passwords should never contain your name, names of your family members, pet names, or any names that are related to your career.

- In order to meet standard complexity requirements, passwords should be at least seven characters in length.

- Passwords should contain a mixture of letters and numbers.

- If possible, do not use any real words or familiar number combinations (such as your phone number). For example, c32at17 is a much stronger password than cat3217.

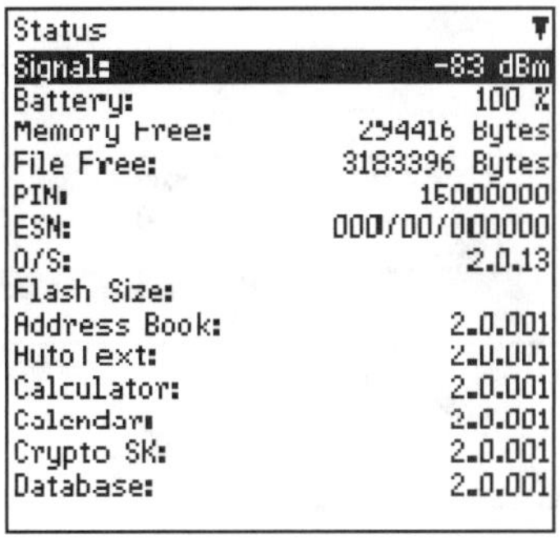

```
Status                     ▼
Signal:               -83 dBm
Battery:               100 %
Memory Free:      294416 Bytes
File Free:       3183396 Bytes
PIN:               15000000
ESN:         000/00/000000
O/S:                  2.0.13
Flash Size:
Address Book:        2.0.001
AutoText:            2.0.001
Calculator:          2.0.001
Calendar:            2.0.001
Crypto SK:           2.0.001
Database:            2.0.001
```

FIGURE 4-17   Status screen

Storage Mode

Let's say you finally get that two-month vacation to Paris and you want to leave your BlackBerry at home. What should you do? The BlackBerry 957 model provides a Storage Mode option whereby the BlackBerry can essentially go into hibernation while you are away for an extended period of time. Storage mode can be used if you will be away from your unit for more than two weeks, and this mode is more than just turning off the unit. Storage mode ceases all internal battery functions, including keeping track of the date and time.

If you want to activate storage mode, just access the Storage Mode option on the Options screen. A message appears telling you that the device will power off to save battery life, as shown in Figure 4-18. Click Yes to this message. A second message will appear, telling you that the BlackBerry will lose track of the current time. Click Yes to this message as well. A third message will appear telling you that a reset will be necessary to bring the unit out of storage mode. Click Yes to this message, and the fourth and final message asks you if you want to enter storage mode. Click Yes, and the BlackBerry will go into storage mode. Store the unit in a cool, dry place while you are away. All of your messages and data will be preserved and ready for you once you return.

Once you're ready to bring the BlackBerry back out of storage mode, you can simply insert the unit into the cradle charger and you'll see the Home screen momentarily. If you send your unit into storage mode with a full battery, you can also bring it out of storage mode by pressing the reset button on the back of the unit (you'll need a paperclip or other small, pointed object to reach the reset

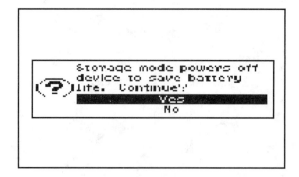

FIGURE 4-18   Storage mode

button). At this point, you will need to reset the date and time and you may need to turn on wireless connectivity by clicking the icon on your Home screen.

TIP   *You can also reset the date and time on the BlackBerry by synchronizing with your PC. See Chapter 5 to learn more.*

If you need to store your 950 BlackBerry, just remove the AA battery. After about 24 hours, the unit will go into a storage mode whereby it will not respond to any keystrokes. To reactive the unit, insert a new AA battery. You'll need to reset the date and time, but all of your messages and data will be preserved while you are away.

4

Chapter 5

Use the BlackBerry Desktop Software

How to...

■ Connect the BlackBerry to a PC

■ Back up and restore BlackBerry data

■ Install and remove applications

■ Synchronize with the PC

The BlackBerry is designed to be the only portable e-mail, Internet, and personal information management system that you need. With the BlackBerry, you can stay on the move while remaining connected. However, the BlackBerry is no island either, and on a periodic basis, you may need to connect the BlackBerry to your PC in order to synchronize the BlackBerry with other personal information management software, install new applications on the BlackBerry, and even back up or restore BlackBerry data. Research In Motion makes all of these tasks easy with the Desktop Manager software, which is included on the CD-ROM that comes with your BlackBerry unit. In this chapter, you'll get a chance to explore the desktop software and see how to install and use it with the BlackBerry.

Installing the BlackBerry Desktop Software

The BlackBerry desktop software is designed to be easy to use and easy to install. The BlackBerry provides you with the Desktop Manager software on CD-ROM and the RIM cradle that connects to your PC right out of the box. Typically, installation of the BlackBerry software on your PC is quick and painless.

Before attempting the installation of the desktop software, however, you should ensure that your system meets compatibility requirements. The BlackBerry Desktop Manager will install and run on the following setups:

■ Windows 95, Windows 98, Windows Me, Windows 2000, and Windows XP with at least 16MB of RAM

■ Windows NT 4.0 with at least 32MB of RAM

■ Macintosh using OS 7 or later and 16 MB or RAM.

As I mentioned in this chapter's introduction, the Desktop Manager allows you to synchronize personal information management (PIM) data on the BlackBerry with applications on your PC using RIM's Intellisync software. For example, I use Outlook 2000 for mail and calendar PIM data. I can synchronize my BlackBerry with Outlook 2000 so that my mail and my calendar data are always in sync between the computer and the BlackBerry.

If you want to synchronize PIM data between your computer and the BlackBerry, you must be using at least one of the supported PIM applications, listed here:

- ACT! 3.0.8/4.0.2
- GoldMine 3.2
- GoldMine 4.0
- GroupWise 5.2/5.5
- Lotus Notes 4.5/5.6
- Lotus Org GS/4.1 Notes
- Lotus Org GS/4.1 PIM
- Lotus Organizer 2.12/97
- Microsoft Exchange
- Microsoft Outlook 97/98/2000
- Microsoft Schedule+Browse File
- Microsoft Schedule+Default
- Microsoft Outlook Express 4.0
- Netscape browser

TIP   *I should note here that some software synchronizes with the BlackBerry better than others. Although all of these will synchronize, some of them are slower. For example, ACT! is much slower than Outlook 2000.*

Once you are ready to install the desktop software, installation is quick and easy. Locate the BlackBerry installation CD-ROM that shipped with your unit, and then follow the steps in "Install the BlackBerry Desktop Software."

TIP   *As with any installation, you should close all programs on your PC before beginning.*

Once the installation is complete, you'll see a desktop icon shortcut to the BlackBerry Desktop Manager as well as an icon in your System Tray, shown in Figure 5-1.

 ... **Install the BlackBerry Desktop Software**

To install the BlackBerry desktop software, just follow these steps:

1. Insert the BlackBerry CD-ROM into your PC's CD-ROM drive.

2. The BlackBerry autostart screen appears. The BlackBerry Installation Wizard tells you to close any open programs and click Next to begin the installation.

3. The Licensing agreement appears. Read the agreement, and click Yes to continue with the installation. If you click No, installation will cease.

4. Enter your name and company name. Click Next.

5. By default, the installation is saved in C:\Research In Motion\ BlackBerry [Internet Edition or Exchange Edition]. You can browse to a different location if desired. Click Next.

6. The programs window appears. By default, the software is stored in your Accessories folder. You can use the scroll bar to select a different storage location if you like.

7. Click Next. Installation of the BlackBerry desktop software occurs.

8. Click Finish to complete the installation. You can also choose to view the ReadMe file from this window and start the BlackBerry Desktop Manager.

FIGURE 5-1   A System Tray icon is added to your system

Connecting the BlackBerry to the PC

Once you've finished installing the BlackBerry software, your next step is to connect the BlackBerry to your PC. The docking cradle that shipped with your BlackBerry unit is used for this purpose. As noted in Chapter 3, the cradle serves as both a BlackBerry charging unit (for the 957) and a connectivity tool. In Chapter 3, you learned to connect the AC power adapter to the cradle connection end in order to charge the battery on the 957. You can leave that AC power connection in place if you like, but in order to synchronize with the PC, you plug the serial port connection end of the cradle to the serial port on your PC. If any other device is connected to the serial port, it must be removed so that the BlackBerry Desktop Manager can detect the BlackBerry unit. As you'll notice, the serial port connection only connects to the PC on one port and in one way. If you need help locating your PC's serial port, refer to your PC's documentation. Once you have attached the cradle to the PC, insert the BlackBerry into the cradle.

If you're using a newer PC, it may be possible that only USB ports are supported. In this case, you will need a USB-to-serial adapter in order to connect the cradle to the USB port. You'll need to install the adapter software on the PC before the BlackBerry will be recognized. You can purchase a USB-to-serial adapter at most computer stores in your area or at online computer stores. Follow the manufacturer's instructions for installation.

Once you have connected the cradle to the PC and inserted the BlackBerry into the cradle, your next task is to configure the Desktop Manager to recognize the BlackBerry. To configure it, just follow the steps in "Configure the Desktop Manager Port."

NOTE   *The maximum speed that data can be transferred between the unit and the PC is 115,200 bps. However, it is possible that your serial connection cannot transmit data this fast. If it cannot, a lower setting will be used. As a general rule, you want to leave the maximum setting enabled so that data will be transferred as quickly as possible between the BlackBerry and the PC.*

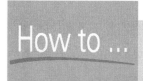 **Configure the Desktop Manager Port**

To configure the Desktop Manager to recognize the BlackBerry, just follow these steps:

1. Double-click the Desktop Manager icon on your PC desktop to open it.

2. The Desktop Manager appears, as shown in Figure 5-2.

3. Click Options | Serial Settings. The Serial Settings dialog box appears, as shown in Figure 5-3.

4. In the Serial Settings dialog box, click the drop-down menu, select the communications port the unit is attached to (typically COM1), and then click the Detect button. A message appears telling to you to make sure that the unit is attached to the cradle. Click OK.

5. Detection occurs. A message appears telling you that the handheld was found, as shown in Figure 5-4. Click OK. You do not need to make any changes for the maximum speed settings at this time. Also, do not click the check box at the bottom of the dialog box unless you want to use USB-to-serial conversion. See the Desktop Manager help files for more information.

6. Click OK to exit the Serial Settings dialog box.

If you have problems getting the Desktop Manager to detect your BlackBerry, check the connection again and make sure that the serial connection is firmly attached. If detection still does not occur, the problem almost always involves the serial port, in that the PC believes some other device is connected to the port. Use Device Manager to make certain that all external devices that are not attached to the computer have been removed, and as always, try rebooting the PC. PC communication with the BlackBerry always works best on COM1, so you may need to remove some other devices or applications using COM1.

5

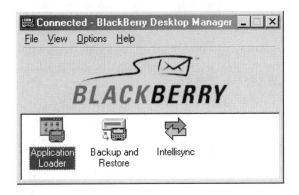

FIGURE 5-2 FIGURE 5-2   The Desktop Manager

There are two other known issues that you might experience when trying to connect your BlackBerry to the PC. Check out the following list if you are having connection problems:

- **Password prompt**   If you are prompted for a password when you connect your BlackBerry to the PC, then you have enabled BlackBerry password

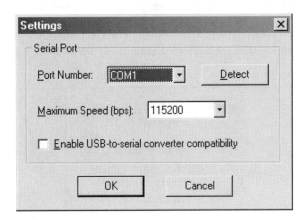

FIGURE 5-3   Serial Settings dialog box

protection in Options (see Chapter 4). Enter the password you configured, or access Options to remove password protection.

■ **Laptop problems**   If you are using the BlackBerry cradle with a laptop, the connection may be broken from time to time if your laptop dynamically reassigns ports. If this happens, just redetect the BlackBerry using the Serial Settings dialog box.

Using the Desktop Manager

Once the BlackBerry desktop software is installed and the BlackBerry is connected to the PC, you're all set to begin using the Desktop Manager software for PIM synchronization as well as backup and application updates. I'll discuss each of these features in the following sections, but before doing so, let's first take a look at what is available on the Desktop Manager interface.

The Desktop Manager interface is a basic and friendly window-and-menu interface with which you are familiar. You see the Application Loader, Backup and Restore, and Intellisync icons in the window through which you can easily access these features. The following four menu options are also available:

■ **File**   Open a desired Desktop Manager feature (such as Intellisync) by selecting the icon in the window and clicking File | Open. Or, you can just double-click the icon in the window. You can also use the File menu to exit the Desktop Manager application.

■ **View**   The View menu allows you to change the appearance of the Desktop Manager. You have two simple options here. First, you can

FIGURE 5-4   Confirmation message

use either large icons or small icons (large are used by default). Second, you can choose whether or not you want to you see the BlackBerry unit's personal identification number (PIN) and status (connected to the Desktop Manager or not). If you choose to use these items, the information appears on the Desktop Manager bottom window border, as shown in Figure 5-5.

■ **Options**   The Options menu allows you to hide the Desktop Manager from your view when it is minimized, and you can access the Serial Settings dialog box, which was covered in the previous section.

■ **Help**   Access the Desktop Manager online help from this menu.

Backup and Restore

The Desktop Manager software contains a feature called Backup and Restore that enables you to back up everything on the BlackBerry or only selected items to a file on your PC. In the event of some problem, you can use the backup file to restore the data on your PC. Backup is one of those items that most of us tend to ignore—until there is a problem, anyway. Most PC operating systems include backup software that is often not used in a way that consistently protects data.

Since the BlackBerry is a portable device, you are always in jeopardy of losing data. The unit may be damaged or stolen (or even lost), and the more you use your BlackBerry, the more important the information stored on the unit will become. You can alleviate any fears of losing information by simply performing a backup

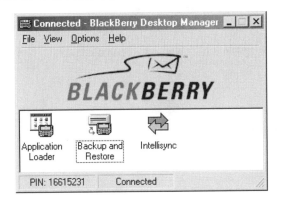

FIGURE 5-5   PIN and status display

and keeping those backup files on your PC. In the event of a problem, you can easily recover any lost information.

If you open the Desktop Manager, you see the Backup and Restore icon. Double-click the icon (or select it and click File | Open) to open the Backup and Restore dialog box, as shown in Figure 5-6. The following sections show you how to use each component of Backup and Restore that is available to you.

Full Backup

A full backup saves everything on your BlackBerry unit to a file on your computer's hard disk. By default, the file is named "Backup-(*yyyy-mm-dd*)," where *yyyy* is the year, *mm* is the month, and *dd* is the date. So, a typical backup filename might be Backup-(2001–07–22). This filename tells you that the backup file was created on July 22, 2001. You don't have to use this default filename, however, as you can easily change it to whatever you want.

To begin a full backup, just click the Backup button in the Backup and Restore dialog box. This opens a typical Windows Save As dialog box, shown in Figure 5-7, where you can select the filename and choose a location on your computer in which to save the file. (You might consider creating a new folder in My

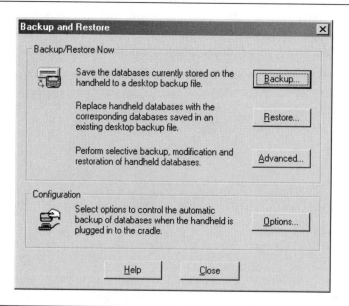

FIGURE 5-6   Backup and Restore dialog box

Documents for this purpose. If you choose a different folder, just remember the folder name and where it is located on your computer.) Also, notice that the backup file will be saved as an .ipd file. This file type is specific to the BlackBerry, so you should not change the extension in order to save the file as some other type. Doing so may prevent you from using the backup file for a restoration.

Once you make your selections, click the Save button. The backup process begins, and you see a status indicator window, as shown in Figure 5-8. From this point, the process is automatic and requires no further intervention from you. Once the backup is complete, you'll notice the .ipd file appears in the Windows location you selected.

TIP | *Subsequent backup operations do not "write over" the previous file. For example, let's say you created a backup job yesterday. When you create one today, the new file is given a different filename—it does not overwrite the old file unless you assign the same name and choose to replace the old file. As you can see, when several different backup files are available, the inclusion of date names as part of the backup files can be very helpful.*

Did you know? Backup Filenames

As you are working with Backup and Restore, it is very important that you use unique names. As you create backup files, you want to be able to distinguish one file from the next, and you also want to know what file is most current. For example, if you created a backup file on Monday and one on Wednesday, and your BlackBerry has a catastrophic failure on Friday, you will want to use the Wednesday backup file in order to restore the most current information to the BlackBerry unit. For this reason, a filename that includes the date is very effective. I recommend that you use the default filename, but if you want to use another naming convention, do consider using one that provides the current date within the name.

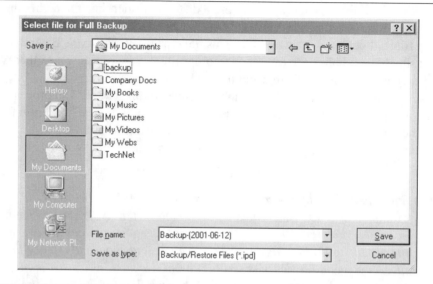

FIGURE 5-7   Saving a BlackBerry backup file

Restoring a Backup Job

In the unlikely event that something happens to your BlackBerry, you can easily perform a restoration. This function will restore all information contained in the backup file you selected. For example, if you performed a full backup, then you can use the file to write all of the backed up information to the BlackBerry in order to restore the BlackBerry to its previous working order.

The Restore feature basically works just like the Backup feature. In the Backup and Restore dialog box, click the Restore button. This action takes you to a typical Windows Select a File dialog box where you can browse for the backup file you want to use for the restoration. Select the file and click open. You see a transfer window, and you may see a message, shown in Figure 5-9, telling you that any current information in various databases will be replaced with the information in the backup file. Once the restoration is complete, you are returned to the Backup and Restore dialog box, and your BlackBerry unit should now be restored and functional.

Performing a Selective Backup

The Backup button on the Backup and Restore dialog box performs a full backup—everything on the BlackBerry is backed up. However, what if you only want to

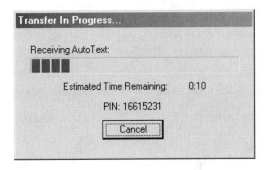

FIGURE 5-8   Backup progress

back up selected items, such as your e-mail or address book? The BlackBerry
Desktop Manager gives you the option to back up only selected items using
the Advanced button in the Backup and Restore dialog box.

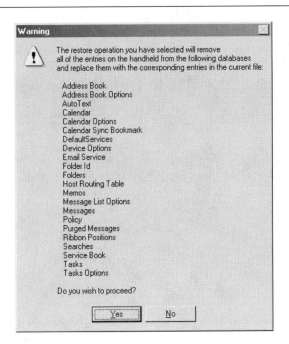

FIGURE 5-9   Warning message

If you click the Advanced button, you see a dual-pane window, shown in Figure 5-10, that lists the contents of the BlackBerry databases and the contents of your backup file on the PC (if one currently exists).

You can perform a few different actions on this window:

- Create a new backup file using the items you select.

- Replace items in a current backup file with updated items from the BlackBerry.

- Delete or edit certain items that currently exist in a backup file.

- Perform a selective restoration.

Each of these actions can be very helpful and important, and I'll show you how to do each of them in the following three sections.

Create a New Backup File with Selected Items   You can easily use the Advanced window to create a new backup file that only contains the BlackBerry items that you select. This feature enables you to create a selective file, such as one that contains your e-mail and addresses. Once you have created it, you can update the

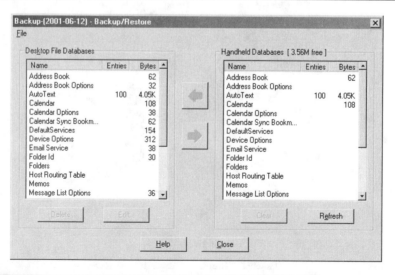

FIGURE 5-10   Advanced Backup window

file as often as you like without having to perform a full backup each time you want to back up e-mail or your address book (or any other item you select). To create a new backup file and perform a selective backup, just follow the steps presented in "Back Up Selected Items to a New File."

 *If you want to transfer several items at one time, select the first item, and then hold down the* CTRL *key and select the additional items that you want. Next, click the transfer button to transfer all of the items at the same time.*

5

Update Items in a Current Backup File   Let's say you have a full backup file, but you only want to update the backup file with folders and your address book. Because of the nature of your business, you want to back up these two items every day, but you do not want to create a new selective backup file for the two items and you do not want to create a full backup file every day. What to do?

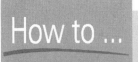 ## Back Up Selected Items to a New File

To back up selected items to a new file, follow these steps:

1. Ensure that the BlackBerry is connected to the PC. In the Backup and Restore dialog box, click the Advanced button.

2. In the Advanced window, click File | New to create a new backup file. Note that the left pane now appears blank and a new default backup name now appears at the top left of the window.

3. In the right pane of the window, select the item that you want to back up and click the arrow button pointing to the left window. The transfer takes place. You can then select another item and click the arrow button to transfer another item. As you can see in Figure 5-11, I have already transferred my Address Book and am now transferring folders.

4. When you're done, click the File menu and click Save to accept the default name given to your new backup file. To change the name, click Save As and give the file the desired name.

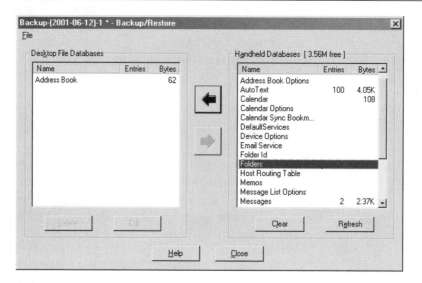

FIGURE 5-11   Selective backup transfer

The Desktop Manager gives you this flexibility by allowing you to replace items in a current backup file with new database files from the BlackBerry. In the same manner, you can create one backup file of selected items, and then update that file over and over as necessary. Both of these features prevent you from having to create multiple backup files—you can just update the ones you have. To update items in a current backup file, follow the steps in "Update Items in a Current Backup File."

Delete or Edit Items in a Backup File   As you may have noticed, the Advanced screen gives you both Delete and Edit buttons for the backup file. You can select any item in the backup file and delete it. You might ask, "Why?" There's a good reason. Let's say that you want to perform a full restoration to your BlackBerry, except for one item, such as the address book. Before performing the full restoration, you can simply delete the address book item out of the backup file. When the restoration is performed, the address book on the BlackBerry will not be altered.

You can also directly edit the address book and AutoText items in the backup file from your desktop. For example, let's say that you want to make a number of changes to the AutoText database. Rather than doing this on the BlackBerry, you can perform the action on your PC, and then just transfer the database to your

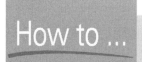 **Update Items in a Current Backup File**

To update items in a current backup file, follow these steps:

1. Ensure that the BlackBerry is connected to the PC. In the Backup and Restore dialog box, click the Advanced button.

2. Click File | Open. In the Windows browse window, locate the backup file that you want to update. Select the file, and then click Open. The file is opened in the left pane of the Advanced window.

3. In the right pane, select the item that you want to update in the backup file, and then click the arrow pointing to the left side of the window. This action replaces the older item in the backup file. Repeat the process as desired.

4. When you're done, click File | Save to save your updates.

5

BlackBerry. To edit the address book or AutoText item, just select the item and click the Edit button. As you can see in Figure 5-12, a familiar window appears in which you can directly make changes to the item and save it into the backup file.

Perform a Selective Restoration   Just as you can selectively back up and update backup items, you can selectively restore items as well. Let's say that you have a full backup file, but you only want to restore the address book on your BlackBerry. No problem—just use the Advanced window to select the address book in the backup file, and then click the arrow pointing to the BlackBerry. A message appears telling you that the BlackBerry's database for that item will be deleted and replaced with the one from the backup file. Just click Yes to continue.

Backup Options

The final button in the Backup and Restore dialog box is the Options button. The Options button opens the Backup and Restore Options dialog box, shown in Figure 5-13, which allows you to schedule backups to occur automatically.

As you can see, you have a few basic options here:

■ You can automatically back up the device every *x* days. Use the menu to select the desired number of days.

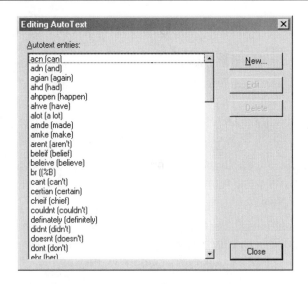

FIGURE 5-12   Edit feature

■ You can choose to back up everything on the handheld, or everything
    except your messages and PIM data.

Simply select the options you want to use and click OK.

Application Loader

The Application Loader is a wizard that allows you to update applications on your
BlackBerry and even remove them if you want. This tool provides an easy way to
update operating system components as updates become available, or to install
additional applications that may be available from third parties.

When you first begin using the Desktop Manager, a dialog box may appear
asking you to update the BlackBerry software to the most current version available
on the CD. You can choose to install the update, or if you are certain that your
BlackBerry has the most current software version, you can choose to ignore the
message. Either way, the process for installing and removing new software on the
BlackBerry functions in the same way with the provided wizard. To learn how to
use this wizard, see "Run the Application Loader."

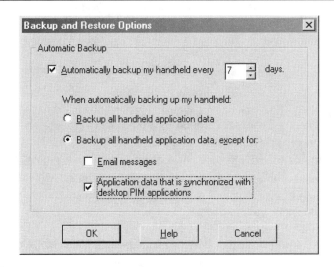

FIGURE 5-13   Backup and Restore Options dialog box

How Often Should You Back Up?

A common question concerns the frequency of backup—after all, how often should you back up data on your BlackBerry? That question is subjective of course, but the idea is to have the most current data backed up at all times so that it can be restored in the case of a failure. Here are a few guidelines that will help you make a decision that is right for you:

- If data changes infrequently on your BlackBerry, back it up once a week.

- If data changes often, back up every three days.

- If data is critical, especially e-mail messages, back up every day.

- If you make a number of configuration changes on the BlackBerry, back it up that day.

Remember, if you want to remove an application from your BlackBerry, just launch the Application Loader again and remove the check beside the application that you want to remove, and then complete the wizard instructions.

Intellisync

Intellisync, which is software developed by Puma Software, is used to synchronize the BlackBerry with applications on your PC. Specifically, the BlackBerry can synchronize with other PIM software, such as Outlook, Lotus Notes, Netscape, and so on. This feature enables you to use PIM software on the PC while synchronizing data with the BlackBerry. Whether you are connected or traveling, you always have access to the same information.

If you are using the BlackBerry in a corporate LAN with Exchange or Lotus Domino, then you probably do not need to configure anything—your BlackBerry is probably already configured to work with the PIM software used by your company. Check with your network administrator to be sure.

If you double-click the Intellisync icon in the Desktop Manager, the Intellisync dialog box appears, as shown in Figure 5-16. The available options are explored in the following sections.

Configuring PIM Applications   Before you can use the Intellisync software, you must configure the desired PIM applications to work with the BlackBerry. The Intellisync window helps you easily configure the supported application(s) for this purpose. The following steps show you how to configure the PIM application for synchronization with the BlackBerry:

1. Ensure that your BlackBerry is connected to the PC, and then open the Desktop Manager.

2. Double-click the Intellisync icon, and then click the Configure PIM button in the Intellisync dialog box.

3. The Configuration dialog box appears, as shown in Figure 5-17. Select the type of application that you want to synchronize with (address book, calendar, MemoPad, or tasks), and then click the Choose button.

How to ...   **Run the Application Loader**

To run the application loader, follow these steps:

1. Open the Desktop Manager and double-click the Application Loader icon.

2. Make sure your BlackBerry is connected to the PC, and then click Next to continue. The wizard initializes the BlackBerry and reads current information.

3. In the next window, shown in Figure 5-14, you see the applications that are currently loaded or available for loading, such as the calculator, MemoPad, and others. Click the check box next to any of these items to install the most current version from the CD, and remove the check beside any item you want removed from the BlackBerry.

4. If you have an additional item you want to install, such as something you downloaded from the Internet, click the Add button and browse for the file. The wizard will look for an Application Loader information file (*.ali). Just select the file, click Open and it will be added to your list of available files for installation.

5. Once your list is complete, just click Next, but do remember that any applications not selected will be deleted from the BlackBerry if they are currently present on the handheld.

6. The next window presents you with two check box options, as shown in Figure 5-15. The first option enables you to erase any application data from the handheld. This feature is helpful if you want to lose old data before performing the upgrade. By default, this option is not selected. The second option erases all applications from the BlackBerry before loading the new applications. This option can help you in the recovery of a failed installation, but is typically not something you should enable unless necessary, so do be careful not to erase applications accidentally. Make any needed selections, and click Next.

7. A summary window appears. Review your settings and click Finish. The transfer occurs, and once it is complete, the BlackBerry system is reinitialized.

5

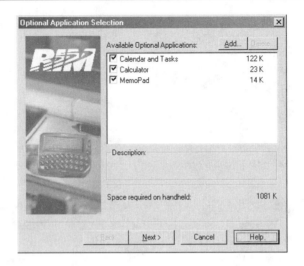

FIGURE 5-14 Install applications

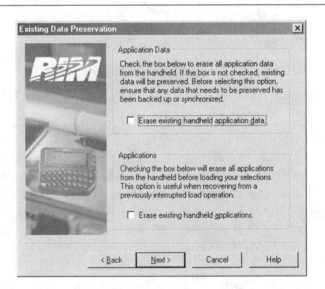

FIGURE 5-15 Additional options

FIGURE 5-16   Intellisync dialog box

4. In the Choose Translator dialog box, select the application that you want to synchronize with. As you can see in Figure 5-18, I use Microsoft Outlook, so I select this option from the provided list.

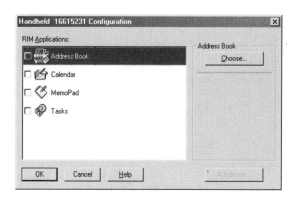

FIGURE 5-17   Select application type

5. Ensure that the Synchronize radio button is selected, and then click OK. You are returned to the Configuration dialog box—notice that the window reports that synchronization will occur with the application you selected.

6. Click the Advanced button, which is now active in the Configuration dialog box, and the Advanced Settings dialog box appears as shown in Figure 5-19.

7. You have a few different options to choose from on the Advanced tabs, as detailed in the following list. Once you're done configuring these Advanced options to your desired settings, just click Close, which returns you to the Configuration dialog box.

   ■ On the Confirmation tab, you can choose to get a confirmation message before any records are changed or deleted. Essentially, you'll get a prompt on the PC screen that you must click for the process to continue. These settings may be helpful, but you will be required to babysit the synchronization process if you click this option.

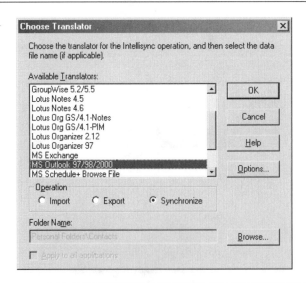

FIGURE 5-18   Select the desired application

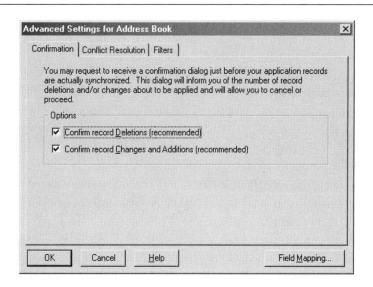

FIGURE 5-19   Advanced Settings dialog box

- Also notice the Field Mappings button at the bottom of the Advanced Settings dialog box. If you click this button, you can make adjustments to the way various database fields between the BlackBerry and the PIM application translate. For example, in an address book, you would want the first name of an entry to correspond to the first name of the entry in the PIM application, and so forth. These mappings just ensure accuracy. Typically, you don't need to change anything here, but you can correct or adjust mappings as necessary.

- If you click the Conflict Resolution tab, you see some options for how synchronization handles information conflicts between the BlackBerry and the PIM application. As shown in the list in Figure 5-20, you can choose for RIM to win or the application to win, as well as other options. By default, you are prompted to make a decision should a conflict occur, and this is a good setting to keep selected. Some PIMs allow the management of multiple databases, so if a conflict is detected, the wrong database may be selected (which can turn into a huge mess). I recommend you keep this setting selected.

- You can use the Filters tab to restrict synchronization. For example, in Microsoft Outlook, you might choose to use a filter that restricts

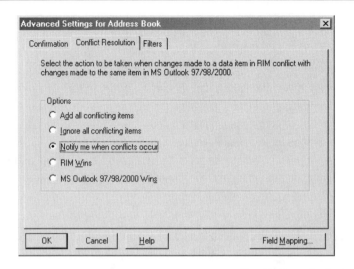

Advanced Settings for Address Book

Confirmation Conflict Resolution | Filters |

Select the action to be taken when changes made to a data item in RIM conflict with
changes made to the same item in MS Outlook 97/98/2000.

Options

- ○ A̲dd all conflicting items
- ○ I̲gnore all conflicting items
- ● N̲otify me when conflicts occur
- ○ RIM W̲ins
- ○ MS Outlook 97/98/2000 Wins̲

[OK]   [Cancel]   [H̲elp]   [Field M̲apping...]

FIGURE 5-20   Conflict Resolution tab

private data, and so forth. You can enable new filters here as needed by
clicking New, entering a filter name, and then creating a condition for
the filter.

8. Click the OK button in the Configuration dialog box to finish.

> **TIP** *The Advanced options may be slightly different, depending on the type of PIM application you want to synchronize with. For example, if you choose calendar, there is an additional tab that asks you about time and date synchronization. These options are self-explanatory. I explore filters and filter creation in other chapters.*

> **TIP** *If you choose to synchronize the BlackBerry's date and time with what is on the PC, make absolutely certain the PC clock is correct. If you synchronize and the date and time are not accurate on the PC, it will disrupt any functions on your BlackBerry that use date and time stamps (such as alarms, e-mail stamps, and so on).*

Synchronizing   When you have configured the PIM applications that you want to
synchronize with, you're ready to actually run a synchronization. Notice that in the
Intellisync dialog box, you have the option to synchronize the date and time on the

Importing and Exporting

5

What do you do if you already have an address book, calendar, MemoPad, or tasks list in a PIM application on your PC, and you want to put that information on the BlackBerry without translating any data from the BlackBerry to the PC or vice versa? This is the reason you are given the option to import or export instead of synchronize. By importing or exporting, you can exchange information between the device and the PC without synchronizing data.

PC with the BlackBerry—an option you can enable if you want by clicking the check box.

When you're ready to synchronize, just click the Synchronize now button. The Intellisync software inspects the synchronization and prompts you to OK it by giving you a report of the number of records that will be synchronized (if you kept the check boxes selected on the Confirmation tab of the Advanced Settings dialog box). Once you accept the changes, synchronization occurs and you see an Intellisync progress window, as shown in Figure 5-21.

TIP

Once synchronization is done, click the View Log button to see a log file of the entire synchronization process and all of files that were synchronized.

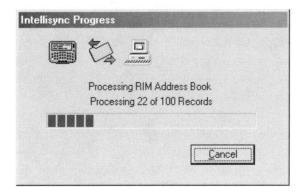

Intellisync Progress

Processing RIM Address Book
Processing 22 of 100 Records

Cancel

FIGURE 5-21   Intellisync progress window

Enabling Auto start   You can enable synchronization to occur automatically when your BlackBerry is first connected to your computer, if you so choose. In the Intellisync dialog box, just click the Auto start button. You'll see two check box options for synchronizing PIM and date and time when the BlackBerry is first connected to the PC. Just click the check boxes to enable these features. If you use the auto-synch option, however, check your import/export configuration, because this is the configuration that will be used each time the unit is connected. In other words, you may only get data moved from the BlackBerry to the PIM and not vice versa. Just check out your settings and make sure everything is correct before using auto-synch.

Part 3

Communicate with the BlackBerry

Chapter 6

Getting Started with E-mail

How to...

- Get connected
- Compose and send e-mail
- Receive and read e-mail

Your BlackBerry is a true e-mail solution; after all, wireless e-mail is the real reason Research In Motion created the first BlackBerry. The good news is that BlackBerry e-mail is easy to use and very powerful. In fact, you can do most of the things with the BlackBerry e-mail application that you can do with your desktop e-mail client. In this chapter, you'll explore network connectivity, and then once you are connected, you can begin sending and receiving e-mail. In Chapter 7, I will dig a little deeper into the options and features of e-mail management. So this chapter and Chapter 7 are your complete references for how to do everything with your BlackBerry's e-mail feature.

Getting Connected with Your BlackBerry

Your BlackBerry contains a wireless radio modem that enables the unit to connect with the wireless network. When you first receive your BlackBerry unit, you will need to turn on the wireless modem and register with a network. If you are using the BlackBerry Enterprise Edition, which works with Microsoft Exchange or Lotus Domino, the radio may already be turned on and the unit registered. Your network administrator will give you specific instructions about what you need to do or not do in order to get connected.

In any case, connectivity involves a three-step process. First, you need to turn the wireless radio modem on if it is not turned on already. On the BlackBerry Home screen, look at the wireless icon. On both the 957 and 950 models, the icon will appear as an airplane if the radio modem is turned on and as a wireless tower if it is turned off. If you need to turn the radio modem on, just roll the trackwheel to select the icon, and then click the trackwheel—that's all there is to it. As you can see in Figure 6-1, the radio modem is currently turned on.

> **TIP** *Remember to turn the radio modem off if you will be out of coverage for an extended period of time or traveling on an airplane. Keeping the modem turned off when not in use will greatly conserve battery power.*

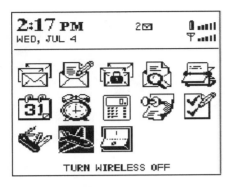

| FIGURE 6-1 | Radio modem is turned on |

The next step to getting connected is to register your unit with the network. This process is easy and basically involves sending a registration notice over the wireless network. Check out "Register Your BlackBerry" for step-by-step instructions

> **TIP** *If the registration process does not seem to be working, you may be out of the network connectivity area. Access the Home screen and ensure that the radio indicator icon in the upper right of the screen shows the icon you expect for connectivity, not an "x."*

Once registration is complete, you may need to activate your account, particularly if you are using the BlackBerry Internet Edition. The process for account activation depends on your service provider. Some have you visit an Internet site and login in order to activate your account, and some require no action at all. Consult your service provider's documentation for details.

Getting Started with E-mail

The BlackBerry contains four Home screen icons, described in the following list, that help you effectively and efficiently use e-mail:

■ **Messages**   All messages that you receive are stored in the Messages screen, and any messages that you have created that are waiting to be sent are stored here as well. You can think of Messages as your inbox and outbox.

 **Register Your BlackBerry**

To register your BlackBerry on the network, follow these steps:

1. On the Home screen, open the Options icon by clicking it.

2. Using your trackwheel, scroll to Network Settings and click the trackwheel.

3. In the Network Settings screen, you see the Roaming Settings option first. Ensure that this setting is correctly set to U.S. or Canada. The Radio setting should be set to On (this is the same setting you adjusted on the Home screen), and finally, you see your current network status, which is probably Inactive.

4. To activate your unit, click the trackwheel and then click Register Now, as shown in Figure 6-2. A message is sent over the network that activates your unit. Once the unit is activated, you will receive an e-mail message confirming your registration within a few seconds.

5. Click the trackwheel and then click Save Options. This returns you to the Options screen. Click the Escape button to return to the Home screen.

FIGURE 6-2 Register Now option

Did you know?

The Case of the Disappearing Registration

Consider this scenario: You register your BlackBerry on the network and all is well. Three days later, it appears that your unit is not registered, so you register the unit once more. A week later, the same thing happens again. What is happening with the registration?

The likely cause of the "disappearing registration" is the application loader. You have probably loaded or unloaded applications that may cause your unit to require re-registration. For some updates, this issue occurs, so the best thing to do is to re-register the unit anytime new applications are loaded or unloaded.

- ■ **Compose**   The Compose option allows you to create and send an e-mail message.

- ■ **Saved Messages**   You can choose to save any message that you receive (or even your own that you are about to send), and these saved messages are stored in the Saved Messages Folder.

- ■ **Search Messages**   The BlackBerry has an excellent search feature that allows you to search messages for keywords, including sender or recipient.

The four icons provide you with an easy place to move around from e-mail to e-mail function. This design works much better than one e-mail program with multiple, confusing menus, as you'll see in the sections that follow. So, let's get started. The next section shows you how to compose and send an e-mail message.

Composing and Sending E-mail

Composing and sending e-mail on the BlackBerry is a real snap. Before I show you the process for composing and sending an e-mail, however, let's consider two important ways that the BlackBerry can send e-mail. The BlackBerry can send e-mail using an e-mail address, such as *myname@myisp.com*, or it can send to another BlackBerry unit using a personal identification number (PIN). The PIN is essentially a unique number given to each BlackBerry unit when it is manufactured. You can locate the PIN on either the back of the BlackBerry case or in your documentation, depending on your model.

Sending e-mail via PIN number only works if you are sending e-mail to another BlackBerry user. Obviously, you must have the PIN of the unit you are sending e-mail to for this to work. Why use a PIN number? After all, an e-mail address is easier to remember. However, e-mail sent via a PIN number is actually faster than e-mail sent using an address because there are less server "hops," or transfers, that must take place before the message is delivered. If you want to use PIN numbers, you can enter them into address book entries, just as you would an e-mail address. In most cases, you will simply use an e-mail address, but if you are communicating with several other BlackBerry users, consider trying the PIN.

To compose an e-mail, select the Compose icon on your Home screen and click it with your trackwheel, or just press C on your keyboard.

SHORTCUT   *Because message composition is a common task on the BlackBerry, you can also compose a message by clicking the trackwheel to bring up menu options and clicking Compose Message when you are in the Address Book, Messages, or Saved Messages screens. This feature also prevents you from having to exit these applications and return to the Home screen in order to send a message; instead, you can do so directly from these folders as well!*

When you open the Compose application, you are taken immediately to your address book, as shown in Figure 6-3. You can learn more about creating address book entries in Chapter 8.

The PIN Is Mightier than the Address

The PIN is mightier than the address—or at least faster when two BlackBerry units are communicating with each other. When you send an e-mail to a BlackBerry user via e-mail address, that e-mail address is resolved into a PIN number. This action may require several servers and takes longer than using the PIN number. Because the e-mail address requires more server "hops," messages are slower. If you want to make things more speedy, try using a PIN number when possible.

| To: |
| [Use Once] |
| Darren Meigs |
| Jeff Gladstone |
| Kay Anderson |

FIGURE 6-3   Address book

6

If the person to whom you want to send an e-mail message is configured with an address book entry, just scroll to that person's name and click the trackwheel. A menu appears. Click the Use Email option (or Use PIN option) to send an e-mail to that person. If you want to send an e-mail to someone who is not in the address book but you do not want to add his or her contact information to the address book, choose the Use Once option, as shown in Figure 6-3. When you click Use Once, a menu appears from which you can choose either Use Email or Use PIN and then enter the e-mail address or PIN number. When you're done, just click the trackwheel and then click Continue.

Once you select the addressee or have entered a Use Once address or PIN, the e-mail composition screen appears, as shown in Figure 6-4. On this screen, you can enter a subject for the message and you can type the message that you want. Maneuver between the Subject line and the message area with the trackwheel.

Allow me to point out two helpful features the BlackBerry provides for e-mail composition. First, you do not have to capitalize the first word of a sentence. The BlackBerry knows when you start a new sentence and will automatically capitalize the first word for you. Also, you do not have to place a period at the end of a sentence. When a sentence is complete, just press the SPACE key two times and a period will automatically be inserted at the end of the previous sentence. These are just two time-saving features the BlackBerry provides for you!

When you are done typing your message, click the trackwheel to see the menu, and then click either Send Message or Save Message. Use the Save Message option if you did not finish typing the e-mail or need to proof it again before sending it.

Did you know?

I Only See the PIN Option—Not the E-mail Address!

When you are attempting to compose e-mail, it is possible that you may only see the option to use a PIN number instead of an e-mail address. This issue can occur for two different reasons:

- You are not registered on the network. You have either not registered or need to re-register due to software changes that have occurred on your BlackBerry or due to some kind of server problem. If you have not registered the BlackBerry or need to re-register, only the Use PIN option appears.

- You previously used a PIN number for the particular address book entry. If you use a PIN number, then the default menu option will prompt you to use the PIN.

Once you click Send Message, it is immediately sent over the wireless network—there is nothing else for you to do. However, if you are out of the coverage area or if wireless connectivity is turned off, the message is placed

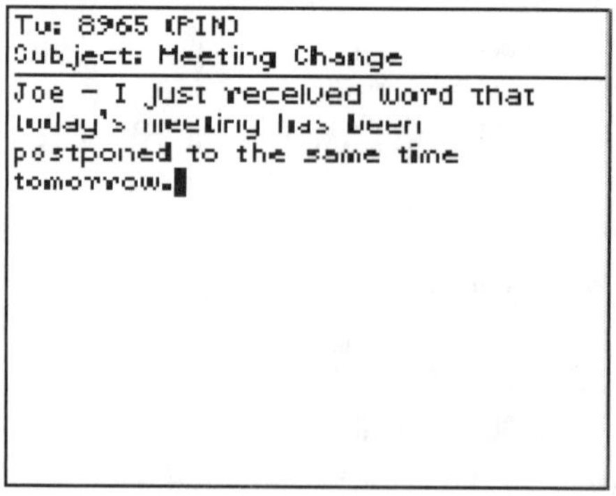

```
To: 8965 (PIN)
Subject: Meeting Change
Joe - I just received word that
today's meeting has been
postponed to the same time
tomorrow.
```

FIGURE 6-4   Composed message

in your Messages folder, where it is stored until your BlackBerry is connected to the network again.

> **TIP** *If messages must be held in the Messages folder until they can be sent, they are automatically sent out once connectivity is established—you don't have to do anything in order to send the held messages.*

Additional Composition Options

The BlackBerry e-mail screen provides you with a simple interface through which you can type an e-mail to another person. However, the BlackBerry also knows that life is not that simple, so some additional messaging options are also available, all of which are found on the menu.

6

If you click the trackwheel, you see several other field options, which are explained in the following bullet list:

■ **Add To**   This option adds another To field so you can send the e-mail to more than one person. In a typical desktop e-mail program, you have one To line on which you can enter multiple addresses. On the BlackBerry, you can only have one address per field line, so if you want to send the e-mail to multiple people, you need to add more To lines, as you can see in Figure 6-5.

> **TIP** *Save battery power! Use the additional To field or the CC or BCC fields, explained in the following bullet list points, in order to send the same message to several people. Sending multiple messages consumes more battery power than sending a single message addressed to several people.*

■ **Add CC**   CC stands for *carbon copy*, a term that is held over from our old typewriter and snail mail days. When someone is CC'd, he or she is given a copy of the message. In terms of e-mail, for all practical purposes, a person who is CC'd receives the message just as anyone in the To field does. Individuals that are CC'd can see who the message was sent to and any other recipients that are CC'd. CC'd recipients can also reply or forward a message, so the end result is that there is little difference between who is on the To list and who is on the CC list. In business, however, the CC field usually means that the message is for information purposes and does not necessarily need a response as it might from the To recipient. To add a CC field, just click the option using the menu and select

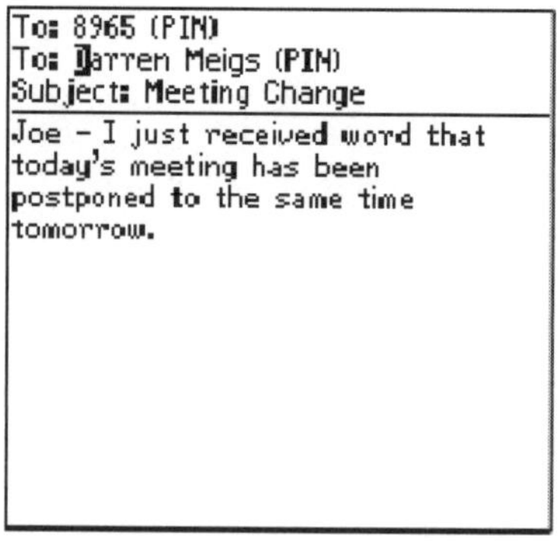

```
To: 8965 (PIN)
To: Darren Meigs (PIN)
Subject: Meeting Change

Joe - I just received word that
today's meeting has been
postponed to the same time
tomorrow.
```

FIGURE 6-5   You can add more To fields.

someone from the address book (or choose the Use Once option), as shown
in Figure 6-6.

■ **Add BCC**   The BCC field, which stands for *Blind Carbon Copy*, has the
same qualities as the CC field in that the recipient can read the message
and see who it was sent to and who was CC'd, but any To or CC'd recipients
cannot see any BCC recipients. Additionally, BCC recipients cannot see
each other either. To add a BCC field, just click the option using the menu
and select someone from the address book (or choose the Use Once option),
as shown in Figure 6-7.

```
To: 8965 (PIN)
Cc: Darren Meigs (PIN)
Subject: Meeting Change

Joe - I just received word that
today's meeting has been
postponed to the same time
tomorrow.
```

FIGURE 6-6   CC field

```
To: 9965 (PIN)
Xcc: Darren Meigs (PIN)
Subject: Meeting Change
Joe - I just received word that
today's meeting has been
postponed to the same time
tomorrow.
```

| FIGURE 6-7 | BCC field |

NOTE   *If you make a mistake and accidentally add someone using the To, CC, or BCC lines, just click the trackwheel to see the menu and click Delete Address. Click Yes in response to the confirmation message that appears, and the address (and field) you added will be removed.*

■ **Attach Address**   You can attach an address to a message, which essentially attaches the address book entry for the address to the message. For example, let's say that you want to send a colleague some contact information for a new client. You have already entered the client's information into your address book. Instead of retyping that information into an e-mail, you can simply attach it to the e-mail, which saves you a lot of time and energy. To attach an address to an e-mail, just follow the steps in "Attach an Address to a Message" that appears after this list of options.

■ **Edit AutoText**   AutoText is a BlackBerry feature that can correct misspelled words and automatically complete common words or even words and phrases that you enter. You can learn all about using and configuring AutoText in Chapter 4.

■ **Options**   The Options menu item that appears when you are composing a message enables you to set a priority for the message. This feature is particularly helpful when you are sending messages to other BlackBerry units. The BlackBerry can recognize messages that are considered of high importance, and depending on your notification configuration (see Chapter 4), the BlackBerry can alert you to the important message. The

BlackBerry only has two Importance settings, which are simply Normal and High. If you want to use the High setting, click the Options item on the menu and then use the trackwheel to change the Normal setting to High, as shown in Figure 6-8. Click the trackwheel again and choose Save Options.

 *Remember, when setting configuration screen options, you can hold down the CTRL key and roll the trackwheel to change the options instead of using the Change Option dialog box.*

 *If you inadvertently include an address attachment that you need to either view or delete, just roll the trackwheel to the attached address in your message, and then click the trackwheel to bring up a menu in which you will see the View Attachment and Delete Attachment options.*

Receiving and Reading E-mail

Your BlackBerry has the capability to automatically receive e-mail. Because of the push networking model used by the BlackBerry, you do not ever have to check your e-mail because it arrives to you automatically. That in and of itself is a great feature because you can spend your time doing other things rather than worrying about checking your e-mail. If you configure the Notify feature in a way that is meaningful to you (see Chapter 4), then the BlackBerry completely takes care of getting your mail—including telling you that it has arrived.

FIGURE 6-8   Importance setting

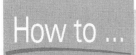 **Attach an Address to a Message**

To attach an address book entry to an e-mail message, follow these steps:

1. When you have finished composing the message, click the trackwheel to bring up menu options.

2. Click Attach Address.

3. The address book entries appear. Scroll to and click the address book entry that you want to attach.

4. In the menu that appears, click Use Address.

5. The address book entry now appears at the bottom of the message, as you can see in Figure 6-9.

6

If you are out of a coverage area or if you have your wireless radio turned off, your e-mail is kept safely on the e-mail server until your unit once again connects with the network. At that time, mail is downloaded to your BlackBerry. Again, this

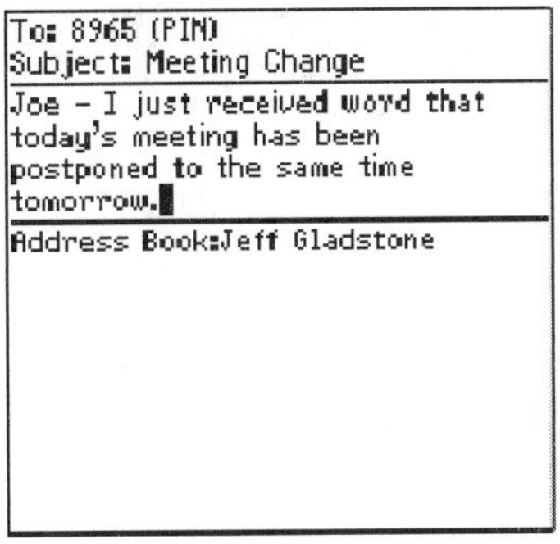

```
To: 8965 (PIN)
Subject: Meeting Change
Joe - I just received word that
today's meeting has been
postponed to the same time
tomorrow.
Address Book:Jeff Gladstone
```

FIGURE 6-9   Attach address

is all done automatically without any intervention from you—and that's great news for all of us busy people.

Once you have received e-mail, click the Messages icon on your Home screen, or just press M on your keyboard. This opens the Messages folder, as shown in Figure 6-10.

From this screen, you can open and read any mail message. Simply use the trackwheel to scroll to the desired message, click the message to see menu options, and then click Open. The message, as well as the sender and subject, is displayed. In order to read the message, use the trackwheel to move around in the message to bring the desired text up on your screen, as shown in Figure 6-11. In some cases, very long messages will be broken into two parts, in which case the end of the first part of the message will display "More available." If you want to read the rest of the message, click the trackwheel to see the menu and choose More. You can then read the rest of the e-mail.

 *The More option does not appear unless the message is long and must be broken into two parts.*

Common E-mail Questions and Answers

Don't worry, your BlackBerry has many additional e-mail features that you get a chance to explore in Chapter 7, but for now I want to address some common

FIGURE 6-10   Messages folder

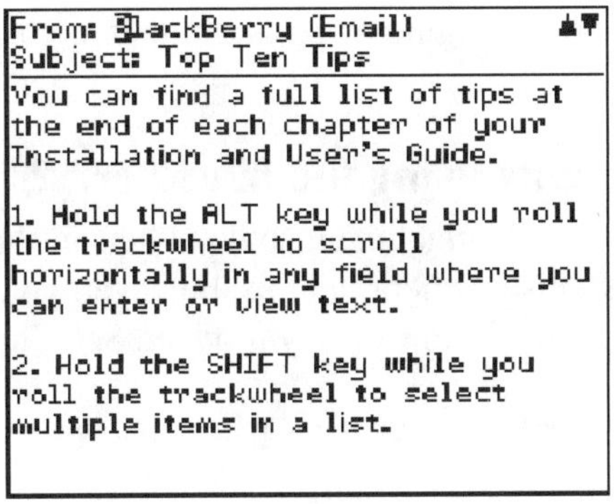

```
From: BlackBerry (Email)        ▲▼
Subject: Top Ten Tips
You can find a full list of tips at
the end of each chapter of your
Installation and User's Guide.

1. Hold the ALT key while you roll
the trackwheel to scroll
horizontally in any field where you
can enter or view text.

2. Hold the SHIFT key while you
roll the trackwheel to select
multiple items in a list.
```

FIGURE 6-11   Read an e-mail message

6

questions people often ask when they start using the BlackBerry. Check out the following sections for Curt's Top questions and answers about BlackBerry e-mail.

I'm Not Connected to the Network. What Will Happen to My Mail?

Relax—your mail will be held on the mail server until your BlackBerry is connected to the network. At that time, the BlackBerry will receive the new mail and notify you if you've configured the Notify feature.

I Need to Compose E-mail on an Airplane, but I Can't Use the Wireless Modem When Flying. What Can I Do?

Federal regulations prevent you from using the BlackBerry's radio modem while you are flying because the signal could interfere with the airplane's communication signals. However, just because you must turn off the radio modem does not mean that you cannot use the BlackBerry. Simply access the wireless icon on the Home screen and turn it off. You can continue to safely use the BlackBerry while on the plane because you are not connected. You can read and write e-mail, and the unit will hold any sent mail until you reconnect. Once you step off the airplane, turn the radio modem back on, and the e-mail that you typed on the airplane will be automatically sent. It's that easy!

Can I Use Any Text Formatting in My E-mails?

Desktop PIMs, such as Outlook or Notes, allow you to select different fonts, colors, and even different theme-based styles. Because the BlackBerry is a text-based handheld, the default font is all that you can use when creating e-mail. In other words, you cannot configure different fonts or colors or use HTML styles in your BlackBerry e-mail.

Can I Send Attachments Using the BlackBerry?

You can send an address book attachment so that you can share an address book entry with someone else. Other than this, however, you cannot send any attachments without the use of a third-party product. See Chaper 14 for details.

Can I Read Attachments Using the BlackBerry?

You cannot read any attachments, with the exception of a native address book attachment, using the BlackBerry. The BlackBerry does not have the capability to open documents or picture files. You can, however, forward an e-mail with an attachment on to someone else, and the attachment will be seen. The forward order occurs on the server's end and the attachment is kept intact. Also, some third-party solutions are now available that allow you to view certain types of attachments. See Chapter 14 to learn more.

Can I CC Several People at One Time?

You can CC or BCC any number of people when composing a message, but you must create a CC or BCC entry for each person. You cannot group e-mail addresses or PINs together and send them under one CC or BCC field.

Can I Include an Auto-Signature?

The BlackBerry does not have an auto-signature feature per se, but you can use AutoText to create a signature. For example, you can enter a signature in AutoText called "Sig" (or whatever) and when you type this word, AutoText will replace it with the signature you entered. See Chapter 4 to learn more about AutoText.

Why Doesn't the BlackBerry Place a Period at the End of My Sentences Automatically?

If you want the BlackBerry to automatically put a period at the end of a sentence when composing an e-mail, just press the SPACE key two times. The BlackBerry will automatically place a period at the end of the previous sentence.

Can I Type Long E-mails?

The BlackBerry was designed for shorter e-mail messages, but it does not restrict you from typing longer e-mails if you wish (and if you love typing long messages with your thumbs). Keep in mind, however, that longer messages require more battery power to send. Say what you need to say, but don't wax poetic either.

E-mail Keyboard Shortcuts

Use the following keyboard shortcuts to save you time and energy as you work with e-mail.

- Press the ALT key and roll the trackwheel to move vertically within the e-mail body or any e-mail field.

- If you are typing in an e-mail field, you can use the SPACE key to automatically insert the "@" and "." characters.

- Press the SPACE key twice to end a sentence, and the BlackBerry will automatically put a period at the end of the sentence and capitalize the first word in the next sentence.

- Enable Key Rate, and you can simply hold down a key in order to capitalize its corresponding letter.

Chapter 7

Managing E-mail

How to...

- Manage e-mail
- Use the Search feature
- Create e-mail filters

As you learned in Chapter 6, the BlackBerry is a real e-mail machine. Designed to be the device that keeps you connected while you are away, the BlackBerry contains most of the same e-mail features as a desktop PIM—all in the palm of your hand. Once you are connected and you begin sending and receiving e-mail, you'll quickly realize that there are many e-mail tasks that you need to perform. In this chapter, I'll describe all of the e-mail management functions available on your BlackBerry so that you can use the BlackBerry to meet all of your e-mail needs.

Managing Messages

In order to help you manage your e-mail, the BlackBerry includes an inbox/outbox feature in the form of the Messages folder, which is available through your Home screen by clicking the Messages icon or pressing M on your keypad. The Messages folder contains a simple text interface where you can see all of the mail that you have received and any mail that is waiting to be sent (such as messages that are held when you are not connected to the network), as shown in Figure 7-1.

From this easy-to-use interface you can perform all of the e-mail actions that you might need. The following sections show you how.

Configuring Options

Before using the Messages folder, you should check out the configuration options that are available to you from this screen. By accessing Options on the menu that appears when you click the trackwheel, you can choose whether or not to show the time and names for e-mail, and whether or not to use a delete confirmation message. The first two are for information purposes. With these options turned on, all e-mail is displayed with a time stamp and the name(s) of the person to whom the e-mail is sent. Under most circumstances, you will want these features enabled—especially if you receive a lot of e-mail.

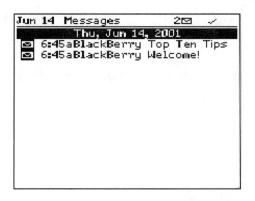

FIGURE 7-1   Messages folder

The last option provides a delete confirmation message. This feature gives you a measure of safety when deleting messages by asking you to confirm deletions. Without this feature turned on, you have no second chance when you click the Delete option.

> **TIP**   *Once you delete a message, it cannot be recovered on the BlackBerry. The Confirm Delete feature can be helpful in preventing accidents, and I strongly recommend that you leave the feature enabled. Some providers have a backup Web site that allows you to back up your e-mail messages. Check with your provider to find out if this additional measure of protection is available to you.*

To learn how to configure the Messages folder options, see "Configure Messages Folder Options."

Marking Messages

If you receive a lot of e-mail each day, you know that sifting through that e-mail and reading each message can be a real headache—especially if you can't keep up with which messages you have read and which messages you have not. The BlackBerry can help keep you organized with its Mark Message feature. This feature allows you to mark a message as either read or unread, thereby ensuring that important messages are reread or given special attention as needed.

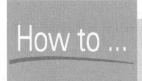 **Configure Messages Folder Options**

To configure Messages folder options, follow these steps:

1. On the Home screen, open the Messages folder by clicking it or by pressing M on your keypad.

2. In the Messages screen, click the trackwheel to see the menu, and then click Options, as shown in Figure 7-2.

3. In the Options screen, click the trackwheel and select any options that you want to change from the menu that appears. (You can also hold down the ALT key and roll the trackwheel to change highlighted item options.) For each item, simply choose Yes or No.

4. When you're done, click the trackwheel to see the menu, and then click Save Options.

To mark a message as either read or unread, simply scroll to the message in the Messages folder, and then click the trackwheel to see the menu for this screen. Next, click either Mark Read or Mark Unread. Messages that are marked as read have an opened envelope icon next to them, while messages marked as unread

FIGURE 7-2   Menu folder options

have an unopened envelope icon beside them. You can change the status of any message (read or unread) at any time by simply reaccessing the menu and changing the mark option.

TIP

You can mark several messages as Read or Unread at the same time by holding down the SHIFT *key and rolling the trackwheel. You can also mark an entire group of messages as Read or Unread by scrolling to the desired date in the Messages folder, clicking the trackwheel, and then clicking Mark Prior Read. All messages prior to the date selected will be marked Read.*

Saving Messages

Think of the Messages folder as a work area. Messages that you receive automatically arrive to this folder, and messages that are waiting on network connectivity to be sent are also held here. From the Messages screen, you read your mail, mark messages as needed, and delete messages you do not want (see the next section). Once you are finished managing messages, however, you also have the option to save messages that you want to keep. These messages are then removed from the

7

Did you know?

Making the Mark Message Feature Count

As with any option or application provided on the BlackBerry, the usefulness of the feature depends on you—after all, e-mail itself isn't very useful if you do not read it! The Mark Message feature provided by the BlackBerry is the same way. The best method is to mark as Unread those messages that you have not finished reading or have not responded to. For example, let's say you're skimming your messages during a cab ride. You read an important message, but you do not have time to respond. One way to recall your attention to this message is to mark it Unread. When you access your Messages folder again, you will remember the message, open it, and have an opportunity to respond. Now this may not seem very important, but if you receive 50+ messages per day, the Mark Messages feature can really come in handy!

Messages folder and placed in a separate folder called Saved Messages, which is accessible from your Home screen by clicking the Saved Messages icon or simply pressing V on your keypad. To save a message, simply select the message that you want to save in the Messages folder, click the trackwheel, and then click Save Message on the menu that appears. In the Saved Messages folder, you'll see your list of saved messages. You can open and read any message that you like, and you can also mark messages in and delete messages from the Saved Messages folder.

Deleting Messages

If you are like me, you tend a get a lot of junk e-mail (unfortunately). This may include advertisements to CC'd messages from colleagues that really don't concern you. You can easily delete messages from the Messages folder that you do not want, and even if you save messages, you can still delete those messages from the Saved Messages folder when they are no longer useful to you. To delete a message, simply scroll to the message you want to delete, click the trackwheel to access menu options, and then click Delete Message. Click Yes in response to the confirmation dialog box that appears, and the message is deleted from the BlackBerry. It is important to note that the BlackBerry does not contain a folder for deleted items. Once you delete a message, it is gone forever and cannot be recovered. Since you cannot recover deleted messages, I strongly recommend that you leave the Confirm Delete option set to Yes in both the Messages and Saved Messages Options screens. This feature will help ensure that you do not accidentally delete a message that you want to keep.

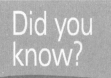

Managing Saved Messages

As you use the BlackBerry, it is important to keep in mind that the Messages folder is designed for incoming and outgoing mail. Think of the folder as a place to quickly read and sort your mail. You can decide what you need and what you don't need while working in the Messages folder. As a general rule of practice, you should try to keep the Messages folder clear from clutter if at all possible. For mail that you want to keep, use the Saved Messages feature so that the mail is moved to the Saved Messages folder. You can then easily access the saved messages and read or respond to them as needed.

You can delete several messages at one time by holding down the SHIFT *key and rolling the trackwheel to select the messages. You can also delete all messages prior to a certain date by selecting the date in the Messages folder, clicking the trackwheel, and clicking Delete Prior from the menu that appears. All messages prior to this date will be deleted. You should, however, use caution and make sure that all messages that you want to keep have been saved before using the Delete Prior feature.*

Searching Messages and Senders

If you access the menu from the Messages folder, you'll see that you also have the option to search messages and search senders. The BlackBerry also contains a Search icon on your Home screen, and I'll discuss these search features a little later in "Searching Messages." For now, however, simply note that you can search for particular messages and even all messages from a particular sender directly from the Messages and Saved Messages folders, just as you can choose to compose messages directly from these locations as well. These menu features allow you quick access to tasks that you need to perform without having to exit and open different applications over and over again.

Did you know?

What Happened to My Messages?

Consider this scenario: You pick up the BlackBerry one morning and begin reading your e-mail while eating breakfast. As you are browsing through your Messages folder, which contains a lot of messages, you notice that some older messages are missing. What happened?

The BlackBerry has to use memory to store messages in the Messages folder. When memory begins to run low, the BlackBerry has to make room for new, incoming messages. To find the room it needs, the BlackBerry begins deleting the oldest messages found in the Messages folder; however, messages stored in your Saved Messages folder are not deleted. In order to avoid the potential message loss, it is important that you keep your Messages folder tidy—delete messages you don't want and save messages that you do want. These housekeeping actions will help ensure that you do not lose e-mail that you might need.

Message Menu Items

You can open and read any message that appears in your Messages and Saved Messages folders. Once you open a message and read it, you can click the trackwheel to see a message menu that provides you with a number of message-specific options. The following list describes these features:

- **Mark**, **Save**, and **Delete**   The Mark, Save, and Delete features are available within the message menu just as they are on the Message folder menu. This feature saves you time so you can manage messages as you are reading (save the good stuff, delete the junk). These three features work in exactly the same way as they do from the folder menu, so refer to the previous sections for more information.

- **Reply to Message**   This feature works just like the Reply option usually available with desktop PIMs. If you want to reply to the sender, just choose this menu option, type your reply message, and send it. This Reply option does not include the original message text in order to conserve transmission time and battery power.

- **Reply to All**   This feature sends a reply to everyone to whom the original message was sent. For example, the person who sent the message will receive the reply as well as any CC'd recipients. This Reply to All option does not include the original message text in order to conserve transmission time and battery power.

- **Forward**   This option forwards the message to another contact. Simply select the option from the menu that appears, and then select the contact in the address book (or use the Use Once option). You can also enter additional information within the e-mail as needed.

- **Reply with Text**   This option replies to the sender, but it includes the text of the original message. Use this option only when necessary because the longer the message, the more battery power consumed.

- **Reply to All with Text**   This option sends a reply to the sender and any CC'd recipients, but it includes the text of the original message. Use this option only when necessary because the longer the message, the more battery power consumed.

■ **Show Qualified Address**   Place your cursor in the To or From field of
any e-mail and click the Show Qualified Address option from the message
menu to see the actual e-mail address of the sender or recipient, such as
you@yourisp.com.

■ **Show Friendly Name**   Place your cursor in the To or From field of any
e-mail and click the Show Friendly Name option from the message menu
to see the first and last name of the sender or recipient.

■ **Add to Address Book**   Place your cursor in the From field of an open
message, click the trackwheel, and choose the Add to Address Book option
to automatically put the contact in your address book. This option does not
appear if the sender is already in your address book. See Chapter 8 to learn
more about the address book.

■ **Next Unread**   This option skips you to the next unread message.

■ **Previous Message** and **Next Message**   Use these options to view the
previous or next message in the message list.

As you might guess, there are also a few keyboard shortcuts you can use when
working with the menu options. If you memorize the keyboard shortcuts presented
in Table 7-1, you'll see that they save you time and trackwheel movements when
reading and managing messages.

Keyboard Shortcut	Description
ALT-ENTER	Move up a page in an open message.
ENTER	Move down a page in an open message.
T	Go to the top of an open message.
B	Go to the bottom of an open message.
N	Go to the next message.
P	Go to the previous message.
U	Go to the next unread message.
R	Reply to a message without text. This option replies to the sender only without retaining the message text.
C	Reply to a message with text. This option replies to the sender only and retains the message text.
F	Forward the message.

TABLE 7-1   Message Keyboard Shortcuts

Editing or Resending a Message

Messages that you send appear in the Messages folder, and even though these messages have been sent, you can still open them and edit and/or resend the message if necessary. This feature is very helpful if you make a mistake or need to send additional information. Also, if you try to send a message when you are in a place where connectivity isn't so great, such as a parking garage, you may need to resend the message when you have good connectivity. In the Messages folder, simply open the message you want to edit or resend, and then click the trackwheel to access the message menu. Click the Edit Message option, and your cursor now appears in the message so that you can make changes as needed. When you're done, simply click the trackwheel to access the message menu, and then click Resend Message to resend the message.

Opening Attachments

If a received message contains an attachment, which as mentioned in Chapter 6 can only be a BlackBerry address book entry, you can choose to open and view that attachment and add the attachment to your address book. The following boxed text, "Open and Save a Viewable Attachment," walks you through the steps.

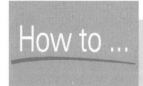 **Open and Save a Viewable Attachment**

If a received message has an attachment in the form of an address book entry, follow these steps to read the attachment and save it to your address book.

1. Open the message that has the attachment.

2. Using your trackwheel, scroll to the attachment so that your cursor is placed somewhere in the name of the attachment, as shown in Figure 7-3.

3. Click the trackwheel to see the message menu and click View Address to view the attachment contact information.

4. If you want to save the attachment, click the trackwheel to see the message menu and then click Save Address.

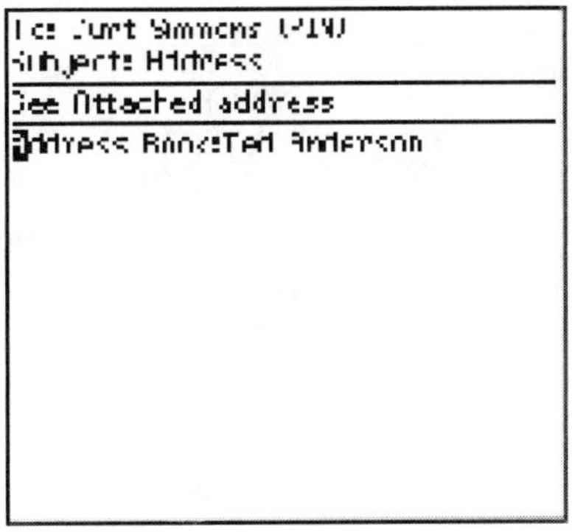

FIGURE 7-3   Message attachment

Inserting Symbols into E-mail Messages

The BlackBerry provides a simple menu, called the Symbols menu, that you can
use when creating new messages (or replying or forwarding messages) so that you
can easily insert common symbols into your e-mails. The Symbols menu provides
you with typical desktop keyboard symbols that do not appear on your BlackBerry
keyboard.

To access the Symbols screen, just press ALT-SPACE. You'll see the Symbols
screen appear, as shown in Figure 7-4.

Use the trackwheel to select the symbol that you want to include, and then
click the trackwheel to insert the symbol into the e-mail. You can also use the
keyboard hot key that appears directly below the symbol to which it corresponds.
For example, if you want to insert < (less than sign), just press D on the keyboard.

Inserting Accent and International Characters

Aside from the Symbols screen, you can also insert accent characters and
international symbols. When you are typing, simply hold down the desired key
on the keyboard and roll the trackwheel to see various accent/character options
you can choose.

TIP   *You can capitalize any letter by holding down the key and rolling the
trackwheel as well.*

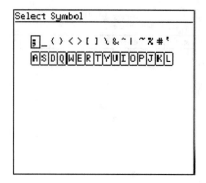

FIGURE 7-4   Symbols screen

Quick Message Keyboard Tips

Aside from the keyboard shortcuts you can use when working with a particular message, you may find helpful these additional keyboard shortcuts:

- Use ALT-U to toggle between marking a message read or unread.

- Use the trackwheel to select a date in the Messages folder, and then simply press the DEL key to delete all messages prior to the date.

TIP   *Be careful! Make sure you want to delete all messages prior to the selected date before you press DEL. Deleted messages cannot be recovered.*

- View all received messages in either Messages or Saved Messages by pressing ALT-I.

- Use ALT-O to view all sent messages in the Messages folder.

Searching Messages

The BlackBerry provides you with a helpful Search feature so that you can easily locate messages by subject or by sender. You can directly access the Search feature from the Home screen by clicking the Search Messages icon or by simply pressing S on the keypad.

When you bring up the Search Messages screen, as shown in Figure 7-5, you see several fields where you can enter text for your search. You are provided with fields for name, subject, message, and show. You do not need to enter search criteria for each field, only the ones you want searched; however, the more information you enter, the more narrow your search will be. Specifically, these fields perform specific searches, as described here:

- **Name**   Enter a name that you want to search for and use the associated In field to specify the location of the name, such as To, From, CC, BCC, and so on.

- **Subject**   Enter keywords in this field to search for a desired subject.

- **Message**   Enter keywords that may appear in the message text.

- **Show**   You can narrow your search to specific types of messages by specifying one of the following options: Received Only, Saved Only, Sent and Received, or Sent only.

FIGURE 7-5   Search Messages screen

You can enter keywords directly into the desired fields, but you can also access the menu on this screen to help you a bit. For example, you can use the menu to select names, clear fields, and even save and recall searches.

For example, let's say that I perform a specific search to locate certain information in the text of certain e-mails, as shown in Figure 7-6.

Once I'm done searching, I decide to save this search for future use, so I click the trackwheel and then click Save Search from the menu that appears. This action opens an additional screen, shown in Figure 7-7, where I can enter a name for the search and designate a hot key (ALT-*N*, where *N* is any keyboard letter) so I can easily perform the same search using the hot key. For example, for my search, I have entered a keyboard hot key of ALT-A. Whenever I want to perform the search, I can just press ALT-A, and the search will be performed and the results returned to me. I can also use the Recall Search feature on the Search Messages menu to select the name of the previously saved search that I want to perform. This feature works well if you do not like using hot keys.

Once you recall a search, you can also edit it. For example, let's say I save a previous search, but now I want to search on a different name than the one I provided in the Name field. No problem—once I recall the search, I simply click the trackwheel and select Edit Search from the menu that appears to make editorial changes to the search as desired.

```
Search Messages
Name: █
     In:                      From: Field
Subject:
Message: configuration sale
access
Shows:              Sent and Received
```

FIGURE 7-6   Example search

7

FIGURE 7-7   Save search

> **NOTE**   *Searches always function best if you are specific in what you want to find. If your search returns no matches, you are probably using too narrow of an approach. Try leaving some fields open or using more keywords.*

Mail Filtering

Depending on your BlackBerry version, you may have available to you some mail filtering and management functions. For those of you using the BlackBerry Internet Edition, you are provided access to a Web site from which you can manage filters and mail transmission. If you are using the BlackBerry Enterprise Edition, consult your documentation or administrator's instructions to see if filtering options are available to you.

For Internet Edition users, check your Internet service provider's documentation to locate the URL you should access to manage your mail online. The URL will be different, depending on your provider. Typically, you will find a URL that gives you a login screen where you enter your username and password. Once you have access to the Web site, you'll see the same screens, or least screens similar to those presented in the following sections.

Checking Out the E-mail Management Site

Once you log in to the Web site provided by your service provider, you will see a
BlackBerry e-mail management screen, as shown in Figure 7-8.

As you can see in Figure 7-8, you have a few different categories from which
you can choose to access different management features:

- **Email Options**   This feature allows you to send a copy of your mail to
  another e-mail address for easy management purposes.

- **Filters**   Use the Filter section to control the messages that are sent to your
  BlackBerry.

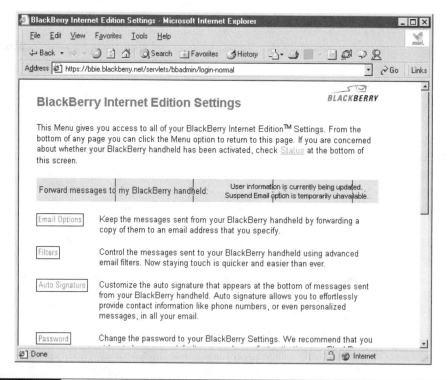

FIGURE 7-8   BlackBerry e-mail management online

- **Signature**   Aside from using AutoText, you can also create an e-mail signature here that is automatically attached to all e-mail messages.

- **Password**   Update your password here.

- **Warranty**   Update warranty information here.

- **Status box**   The status box lists the current status of your handheld. This is the same screen you access to activate your BlackBerry.

The Signature, Password, and Warranty features of the site are self explanatory—just click on them to learn more. The Email Options and Filters features are considered in the next two sections.

Email Options

The Email Options screen (which actually displays just one option) allows you to forward a copy of all mail to another address. This feature is helpful if you want to maintain a copy of your mail in another location, such as at a different ISP address or even a free Web account (for example, a Netscape, Hotmail, or Yahoo mail account). As you can see in Figure 7-9, you just need to enter the address where you want mail forwarded and click OK.

Filters

The Filters option allows you to control what e-mail is actually sent to your BlackBerry. As you can see in Figure 7-10, you essentially create a desired filter, and then apply some action to the filter. For example, in Figure 7-10, you see a default filter for both To and BCC and one for CC. By default, if a message is addressed to you or you are BCC'd on a message, that message is sent to your handheld. If you are CC'd, only the message header is sent to you. You can change these filters by clicking the Edit button, delete filters by clicking the Delete button, and create new filters by clicking the New button.

To learn how to create a filter, see "Create a New Filter."

Finally, you'll also notice at the bottom of the Filters screen that you have a drop-down list that lets you specify what happens if none of the filters apply to a message. By default, if no filter applies to a message, then the message is sent to your handheld. You can use the drop-down menu to change this default behavior,

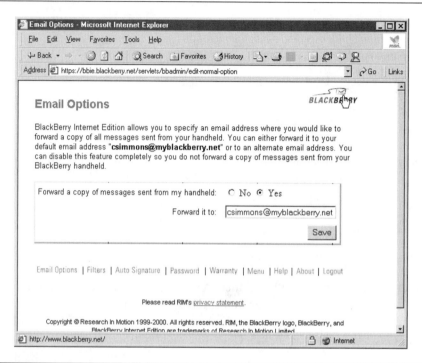

Email Options - Microsoft Internet Explorer

File   Edit   View   Favorites   Tools   Help

Back   •   Search   Favorites   History

Address https://bbie.blackberry.net/servlets/bbadmin/edit-normal-option

BLACKBERRY

Email Options

BlackBerry Internet Edition allows you to specify an email address where you would like to forward a copy of all messages sent from your handheld. You can either forward it to your default email address "**csimmons@myblackberry.net**" or to an alternate email address. You can disable this feature completely so you do not forward a copy of messages sent from your BlackBerry handheld.

Forward a copy of messages sent from my handheld: ○ No ● Yes

Forward it to: csimmons@myblackberry.net

Save

Email Options | Filters | Auto Signature | Password | Warranty | Menu | Help | About | Logout

Please read RIM's privacy statement.

Copyright © Research In Motion 1999-2000. All rights reserved. RIM, the BlackBerry logo, BlackBerry, and BlackBerry Internet Edition are trademarks of Research In Motion Limited.

http://www.blackberry.net/   Internet

FIGURE 7-9   Forward Mail option

but be careful about being too restrictive. The idea with filters is to control mail coming to your BlackBerry, not stop it from coming to you.

TIP

Once of the cool things about filters is that you can use the Level 1 notification feature to make sure you quickly get e-mails from a certain person. Even if this person does not designate a message as high priority, you can use the Level 1 feature to make it a priority.

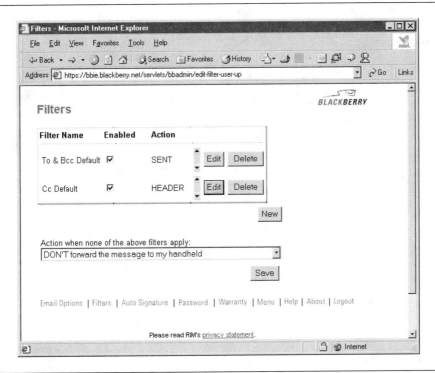

FIGURE 7-10   Default filters

How to ... Create a New Filter

To create a new filter, follow these steps:

1. Log in to your BlackBerry Internet site and click the Filters link.

2. In the Filters screen, click the New button.

3. The New Email Filter screen appears, as shown in Figure 7-11. Enter the desired information to create the filter. Be sure to give the filter a friendly, recognizable name and include parameters. For example, in Figure 7-11, I am blocking all mail from Janice, no matter whether the message is to me or if I am BCC'd or CC'd. Use the Action drop-down menu at the bottom of the screen to select one of the actions described here:

   - Don't forward the message to my handheld

   - Forward the message to my handheld

   - Forward message with LEVEL 1 notification

   - Only send the header to my handheld

When you are done, just click the Save button and the new filter will appear in your list.

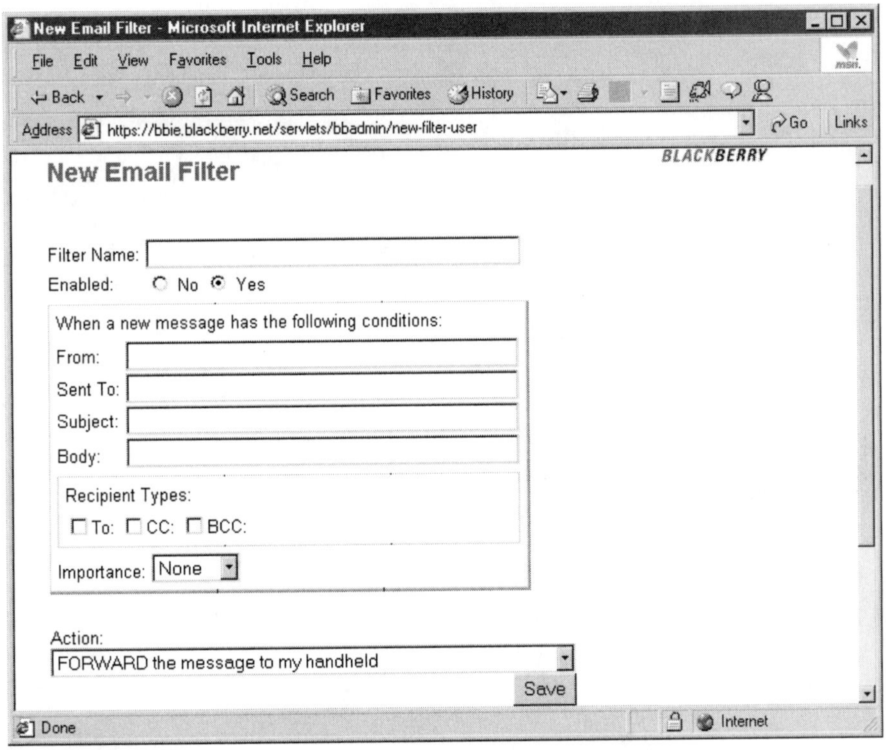

FIGURE 7-11 New Filter options

Chapter 8

Use the Address Book

How to...

- Configure the address book
- Create new address book entries
- Manage address book entries
- Create address filters for Intellisync

The BlackBerry address book is just like an address book that you might keep at your desk—it is designed to hold all kinds of contact information about other people. Using the address book, you can easily recall e-mail addresses, phone numbers, pager numbers, and basic information about each person. Are you attending a conference and need to add some new contacts to your list? No problem, your BlackBerry is in your pocket. Are you on the road and need a phone number quickly? No problem, your BlackBerry is always with you. In this chapter, you'll explore the BlackBerry address book and learn how to do everything with this very helpful piece of software.

Getting to Know Your Address Book

The address book is easily accessible from your Home screen. On the 957 model, the Address Book icon looks like a Rolodex (as shown in Figure 8-1), and on the 950 model the Address Book icon looks like an open book (as shown in Figure 8-2).

FIGURE 8-1   Address Book icon on the 957

FIGURE 8-2   Address Book icon on the 950

On either model, just use the trackwheel to scroll to the Address Book icon, and then click it to access the address book.

Once you open the address book, you see a listing of the current addresses you have entered or that have been synchronized from your PIM desktop application (see Chapter 5). Contacts are listed by name in alphabetical order, as shown in Figure 8-3. If you have not added any contacts to the address book, you will see a No Addresses entry.

Every action you want to perform in the address book is handled by clicking the trackwheel to see the address book menu. I will describe all of the items listed in this menu, but let's first take a look at Options. Options provides three settings you can use to determine how the address book behaves. The default settings are all that you probably need, but you may find changes to these settings helpful.

8

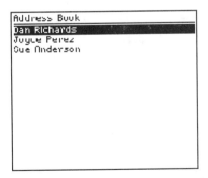

FIGURE 8-3   Address book contact entries

Click the trackwheel while you are in address book and click Options. You see Sort By, Confirm Address Delete, and Allow Duplicate Names settings, as shown in Figure 8-4.

The Sort By setting allows you to change the manner in which addresses are listed when you first open the address book. You'll notice that by default, addresses are sorted in alphabetical order based on first name. This may not be very practical to you, so you also have the option to list addresses by last name or by company. The option to list addresses by last name is self-explanatory. In the case of organization by company, the company name is listed first, followed by the actual contact's name, as shown here:

Gadgets, Inc., Standton, Rusty
Gadgets, Inc., Wilkinson, Susan

This setup can be helpful if you are doing work for several different companies (or vice versa) and you want to see all of the contacts from one company in a block. Just use the trackwheel to scroll through the company names until you find the company you want, and then you can drill down to the actual addressee that you want.

Aside from the Sort By setting, you can also choose to confirm address deletions or allow duplicate names. By default, both of these settings are enabled. The Confirm Address Delete option, when enabled, gives you a message each time you choose to delete an address from the address book, as shown in Figure 8-5.

As a general rule, you should leave the Confirm Address Delete option enabled. Sure, it means an additional scroll and click, but when managing a bunch

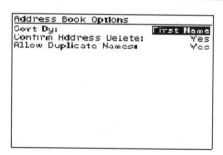

FIGURE 8-4 Address book options

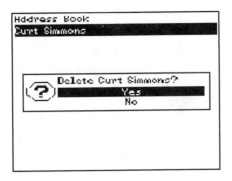

FIGURE 8-5   Confirm deletion message

of addresses, it is very easy to accidentally delete an address (such as when the taxi hits a bump and your fingers slip on the trackwheel). Without the confirm deletion message, you have no protection from accidental deletions, so I recommend that you leave this setting enabled.

> TIP
>
> *Remember, if you accidentally delete an address, you must completely reenter it or synchronize with your desktop PIM application so the address can be rewritten. The BlackBerry does not provide you with an Undo feature.*

The final option, Allow Duplicate Names, enables you to have multiple entries that contain the same first and last name. The only problem with this setting is that only the names are displayed, so if you have two Sue Wilkinson entries, they will look identical in the address list. The names are alphabetized based on e-mail address, but the listing does not show the e-mail address, so you just have to know which is which. This isn't too difficult with only two names, but if you have more, it can get confusing because you would have to memorize the e-mail address of each duplicate name to know which one you would want to use. Another workaround is to list the Address Book contents by company so you can differentiate between the names by company (if they work for different companies). At any rate, you can consider this setting and determine if you want to use it or not. Changing any of these settings is easy—just follow the steps in "Edit Address Book Options" to edit these entries.

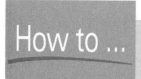 **Edit Address Book Options**

To edit address book options, just follow these steps:

1. In address book, click the trackwheel to see the menu, and then click Options.

2. In the Sort By field, click the trackwheel to see the menu, click Change Option, and use the trackwheel to scroll through the provided options. As a shortcut, you can also use the SPACE key on the 957 or the SYMBOL key on the 950 model to just scroll through the options directly from the Options screen (this bypasses the menu). Either way, select the option that you want by clicking it.

3. Roll the trackwheel to move to the Confirm Address Delete option or the Allow Duplicate Names option, and then use the menu or the SPACE/SYMBOL keys to select the desired option.

4. When you're done, click the trackwheel and choose Save Options from the menu. Your options go into effect immediately, and you are returned to the address book screen.

Creating Address Book Entries

Once the address book looks and acts the way you want, you can begin adding address entries. Address book entries are easy to add, and you have a number of field options so you can add as little or as much information about your addresses as you like. When you create a new address, you are given a list of items for which you can enter descriptions:

- Addressee's first and last name
- E-mail address and PIN number
- Title
- Company

- Work, home, mobile, pager, and fax numbers

- Addresses (two lines provided)

- City, state/province, and ZIP/postal code

- Country

- Notes

TIP *Fields that require numbers, such as PIN, automatically allow you to press the number keys without using the ALT key. Phone number fields also support the – (minus sign), + (plus sign), × (multiplication sign), . (period), and , (comma) without having to hold down the ALT key.*

To create an address, you simply populate these fields as desired. In order to create the address, you only need to enter one entry (such as a first or last name, or just an e-mail address), but typically you should enter at least the first and last name and an e-mail address for your contact. Of course, you can populate every field on every address if you like—the BlackBerry is flexible and the choice is completely yours.

One item that I would like to point out concerns e-mail addresses. You are allowed to enter up to three e-mail addresses per address entry. This feature is helpful for including contact information for individuals who have both corporate e-mail and personal e-mail addresses. By default, the address book entry area only gives you one e-mail address field. You can add up to two additional fields by clicking the trackwheel to see the address book menu, and then clicking Add Email. If you create an entry that has more than one e-mail address, you are prompted to select the e-mail address you want to use when composing a message to that person. To create a new address, follow the steps in "Create a New Address Book Entry."

TIP *If you try to exit the address you are entering without saving it, you'll be prompted to save the entry. This feature prevents you from accidentally losing information you are currently working on.*

8

Create a New Address Book Entry

To create a new address book entry, just follow these steps:

1. In the address book, click the trackwheel to bring up the address book menu, and then select New Address.

2. The New Address screen appears. Populate the fields, using the trackwheel to navigate and pressing the ENTER key to enter information after you've typed it. Remember, you only have to populate the fields that you want—you can skip around between fields as needed. Figure 8-6 gives you an example of a working entry.

3. If you need to enter more than one e-mail address, click the trackwheel to see the menu, and then click Add Email. A new e-mail field appears, and you can populate it with a second address. Repeat this process to add a third e-mail address if you like.

4. Use the Notes field to enter any information that is relevant, as shown in Figure 8-7. The BlackBerry gives you plenty of room to type information, so feel free to put in as much as is needed. Also, refer to "Using the Notes Field," which follows shortly, for more information.

5. Once you're done, click the trackwheel to see the address book menu and click Save Address.

Managing Addresses

Once you have created entries for your address book, you can easily view and manage the addresses at any time. These tasks are quick and simple, and the following sections describe them for you.

Viewing Addresses

You can view address information that you have entered quickly and easily at any time. In the address book, scroll through the list of addresses, highlight the address you want to view, click the trackwheel to see the address book menu, and select

```
┌─────────────────────────────────────┐
│New Address                        ▼  │
│First: Ted                            │
│Last: Anderson                        │
│Email: tanderson@trintron.ca          │
│PIN: 45470905                         │
│Title: Manager                        │
│Company: Trintron Graphics            │
│Work: 704 655 0905                    │
│Home: 704-825-7144                    │
│Mobile: 685-926-1619                  │
│Pager: 685-562-1285                   │
│Fax: 70-665-5589                      │
│Address1: P.O. Box 70945205           │
│Address2: 3004 Stanton Ave            │
│City: Dallas█                         │
└─────────────────────────────────────┘
```

FIGURE 8-6   Example entry

View Address. This feature opens the address screen and organizes the information you entered for the address in an easy-to-read format, as you can see in Figure 8-8.

You can scroll through the information in the entry by using the trackwheel. When you're done, just click the trackwheel and click cancel.

8

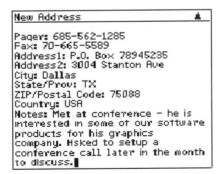

```
┌─────────────────────────────────────┐
│New Address                        ▲  │
│Pager: 685-562-1285                   │
│Fax: 70-665-5589                      │
│Address1: P.O. Box 78945235           │
│Address2: 3004 Stanton Ave            │
│City: Dallas                          │
│State/Prov: TX                        │
│ZIP/Postal Code: 75088                │
│Country: USA                          │
│Notes: Met at conference – he is      │
│interested in some of our software    │
│products for his graphics             │
│company. Asked to setup a             │
│conference call later in the month    │
│to discuss.█                          │
└─────────────────────────────────────┘
```

FIGURE 8-7   Populated Notes field

Using the Notes Field

The Notes field is an open-ended entry that allows you to include essentially any information that is helpful to you. For example, you might include such information about the contact in this section as "works from home on Tuesdays and Thursdays," or general information about who the person is, where you met him or her, what business needs are important, and so on. The Notes field can contain static information that always stays in the address book entry, or it can hold temporary information. I use this field to keep track of new people I meet when I'm on the road. I put notations about each person in this field so I can keep up with "who is who" and have a frame of reference for each person when I get home. The options are quite endless, so use this field to meet your needs.

Editing Addresses

Address information for your contacts is likely to change from time to time, and the BlackBerry allows you to edit address book entries so that you do not have to delete the old entry and create a new one each time some information changes.

To edit an address book entry, simply scroll through the list of addresses, select the one you want, click the trackwheel, and then click Edit Address on the menu

FIGURE 8-8   View address book entry

that appears. This opens the same screen as you see when first creating the address. Simply scroll through the fields and make the necessary changes to the affected entries. When you're done, just click the trackwheel to bring up menu options and click Save Address.

NOTE

If you want to remove a field entry, just scroll to the field, click the trackwheel, and then select the Clear Field option on the menu that appears. This is particularly helpful for longer addresses and the Notes field, where you may have a lot of information to remove or replace.

Deleting Addresses

You can easily delete addresses that you no longer need from the address book. Keep in mind that as long as you do not change the Confirm Address Delete option on the Options screen, you will be prompted for confirmation each time you delete an address. Again, this provides you with a safety net, and should strongly consider leaving this option at the default setting.

8

To delete an address that you no longer want, just scroll to the address in the address book screen, click the trackwheel, and then click Delete Address. Click Yes in response to the confirmation message that appears, and the entry is immediately removed from your address book.

Searching the Address Book

Over time, you will accumulate a lot of addresses. Sure, you can use the trackwheel to scroll to the one you want, but what if you have a hundred entries or more? Quickly getting to the address you want can get a little annoying, but if you know at least part of the name of the person you want to contact, you can quickly find the address. When you open the address book, just begin typing the person's name on the keyboard. The address book will begin suggesting names for you. For example, if you want to find someone named Malone, Jennifer, just type Mon and all names that include "Mon" will quickly appear, with all other entries vanishing from view. You can then quickly select the one that you want. The search feature searches through first names, last names, and company names in that order to match your search criteria, so always try to use the first name or first initial when typing. Remember, the more specific you are, the fewer returns you will get and the faster you can find what you want.

Composing Messages

Whenever you want to compose a message, the address book automatically opens so you can select the address book entry that you want. You can also use the Use Once feature in order to manually enter the e-mail address. Note that the Use Once option is always at the top of the list. If you scroll deep into your address book and then want to return to Use Once, just press U on your keypad, and you will be returned to the top. When you are using the address book, you can also scroll to the address that you want to send mail to and simply click the trackwheel to open the menu, and then click Compose Message.

Filtering Address Book Entries During Synchronization with PIM Applications

In Chapter 5, you learned about the BlackBerry desktop software, which uses Intellisync to synchronize information on your BlackBerry with information on your PIM applications, such as Lotus Notes, Outlook, Netscape, and so forth. I'll not repeat the usage information here, but I do want to call your attention to the filtering functions that are available when synchronizing address book data between the BlackBerry and a PIM application.

The filtering feature allows you to prevent the synchronization of some address book field options. For example, let's say that you are using Lotus Notes, but you do not want some items in your PIM application to transfer to the BlackBerry. You can use the filtering functions to prevent the transfer of this kind of data.

In order to set up filters, you must first configure the BlackBerry Intellisync software to synchronize with the PIM application of your choice. See Chapter 5 for step-by-step instructions. Once the PIM application has been selected, you want to visit the Advanced properties pages. Open the BlackBerry desktop software and double-click Intellisync. Next, click the Configure PIM button. This action opens the Configuration dialog box showing what PIM applications your BlackBerry is configured to synchronize with. Select the Address Book option, shown in Figure 8-9, and then click the Advanced button.

You see the Advanced Settings for Address Book dialog box. Click the Filters tab. As you can see in Figure 8-10, no filters are selected in this window by default. Depending on what PIM application you are using, some option may already be available to you; regardless, you can easily create new filters as needed. Before doing so, make sure you back up your BlackBerry, just in case something goes wrong.

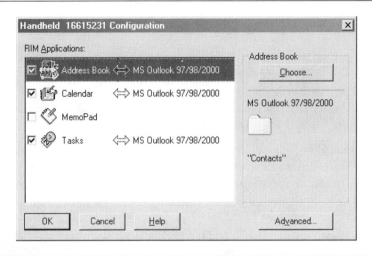

FIGURE 8-9 PIM application configuration dialog box

8

The following section, "Create an Address Book Filter," shows you how to create a new filter.

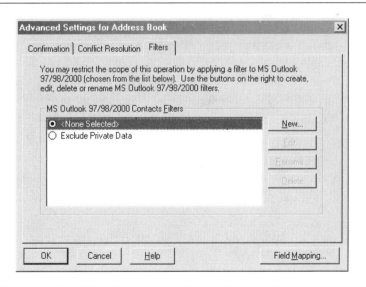

FIGURE 8-10 Filters tab

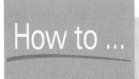 **Create an Address Book Filter**

To create a new address book filter, just follow these steps:

1. On the Filters tab, click the New button.

2. In the Filter Name dialog box, enter a friendly, recognizable name for the filter that you want to create, as shown in Figure 8-11. For example, I do not want "body" information, which is essentially Notes in Outlook 2000, to be transferred to the BlackBerry. If you're not sure what fields you want to create filters for, click the Field Mappings button on the Filters tab to see how BlackBerry address book entries are mapped to entries in your PIM application. Enter the name and click OK.

3. In the dialog box that appears, make sure the Conditions tab is selected. You have a few actions to perform here:

   ■ First, click the Field drop-down menu and select the field for which you want to create a filter. The field names will vary, depending on your desktop PIM application. You can see in Figure 8-12 that I have selected Body because I do not want any body text, or notes, to be transferred to the BlackBerry.

   ■ Next, choose an operator value for the filter. You have the options of "starts with," "contains," "does not contain," "equals," "does not equal," "is empty," "is not empty," "is between." Since I do not want any body information transferred, I am selecting "is not empty." This setting tells Outlook not to transfer information for entries in which this field is not empty.

   ■ Depending on your value selection, you may need to enter a value in the Value field as well. For example, if you use the "starts with" operator, you need to enter the value for the filter, which can be a letter or combination of letters, depending on what you want to filter.

   ■ Click the Add to List button and repeat the process of adding more operators and values as needed for this particular filter.

4. Click on the Rules tab to see the options shown in Figure 8-13. By default, the "all rules must be met" option is selected, and you see your filter configuration listed. If you have only one operator, then you don't need to do anything here. If you have more than one operator or value, you can determine if all conditions (all operators and values) must be met before the filter is applied, or if only one condition must be met before the filter is applied. Once you're done, click OK. This returns you to the Filters window, and you see that your new filter is selected for use. You can return to this window and edit or delete the filter at any time.

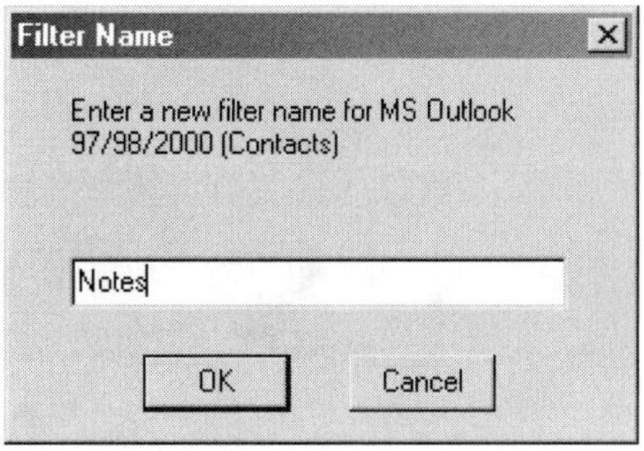

8

Filter Name   ☒

Enter a new filter name for MS Outlook 97/98/2000 (Contacts)

Notes

OK   Cancel

FIGURE 8-11   Filter name

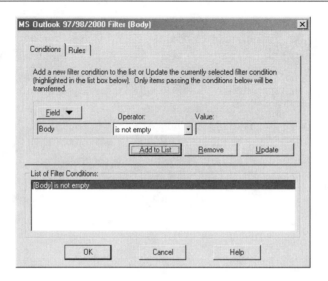

Conditions tab

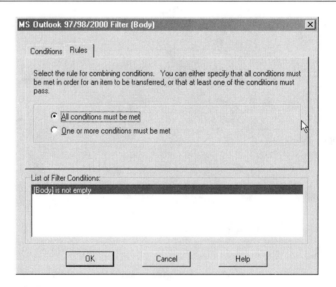

Rules tab

Chapter 9

Browse the Wireless Internet

How to...

- Get set up with the GoAmerica service

- Install the browser

- Surf the Internet

- Use the Go.Web browser features

The Internet is an ever-changing, always-growing animal. What began only a few years ago as a networking tool for super computer geeks has become vitally important to our culture and frequently to our businesses. Because the Internet is so important, the wireless community began realizing that the Internet needs to be everywhere, not just tied down to a modem and a computer. With this thought in mind, web sites began initiating a protocol that would enable their sites to be viewed on wireless devices, such as PDAs, Internet-ready phones, and even pagers. This service is becoming increasingly popular, and you can expect the trend to continue as the Internet becomes more and more important in all of our lives.

The BlackBerry supports the use of the wireless Internet through third-party offerings. This means that the BlackBerry you purchased does not come equipped with a web browser or other software that enables you to browse the Internet. You first must purchase a third-party Internet service that will enable your BlackBerry to surf the wireless World Wide Web. The most popular Internet service for the BlackBerry is the GoAmerica wireless Internet service, which is explored in this chapter. However, you can also use the PocketGenie, which is explored in Chapter 13, so be sure to check out that chapter. I'll also briefly discuss BlackBerry paging in Chapter 13 as well. So, are you ready to surf? Then let's get started.

The BlackBerry and the Internet

Before I get into the specifics of the GoAmerica wireless web service, let's first consider how the BlackBerry functions on the Internet. The Internet is made up of HTML pages that are read and displayed in web browsers, such as Internet Explorer and Netscape Navigator. The HTTP protocol is used to transfer these web pages to and from one location to the next. The Internet has become a rich landscape of graphics and multimedia, enabled by people like you and me, that you've probably come to love (or hate, depending on how fast your Internet connection is). All of this is, of course, great, but how does the BlackBerry handle it?

Because wireless devices such as the BlackBerry do not have the capability (at the moment) to use typical web browsers like Netscape and IE, you have to use an application written especially for them. This is true of any Web-enabled PDA, device, pager, or phone. These browsers work somewhat differently, and they do not have all of the features that one might find in a typical computer browser. The browsers are lightweight in terms of memory and hard disk storage, and they are able to retrieve and display pages from the Internet specifically for the wireless device.

So, you may be wondering if you can see all those pictures and multimedia graphics on a wireless device. The answer is no. Because wireless devices such as the BlackBerry do not have the advanced processing power of a computer, they cannot display all of the graphics you see on a typical web page. Instead, wireless device browsers rely on a text-based display that does not use any graphics. You'll still see links and you may even see some basic line graphics, but that's about it. You can't download pictures, documents, or programs. However, the same information is there, and if it's information you're going after, you will like what you see. In fact, you can get all kinds of information while you are on the move, or just use the Internet to pass the time. For example, you can:

- Access a variety of news sites

- Find information about a city you are in

- Get entertainment news and local information

- Shop

- Access fun sites to pass the time

- Get stock market quotes and news

In fact, you can do just about everything on the wireless Internet that you can do on the wired Internet, without all of the graphics. Now, I'm not one to tell you that the wireless Internet is perfect, because it's not. In fact, it is dependent on your coverage area, just like your e-mail, and my experience has shown that the wireless Internet can be slow. But overall, you just can't beat access to information anywhere, any time, and that's why I love it.

The GoAmerica Web Service

GoAmerica, which you can visit online at http://www.goamerica.com, is a wireless Internet service provider. This means that they focus on providing the

Did you know?

The Wireless Internet and Protocols

As I mentioned, typical web sites use Hypertext Markup Language (HTML) and Hypertext Transfer Protocol (HTTP) to display and move around web pages. While some wireless web browsers use HTML, most use the Wireless Access Protocol (WAP). web sites must be WAP enabled for them to be viewed on wireless devices, and the WAP protocol is used to retrieve those web pages and display them on your wireless device. As you are using the wireless Internet or having discussions about it, you may hear the WAP term from time to time, so just remember that WAP refers to a communication method that allows web site content to be displayed on your BlackBerry or other wireless Internet-ready device.

tools necessary for wireless devices to access and use the wireless Internet. Wireless Internet providers are just like wired providers—you pay them a monthly access fee to use the Internet with your wireless device, and in turn, they provide the service and software you need to surf the Internet.

GoAmerica is a leading wireless provider and the most popular BlackBerry ISP. If you plan on connecting to the wireless Internet, the odds are good that you will choose GoAmerica as your ISP, although in all fairness other ISPs are available as well (see Chapter 13). The GoAmerica tools and the access to the Internet you will receive are great, and you'll be happy to part with the monthly access fee.

In order to use the GoAmerica browser and web service, you must sign up with GoAmerica, after which they will create an account for you. As you can see in Figure 9-1, Go.Web supports the BlackBerry, and once you purchase an account, you can download the Go.Web browser and install it on your BlackBerry, just as you would any other application. Depending on your service provider, however, the browser may already be installed and configured for you, so just check out your network provider documentation before doing anything.

TIP   *See Chapter 5 to learn more about installing applications on your BlackBerry. Also, see Chapter 14 to learn more about downloading BlackBerry applications.*

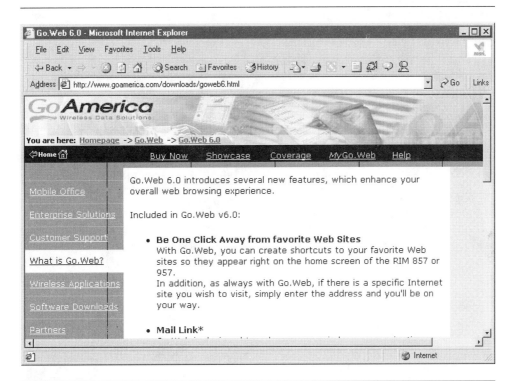

You can sign up for the GoAmerica service at the GoAmerica web site. You can even purchase a BlackBerry there as well. Setup for the service will cost you about $25. If you want a kilobyte-limited service, it will cost you around $10 a month; unlimited service will cost you around $20 a month (I recommend the unlimited). Overall, setup and installation is quite easy. You can download the GoAmerica web browser from http://www.goamerica.com/downloads. Once the download is complete, you'll need to install it on your BlackBerry. The steps in "Install the GoAmerica Web Browser" walk you through the installation process.

Getting Started with GoAmerica

The GoAmerica browser is a full-featured browser that makes using the wireless Internet on your BlackBerry a real snap. Once the GoAmerica browser has been installed, you can access it directly from your BlackBerry's Home screen through

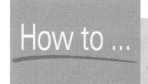

Install the GoAmerica Web Browser

To install the GoAmerica Web Browser, just follow these steps:

1. Double-click the GoAmerica installation icon that appears once the download is complete.

2. Click Next on the GoAmerica Welcome screen that appears.

3. Read the End-User License agreement and click Next.

4. The Choose Destination Location window shown in Figure 9-2 appears, through which you choose the directory destination on you computer. The default is fine, or you can change it using the Browse button if you like. Click Next.

5. A software confirmation window appears, letting you know that the software detected your BlackBerry software. Click Next.

6. The Programs Folder window appears. By default, the BlackBerry software is installed in Accessories. Click Next.

7. The files are copied to your computer. Click the Finish button to complete the installation.

8. Place the BlackBerry on the cradle and use the Desktop Manager to perform a complete backup of the BlackBerry. See Chapter 5 for step-by-step instructions.

9. Open the Application Loader on the Desktop Manager.

10. In the selection window, choose the GoAmerica browser, as shown in Figure 9-3, which will now appear as an option.

11. Complete the steps in the wizard and the GoAmerica browser will be installed on your BlackBerry.

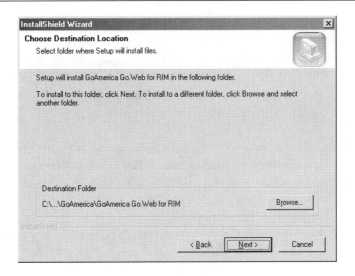

FIGURE 9-2   Choose Destination Location window

9

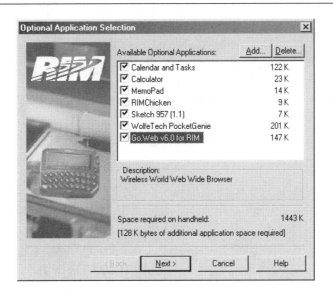

FIGURE 9-3   Select the GoAmerica browser

the GoAmerica icon. If you scroll to and click the icon for the first time, you see the Click here to start screen, shown in Figure 9-4.

Click the start button. At this point, connectivity begins and security keys for your unit are generated. Once this process completes, the download of information occurs. Notice that as the download is occurring, you see an arrow in the upper-right corner noting the transfer of information, and the signal strength appears in the lower-right corner. Once the download is complete, you see the Go.Web home screen, shown in Figure 9-5.

The Go.Web home screen, which is referred to as the main menu, provides you with different categories of Internet sites that you can browse and access, or you can access whatever site you want by entering a URL. Before getting into the different categories that are available to you, however, let's first spend a moment looking at Go.Web browser navigation.

You'll quickly see that the Go.Web browser works just like any other BlackBerry application. You use the trackwheel to scroll to and click the items that you want. You also click the trackwheel to see an options menu, as shown in Figure 9-6. Using this menu, you can easily maneuver around and get to the screen you need. Notice that the Back option is available in Figure 9-6. The Back (and Forward) features available on this menu enable the browser to act more like a desktop browser. In fact, there are a number of possible menu options that may

FIGURE 9-4   GoAmerica start screen (Copyright, 2001, GoAmerica, Inc. All rights reserved)

appear, depending on what you are doing with the BlackBerry. The following list
outlines the possible options:

- **Hide Menu**   Closes the menu without making any selections.

- **Back**   Returns you to the previous web page screen.

- **Forward**   Moves you to the web page screen you moved back from.

- **Goto Link**   Takes you to the current link you have selected. You can also
  just simply press ENTER or click the trackwheel when a link is highlighted
  to move to the link (which is a lot faster than using the menu).

- **Refresh**   Reloads the web page from the Internet to make certain you
  have the latest information.

- **Add Mark**   Creates a bookmark of the current page. You can then use the
  bookmark to easily return to the web page. See "Create a New Bookmark"
  later in this chapter.

- **View Marks**   Enables you to see a list of all bookmarked pages.

- **View MobileClips**   Enables you to customize information that you see
  and view in an online GoAmerica library of MobileClips (discussed in
  more detail later in "Using MobileClips").

- **Mail Link**   Enables you to send the URL of the current web site in an
  e-mail message. See "E-mail a URL" later in this chapter for step-by-step
  instructions on how to e-mail URLs.

9

- ■ **Go.Web Home**   Returns to the Home menu screen, shown earlier in Figure 9-5.

- ■ **Check/Uncheck**   Add or remove a check from a check box. You can also just click check boxes with your trackwheel to get the same results.

- ■ **Show List**   See a list of menu options from a drop-down box that appears on a web page. You can also just click the drop-down box to see the options.

As you see, a number of menu options simply repeat what you can do with the trackwheel. This is typical for BlackBerry applications and is a feature that makes your work with the BlackBerry easier.

Accessing Web Sites

The GoAmerica browser comes to you with a list of default categories that you can see on the main Go.Web menu (refer back to Figure 9-5). These menu options provide you with a default listing of web sites that you can easily access, or you can access your own. In this section, I'll give you a quick review of the categories and web sites that are available from the Go.Web menu. Note that you may have additional categories and/or sites available that may have been added since the writing of this book.

FIGURE 9-6   Go.Web Options menu (Copyright, 2001, GoAmerica, Inc. All rights reserved)

Once you click on a category, you can see the subcategories available under that category as well as the other categories. In other words, the browser makes it easy for you to move from category to link on one screen, as shown in Figure 9-7.

GoAmerica Services

The GoAmerica Services category provides you access to information about GoAmerica as well as help for several of its services, as detailed in the following text.

GoAmerica News

GoAmerica News, shown in Figure 9-8, gives you information about GoAmerica. Essentially, all you can access here are press releases from GoAmerica, but it's a good link to follow if you want to stay up-to-date with what is available for the service or coming in the future.

Go.Web POP3 Access

If you are using GoAmerica as your e-mail provider (which is typical for BlackBerry Internet Edition customers), you can access your e-mail online using this link. Just login with your username and password to access your account.

9

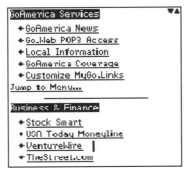

FIGURE 9-7   Categories and links (Copyright, 2001, GoAmerica, Inc. All rights reserved)

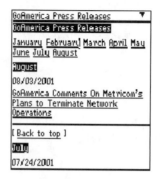

Local Information

Local Information is a great tool to access because it lets you quickly find information about the area you are in. Using the wireless network, the Internet can return information about the area where you are currently using your BlackBerry. As you can see in Figure 9-9, the Local Information feature tells you where you are (or near) and gives you links for local weather and restaurants.

GoAmerica Coverage

The GoAmerica Coverage option allows you to enter a ZIP code and find out if there is current network coverage for that ZIP code. This is a handy feature to use if you will be traveling and want to make sure you remain in one of the coverage areas.

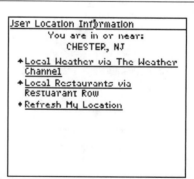

Customize MyGo.Links

This feature gives you access to a number of different aspects of the GoAmerica web site. You can get help from the web site and access information specific to the BlackBerry. You'll need to log in with your username and password to access the bulk of the features available through this link.

Business & Finance

Keep up with your business and what is happening in the financial world while you are on the go. Your Go.Web browser gives you predefined links to several popular online financial and business sites. The following sections tell you what is predefined in the Business & Finance category.

Stock Smart

The Stock Smart web site, shown in Figure 9-10, is a monitoring site where you can watch any number of stocks and even get live quotes over the Internet. You can check out the most active stocks on NASDAQ and find information about stock "winners and losers." Overall, if you need to keep track of certain stocks by getting quotes online, this a great site to use.

USA TODAY Moneyline

USA TODAY Moneyline is a division of USATODAY.com and provides news and information about finance and business. If you click the USA TODAY

| FIGURE 9-10 | Stock Smart |

Moneyline link, you see the home screen shown in Figure 9-11. From here, simply click the links that are of interest to you. Be sure to sign up for the e-mail newletter!

> **TIP** *As you browse the available web sites, be sure to use the Back and Forward options on the menu to easily move from page to page.*

VentureWire

VentureWire, shown in Figure 9-12, is a general news and financial site that provides you with all kinds of business-related information. Access this site to see top financial headlines. There's a helpful search feature you can use to locate the information you are looking for.

TheStreet.com

TheStreet.com is a financial information site that is similar to the other sites provided under this category. At this site you'll find quick access to headlines, as you can see in Figure 9-13. Just click any link to learn more.

> **NOTE** *Keep in mind that particular pages within any of these web sites can be marked and added to your list of bookmarks so you can easily access them when you want. Bookmarks are explored in more detail later in "Using Bookmarks."*

FIGURE 9-11   USA TODAY Moneyline

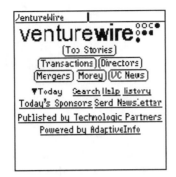

FIGURE 9-12   VentureWire

News

The News category provides access to a number of popular web sites that let you keep up with the current news headlines and information. Use these sites for general news topics, and keep in mind that some of them do have business-related news that can be readily accessed from the news site's home screen. The following sections show what default link options are available to you.

FIGURE 9-13   TheStreet.com

ABCNEWS.com

ABC News is, of course, a world leader in news and information, and you can easily access the ABCNEWS.com site via your BlackBerry. As you can see in Figure 9-14, you can access the current headlines, business news, science, travel, technology, and other news categories. Of course, there is a wealth of information here, so check it out.

MSNBC Mobile

Like ABCNEWS.com, you'll get full access to all kinds of news and information at MSNBC Mobile. You find easy access to information here, including top stories in all kinds of categories. Figure 9-15 shows the MSNBC Mobile home page.

The New York Times

Known for excellence and quality in journalism, the New York Times is available on the wireless Internet, as shown in Figure 9-16. As you can see from the home page, you can access a couple of different category links to easily get to the news that you want.

The Wall Street Journal

Known as a world leader in business and economic news, the Wall Street Journal is available in an interactive edition via Go.Web. Read headlines, find out specific

FIGURE 9-14   ABCNEWS.com

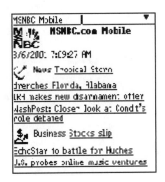

FIGURE 9-15   MSNBC Mobile

business news, and keep up-to-date while you are on the move. The wireless version
of the Wall Street Journal is shown in Figure 9-17.

USA TODAY Nationline

USA TODAY Nationline, a division of USA TODAY.com, provides you with all
kinds of national and sports news with easy links for you to find what you want.
You can also sign up for their free e-newsletter from the home page, shown in
Figure 9-18.

FIGURE 9-16   The New York Times

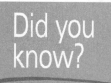

The Wireless Internet vs. the Wired Internet

So you're looking at wireless Internet sites and notice there is some resemblance to the wired version. For example, ABCNEWS.com looks about the same on the wireless Internet as it does on the wired one. Are you getting the same information? Are you getting less information?

Remember that wireless Internet data is text-based and does not include all of the graphics. However, the actual information you are reading should be the same on the wireless Internet as it is on the wired Internet. Some sites may not give you as much information or links to everything, but this is quickly becoming a thing of the past. You can rest assured that when you access information on the Internet via your BlackBerry you are getting up-to-date, complete data, just as you would on the wired Internet.

Excite News

Excite, the popular online search engine, provides a news and information page that is available from your BlackBerry. You'll find basic links to news, sports, and even classified pages.

```
What's News                 ▼
Monday, August 6, 2001
10:03 a.m. EDT
The Wall Street Journal
Interactive Edition
What's News | Asia | Europe
Technology | Markets Update
ECHOSTAR MADE an unsolicited
$30.4 billion stock bid for rival
satellite broadcaster Hughes
Electronics. The offer, made in
the form of a public letter to the
board of General Motors, Hughes's
parent, is intended to lure the
```

FIGURE 9-17   The Wall Street Journal

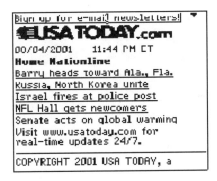

CNET News.com

CNET is a popular online source for all things computing. You can find information here about the computer industry, what's new and upcoming, and yes, you'll find plenty here about wireless devices as well. The CNET home screen is displayed in Figure 9-19.

ZDNet.com

ZDNet, shown in Figure 9-20, is another popular online source for news and information about the computing industry. You can find all kinds of information

FIGURE 9-20   ZDNet.com

on this site about wireless devices as well as plenty of reviews and articles. It's a great resource to keep in mind, and I use it all the time.

Wired News

The Wired News site provides you with more new on computing, business, culture, politics, and a variety of other news topics. News is organized into categories for easy browsing and viewing.

Sports

Of course, you don't want to be away from the computer or television too long and lose track of your favorite games and sports teams. Don't worry, Go.Web enables you to keep track of the latest sports scores and news no matter where you are. You'll find easy access to two different sports sites, which are described in the following sections.

ESPN

ESPN is the most popular Internet site for sports news and reports, as shown in Figure 9-21. Visit this online mobile source and easily access different categories of information. Be sure to check out the top stories so you can stay abreast of the latest news in sports.

The Sporting News

The Sporting News is another online news source for what's hot in sports. You can quickly access sports headlines here, but the site is not as comprehensive as ESPN.

FIGURE 9-21   ESPN

Travel

As you might guess, the Go.Web browser provides you with a travel section so you can easily use the BlackBerry to get information while you are on the road. You'll find the following sites, which are directly provided for you, valuable resources as you travel.

MapQuest

MapQuest is a very popular online travel site where you can enter destination information and then get driving directions as well as general area maps. You'll find the same functionality on the wireless web as you have on the wired web, with more text instructions of course. You'll use this one as you travel, so get familiar with it!

10Best.com

10Best.com allows you to select a city, and then find out all kinds of information about that city, such as dining guides, local attractions, hotels, and many other items. This is an easy-to-use, helpful site that you will enjoy. As you can see in Figure 9-22, I have pulled up information for Dallas, Texas.

Frommer's City to Go

Frommer's City to Go allows you to choose a region and locate information about cities in that region. The site then provides you with categories for dining, lodging, entertainment, nightlife, and so on. The site is easy to use and provides a lot of information.

FIGURE 9-22   10Best.com

Restaurant Row

The Restaurant Row site provides you with location categories so that you can search for restaurants by their distance from you, or you can perform advanced searches to find the kind of restaurant that you want. If you are on the move and looking for a good place to eat, this is a quick-and-easy Internet site to use.

USA TODAY Travel Tips

USA TODAY Travel Tips is another division of USA TODAY.com. You can get information here about travel destinations, hot spots, problems spots, and general-travel related news. Check it out!

Weather

After the Travel category you'll find the Weather category. Designed for the mobile user, this site can help you find out about weather conditions in your area and the areas you are traveling to.

Weather.com

Weather.com is a popular online site for locating weather conditions by city, state, and even area code. Just use the easy search features to find current weather conditions and reports for the desired area. The features provided enable you to search for weather conditions in a particular state, city, or area code, or you can access the site to read general weather-related news. Either way, it's a very valuable site to have in the palm of your hand. In Figure 9-23, you can see that I have pulled up the weather report for Copper Mountain Resort in Colorado.

FIGURE 9-23   Weather.com

Living

The Living category encompasses a number of different sites that are related to culture and lifestyles. The sites you'll find here provide fun and information on a variety of topics, as described in the following sections.

USA TODAY Lifeline

The USA TODAY Lifeline site, which is simply another division of USA TODAY.com, provides Hollywood information and related articles. This is a great site to access if you need a little leisure reading while you are waiting on your plane.

Yahoo! Movies

Get information on the latest and greatest in the movie world at Yahoo! Movies. This site has an easy-to-use interface that allows you to find the movie you want and read all about it.

AstrologyIS.com

Find your latest horoscope at this astrology site, which features an easy-to-use interface where you can enter your birthday and find the day's current reading.

Shopping

You can shop for items on the wireless Internet, just as you can on the wired Internet. The BlackBerry supports encryption standards that make the transmission of your credit card and other personal information safe. So, while you're waiting on the plane or stuck in traffic, check out these fun shopping sites.

Edmunds2Go!

Interested in buying a new or used car? You can find the information you need at the Edmunds2Go! wireless site, shown in Figure 9-24. Find vehicle prices and reviews and even locate a particular dealer near you. The site is simple and quick and gives you a wealth of information.

Snaz

You can locate all kinds of products through various Snaz stores on your mobile device, the home screen for which is shown in Figure 9-25. Browse, shop, buy— it's all easy and safe. Find gifts and seasonal specials, and even search the site for a particular product. It's a great site to visit.

BarPoint Shopper

BarPoint Shopper is a general shopping site that enables you to search for a product by UPC code, or you can perform a general search and locate the product you need. Then, through secure online ordering, you can easily buy that product—all while you are on the move. BarPoint's home page is shown in Figure 9-26.

FIGURE 9-24   Edmunds2Go!

FIGURE 9-25   Snaz

Search

You can use search engines on the wireless Internet just as you can in the wired world. Go.Web provides you direct access to Google, Alta Vista, and 555–1212.com. Use these sites to search for keywords and find the information you need.

FIGURE 9-26   BarPoint Shopper

Using the Browser's Features

Now that you have explored the categories and default web sites that your Go.Web browser provides, it's time to go a little deeper and take a look at the other features of the browser and how you can really use the options available to get around the Internet. The following sections explore these features and show you how to use them.

E-mail a URL

One of the items on your options menu enables you to send a URL. This means that you can surf the Internet, find a web page you like, and then send that web page via a URL link in an e-mail message that you choose. This simple feature makes sharing links really easy. The following text, "E-mail a URL," gives you the steps you need to use this feature.

> **TIP**   *If you receive a message with an attached URL, your Go.Web browser can automatically open the link and display it for you.*

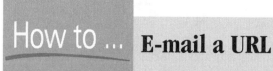

How to ... E-mail a URL

To e-mail a URL, follow these steps:

1. Use the Go.Web browser and locate the page that you want to e-mail.

2. Click the trackwheel to access the menu options, and then click Mail Link.

3. Your address book opens. Select the recipient you want, or select the Use Once feature to enter the recipient's e-mail or PIN.

4. The message window appears. Type a subject and message if desired, and then send the message.

How to ... Create a New Bookmark

To create a new bookmark, follow these steps:

1. Using the Go.Web browser, locate the web page that you want to bookmark.

2. Click the trackwheel to access the menu, and then click Add Mark, as shown in Figure 9-27.

3. In the name box that appears, as shown in Figure 9-28, enter a friendly name for the bookmark, and then click the trackwheel. The bookmark is saved in your bookmarks list.

Using Bookmarks

Bookmarks give you a quick-and-easy way to keep track of web pages that you want to revisit. Instead of having to remember the URL of a certain web page, you can bookmark it. Later, when you want to revisit the page, you access your bookmarks and simply select the bookmark for that page from a list. Setting up and managing bookmarks is easy.

9

FIGURE 9-27 Click Add Mark (Copyright, 2001, GoAmerica, Inc. All rights reserved)

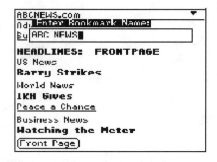

FIGURE 9-28   Enter a friendly name (Copyright, 2001, GoAmerica, Inc. All rights
reserved)

In order to create a bookmark, just follow the steps in "Create a New
Bookmark."

As you surf the wireless Internet, you will bookmark sites that you want to
remember and use the bookmarks page to easily access those sites. Bookmarks are
saved to your BlackBerry Home screen by default, so when you open the Go.Web
browser, you can quickly and easily go to the desired bookmark. When you save a
bookmark, you can choose for the bookmark not to be saved to the Home screen, in
which case it is available from the bookmarks menu. In either case, those bookmarks
may begin to pile up, and some sites you once used will no longer be needed.

You can easily remove bookmarks that you no longer need. When you are in
the Go.Web browser, simply click the trackwheel to see the menu, and then click
View Marks. This takes you to the bookmarks page, as shown in Figure 9-29. Roll
your trackwheel to select the bookmark you no longer want, click the trackwheel,
and then click Delete Mark.

FIGURE 9-29   Bookmarked sites (Copyright, 2001, GoAmerica, Inc. All rights
reserved)

How Should Bookmarks Be Named?

By default, the URL name of a page, such as ABCNEWS.com, is used for the bookmark name. However, you can change bookmark names to whatever you want. Often, people use common names such as "ABC News" or just "news" for such a site. There is no right or wrong, of course, but the point is to provide a recognizable name that helps you remember the actual web site. It's okay to use a URL as the name, as long as the URL is descriptive and you will know what web site the URL refers to when you later access the bookmark list. In short, make the names meaningful and useful to you.

Using MobileClips

MobileClips is an online service that makes getting content faster and easier using the BlackBerry. With MobileClips, you can define the content that you want, or you can get content from the Go.Web site and download it from the MobileClip library. These MobileClips are like links in a way, but they provide some additional functionality that you may find useful.

Let's consider an example. While in the Go.Web browser, click the trackwheel to see the menu, and then click View MobileClips. The My MobileClips screen comes up, and it lists any current MobileClips you have configured, as you can see in Figure 9-30.

9

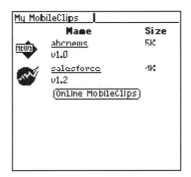

You can access your currently configured MobileClips or you can access the Go.Web online database of MobileClips by clicking the button. This takes you to a Go.Web page that enables you to browse different categories of MobileClips and find something that you want, as shown in Figure 9-31.

You can browse the categories and available MobileClips, and when you find something you want, you can easily add it to your MobileClips library. For example, in Figure 9-32, I have added the UPS tracking tool. Now I can keep up with my UPS packages no matter where I am.

MobileClips are just like bookmarks in that you can easily go to the MobileClips page and delete any mobile clip that you no longer want, and you can always add new ones as desired. You'll find this feature easy to use and a real time-saver for getting the information that you need.

Manually Accessing a URL

The default categories and web sites provided by the Go.Web browser give you a rich landscape of web sites you can access on your BlackBerry. However, what if you want to access a web site that is not listed as a default option? First off, the web site you want to access must support WAP or you will not be able to access it from the Go.Web browser. If the site does support WAP, you can easily access it by entering its URL. Here's how: On the Go.Web home screen, scroll to and click the Open URL option, and then type the URL (such as www.amazon.com), as shown in Figure 9-33. You can then access the web site just as you would on a computer browser.

FIGURE 9-31   Online MobileClips (Copyright, 2001, GoAmerica, Inc. All rights reserved)

UPS package tracking

> TIP *You can access secure web sites by choosing the HTTPS drop-down menu option that appears before the URL entry box.*

Go.Web Browser Configuration

The Go.Web browser installs easily and painlessly on your BlackBerry, and under most circumstances, you don't have to worry about browser setup. However, there are configuration options you should know about in case you ever need to make any configuration changes.

From the BlackBerry Home screen, click the Options icon. You'll see the Go.Web option. Click the option to open the Go.Web Preferences page. You'll

FIGURE 9-33 Manually enter a URL (Copyright, 2001, GoAmerica, Inc. All rights reserved)

see some changeable options, and a number of which cannot be changed, as shown in Figure 9-34. The following preferences are configurable:

■ **Images**   By default, friendly line images can be displayed. Your other option is to display no images, which may make your surfing experience faster.

■ **Format Tables**   Yes is enabled by default, and you'll have a much clearer surfing experience if you leave this option set to the default.

■ **Device Emulation**   The Go.Web browser can act like a browser or a phone—leave the option set to Browser.

■ **Language**   The options are English or French.

■ **Maximum Page Size**   This option determines how many bytes can be displayed on one page. The default is 12,000, and this is a good setting.

■ **Flash Link**   Active links will flash on your screen if you set the option to Yes.

■ **Cache Used/Max**   The Go.Web browser caches pages by default to help with your surfing experience. You should leave these settings alone.

■ **Reset Security**   This feature clears and resets the browser security keys. Try this option if you are having problems connecting using the browser, but seem to have general connectivity otherwise.

FIGURE 9-34   Go.Web preferences

Part 4

Personal Management Tools

Chapter 10

Manage Your Business and Life with the BlackBerry Calendar

How to...

- Distinguish the various BlackBerry calendar components
- Manage appointments
- Perform calendar synchronization

Several years ago, the concept of calendar data and time management with electronic calendars, especially in desktop PIMs, became popular and common in corporate environments. The same is true today—all kinds of applications provide complex calendar support, and some applications are written with calendar management in mind. The BlackBerry steps up to this plate by supporting both its own calendar feature as well as synchronization with desktop PIM calendars. Indeed, in some corporate environments, calendar synchronization can also occur wirelessly with no effort from you. In this chapter, you get to explore the BlackBerry's calendar. You'll learn how to use it to meet your needs and the methods of synchronization with your desktop PIM.

Getting to Know the BlackBerry Calendar

The BlackBerry calendar is available directly from the BlackBerry Home screen. On the 957 model, the Calendar icon looks like a flip-top calendar, and on the 950 model, the Calendar icon consists of the number 31 inside of a box. You can scroll to and click the icon to open the calendar, or you can just press L on your keypad. Aside from this point, the calendar feature on the two models functions in basically the same way. The BlackBerry calendar has four different views, which are explored in the following sections.

Day View

The Day view, shown in Figure 10-1, gives you an hourly look at the entire day. By default, the day begins at 9:00 A.M. and ends at 6:00 P.M., but you can change these settings by adjusting the Calendar Options feature (which I discuss later in this chapter). For each hour of the day, you can enter appointments or even multiple appointments, which you will have a chance to explore in the section "Creating a New Appointment," later in the chapter.

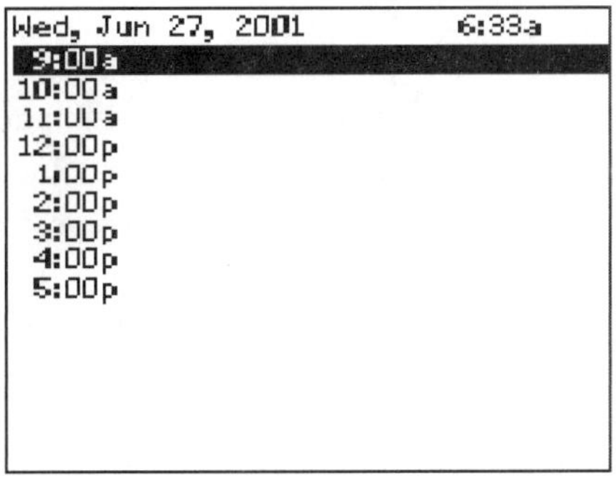

Wed, Jun 27, 2001
6:33a
9:00a
10:00a
11:00a
12:00p
1:00p
2:00p
3:00p
4:00p
5:00p

FIGURE 10-1 Calendar Day view

Week View

The Week view, shown in Figure 10-2, gives you a column for each day of the week (shown at the top of the view) and rows for each hour that constitutes a day (shown running down the left side of the view). The Week view is especially helpful when you need to compare appointments throughout the week or just need to gain an overall outlook of the week's events.

Wed, Jun 27, 2001
6:42a
Jun
2001
S 24
M 25
T 26
W 27
T 28
F 29
S 30
9:00a
10:00a
11:00a
12:00p
1:00p
2:00p
3:00p
4:00p
5:00p

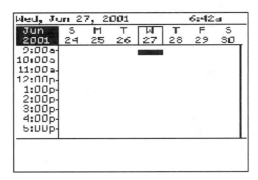

FIGURE 10-2 Calendar Week view

Month View

The Month view, shown in Figure 10-3, gives you a look at the calendar month. On the 957 model, you can see the current month and the upcoming month on the screen. On the 950 model, only the current month is visible due to the screen size.

 Use the trackwheel to scroll through the month to advance to the next month. The BlackBerry will show you any month you want.

Agenda View

The Agenda view, shown in Figure 10-4, gives you an agenda for the day so that you can see your appointments. This is similar to the Day view, but only the appointments are shown instead of each hour of the day.

Configuring Calendar Options

The BlackBerry calendar has a few simple options that you can configure in order to meet your needs. Specifically, you can determine what day of the week the calendar begins on and the start time and end time of each day. These options are easy to configure, and the section, "Configure Calendar Options," shows the steps.

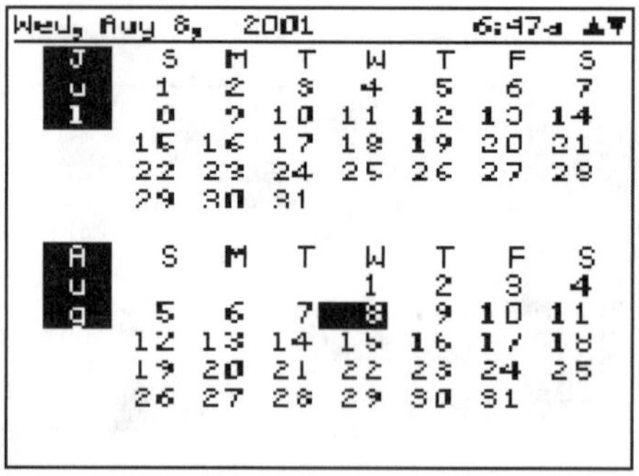

```
Wed, Aug 8,  2001              6:47a
   J    S   M   T   W   T   F   S
   u    1   2   3   4   5   6   7
   l    8   9  10  11  12  13  14
       15  16  17  18  19  20  21
       22  23  24  25  26  27  28
       29  30  31

   A    S   M   T   W   T   F   S
   u                1   2   3   4
   g    5   6   7   8   9  10  11
       12  13  14  15  16  17  18
       19  20  21  22  23  24  25
       26  27  28  29  30  31
```

FIGURE 10-3   BlackBerry Month view

```
┌──────────────────────────────────────┐
│Wed, Jun 27, 2001          6:51a       │
│          Wed, Jun 27, 2001            │
│█9:00a ♦Training Meeting████            │
│ 9:00a ♦Client Site Meeting            │
│ 10:00a                                │
│ 10:00a  @Conf room B                  │
│                                        │
│                                        │
│                                        │
│                                        │
│                                        │
│                                        │
└──────────────────────────────────────┘
```

FIGURE 10-4   BlackBerry Agenda view

Managing Appointments

The obvious purpose of the calendar, aside from just looking at the date, is to set appointments. Using the calendar, you can set appointments throughout the day, week, or month, and the BlackBerry will keep track of those appointments and remind you of them as they are coming up. You can see that this is a powerful tool when you consider the BlackBerry is designed to travel with you wherever you go. You don't need a paper calendar in order to keep up with your schedule— the BlackBerry can do it for you and even sound an alarm 15 minutes before an appointment occurs as a reminder.

The following sections show you how to create and manage appointments so you can make the best use of the BlackBerry calendar.

Creating a New Appointment

You can create a new appointment at any time and from any calendar view (Day, Week, Month, Agenda). By creating a new appointment, you specify information about that appointment so that the BlackBerry can add the appointment to your calendar and keep track of it for you.

10

Configure Calendar Options

To configure the calendar options, just follow these steps:

1. In the Home screen, scroll to and click the Calendar icon, or just press L on your keypad. The BlackBerry calendar opens.

2. Click the trackwheel to see the menu, and then scroll to and click Options. The Options screen appears, as shown in Figure 10-5. As you can see, you can determine the day of the week the calendar begins on and the start and end times for each day.

3. To set the day in which the calendar begins, use the trackwheel to select the option, click the trackwheel, and then click Change Option. Adjust the day of the week as desired in the dialog box that appears. You can also press the ALT key and roll the trackwheel to change the day, which bypasses the menu feature (this is usually faster). The beginning day starts the calendar on that particular day and extends through the week. For example, let's say that due to my work schedule, I want to start the calendar on Thursday of each week. If I specify the beginning day as Thursday, in my calendar I will see the weeks as Thursday through Wednesday instead of the typical Sunday through Saturday, as shown in Figure 10-6.

4. The start and end times for each day are set to 9:00 A.M. to 6:00 P.M. by default. You can change these according to your work schedule using the same scroll-and-click or ALT key methods described in Step 4 for the beginning day specification.

5. Once you are done, just click the trackwheel to access the screen menu and click Save Options.

FIGURE 10-5   Options screen

To add a new appointment, simply click the trackwheel while in any calendar view and click New Appointment. The New Appointment screen appears, as shown in Figure 10-7.

This screen presents the following field options:

- **Subject**   You can enter a subject for the appointment here. Your subjects should be descriptive, yet brief.

- **Location**   You can enter a location for the appointment here, such as Conference Room A, Jim's office, and so on.

- **Date**   Enter the start date in this field. By default, today's date is listed.

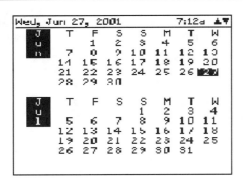

FIGURE 10-6   Calendar beginning day changed to Thursday

10

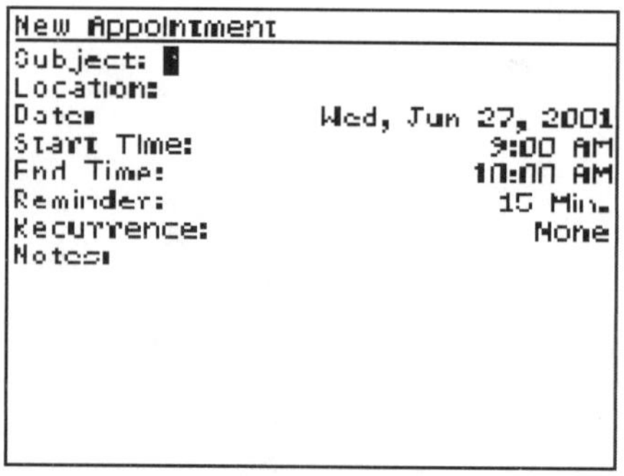

```
New Appointment
Subject: ▌
Location:
Date:                    Wed, Jun 27, 2001
Start Time:                       9:00 AM
End Time:                        10:00 AM
Reminder:                         15 Min.
Recurrence:                          None
Notes:
```

FIGURE 10-7   New Appointment screen

- **Start Time**   Enter the start time of the appointment here. By default, the current time, rounded to the next hour is shown here. (For example, if it is 8:20 A.M., the appointment will show 9:00 A.M.)

- **End Date**   Enter the date the appointment ends.

- **End Time**   Enter the time the appointment ends. The default is an hour after the start time.

- **Reminder**   The BlackBerry can notify you before the appointment occurs. By default, the reminder occurs 15 minutes before the appointment. You can change this value, however, to 30 minutes, 1 hour, 2 hours, 4 hours, 8 hours, 1 day, and so on. You can also turn this option off if you don't want to use it at all.

- **Recurrence**   The recurrence feature allows you to set up a recurring appointment. For example, if you have a staff meeting every morning at 8:30, you don't have to individually enter each morning's appointment— you can just enter it one time and configure the appointment to be a recurring one.

- **Notes**   Enter any information about the appointment you want in this section.

To configure an appointment, simply roll the trackwheel and/or use the ALT key to move between fields and enter or change information as needed. For example, as you can see in Figure 10-8, I have a meeting in conference room C that runs

```
┌─────────────────────────────────┐
│ New Appointment                 │
│ Subject: Payroll Meeting        │
│ Location: Conference Room C      │
│ Date:           Wed, Jun 27, 2001│
│ Start Time:            10:00 AM  │
│ End Time:              11:30 AM  │
│ Reminder:               30 Min.  │
│ Recurrence:               None   │
│ Notes: Bring reports from last  │
│ month's meeting.▇               │
│                                 │
│                                 │
│                                 │
│                                 │
└─────────────────────────────────┘
```

FIGURE 10-8   New appointment

from 10:00 A.M. to 11:30 A.M. I have reminder set for 30 minutes beforehand and a few notes about the meeting.

If you want to specify a meeting as recurrent, scroll to the Recurrence field, click the trackwheel to bring up the menu, and then click Change Option. You see the Set Recurrence screen, as shown in Figure 10-9. Depending on how you want the appointment to recur, use the trackwheel to change the recurrence pattern. For example, you can choose Day, Week, Month, and Year options. Depending on which option you select, the screen changes to give you additional options as needed. For example, if you choose the Week option, as shown in Figure 10-9, you can choose for the appointment to occur every week, every other week, every third week, and so on, and you can specify the day of the week on which the

10

FIGURE 10-9   Recurrence pattern

appointment should recur. Once you are done, click the trackwheel and click Save Recurrence.

Once you are done configuring your appointment, click the trackwheel and click Save Appointment on the menu that appears.

Viewing Appointments

Once you create an appointment, it appears in the four different calendar views. For example, as you can see in Figure 10-10, the Day view lists the day's appointments based on the times in which they occur. You can see the subject, and if you have set a reminder, a little bell appears next to the appointment. You can also see that a bracket appears showing the amount of time the appointment consumes. For example, as shown in Figure 10-10, the Sales meeting is only one hour, but the marketing meeting is three hours (looks like I'll need a lot of coffee for that one).

In the Week view of appointments, you see grids blocked out on the calendar according to the date and time that they occur. If you have multiple meetings back to back, you will see a line dividing each block according to time. For example, as shown in Figure 10-11, on Friday I have an 8:00 A.M. meeting, a 9:00 A.M. meeting, and then a 10:00 A.M. to 1:00 P.M. meeting. A line divides each meeting block so I can tell how long the meeting will last.

Using the trackwheel, you can scroll to appointment blocks on the grid to display the subject and start/end times for the appointment in the bottom screen area.

FIGURE 10-10   Day view of appointments

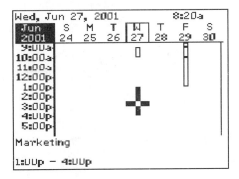

| FIGURE 10-11 | Week view of appointments |

> **TIP** *You can maneuver vertically through the appointment grid by simply using the trackwheel. If you want to maneuver horizontally, hold down the* ALT *key and roll the trackwheel.*

In the Month view, shown in Figure 10-12, the current day is highlighted (boxed) by default. For each day that has appointment(s), a black bar appears next to the day. A short bar represents short meetings and longer meetings are indicated by a longer bar. If the meeting consumes the entire day, the date is highlighted. This view is an excellent way to get a broad look at your schedule.

| FIGURE 10-12 | Month view of appointments |

10

The Agenda view gives you a list of dates with appointments for each date. The appointment times and locations (if configured) are also listed in this view, shown in Figure 10-13.

In any of these views, you can get the details about the appointment by simply scrolling to the appointment, clicking to bring up the associated menu options, and clicking View Appointment. This opens the same appointment screen you saw when you created the appointment initially.

NOTE   *You cannot make any changes to appointments when you use the View Appointment feature. If you need to edit an appointment, see the section "Editing an Appointment" later in this chapter.*

Finally, the menu gives you some additional viewing options that just help you maneuver through appointments. In any calendar view, click the trackwheel to see the menu. You can choose the options Next, Previous, Today, and Go to Date. The Next and Previous options allow you to easily move backward and forward through a list of appointments. The Today option allows you to zero in on the current day's appointments, and the Go to Date option allows you to choose a date that you want to view. When you choose Go to Date, a dialog box appears where you can enter the date that you want, as shown in Figure 10-14.

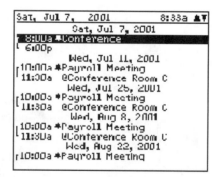

FIGURE 10-13   Agenda view of appointments

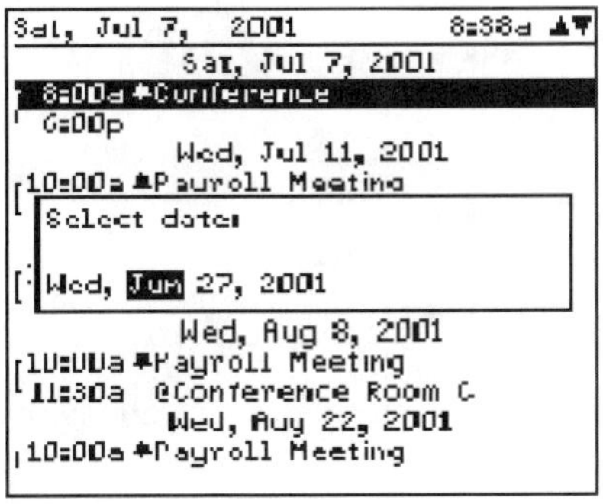

```
Sat, Jul 7,  2001            8:38a ▲▼
            Sat, Jul 7, 2001
  8:00a *Conference
  6:00p
           Wed, Jul 11, 2001
 10:00a *Payroll Meeting
   Select date:

 Wed, Jun 27, 2001
           Wed, Aug 8, 2001
 10:00a *Payroll Meeting
 11:30a  @Conference Room C
           Wed, Aug 22, 2001
 10:00a *Payroll Meeting
```

| FIGURE 10-14 | Go to Date feature |

Editing an Appointment

Unfortunately, changes in life are inevitable (as are mistakes), and the BlackBerry wouldn't be much help if you could not make changes to appointments you've created. If your schedule is like mine, it is not unusual for several appointments to change in any given week and sometimes in any given day. Fortunately, the BlackBerry is very forgiving, and you can make appointment changes quickly and easily. To make changes to an appointment, just follow the steps in "Edit an Appointment."

Did you know?

Which View Should I Use?

The calendar view options are just that—options you can use to get information or gain a perspective about your appointments. For your daily routine, the Day view and the Agenda view will be the most helpful to you because the line item information is specific and easier to read. If you need to get an overall look at your week, use the Week view. You can roll over appointments and see details for those appointments at the bottom of the screen, but this view is best for examining an entire weekly schedule. Finally, the Month view is helpful when planning appointments because it gives you a quick look at the entire month.

10

 **Edit an Appointment**

To edit an appointment, follow these steps:

1. Open the calendar from the Home screen.

2. Select a desired view (preferably the Agenda view or Day view so you can see more details about the appointment).

3. Scroll to and select the appointment you want to change. Click the trackwheel and click Edit Appointment on the menu that appears.

4. The Edit Appointment screen appears, which is the same screen you used when you first created the appointment. Use the trackwheel or ALT key methods to edit the desired fields.

5. When you are done, click the trackwheel and click Save Appointment on the menu that appears. Your changes are updated.

Deleting Appointments

Just as appointments change, they are also cancelled from time to time, and you may need to delete appointments that are no longer relevant. The deletion can be one specific appointment, or you can delete all of the appointments in any given day.

 *The BlackBerry does not delete any of your appointments, even after they have passed. The calendar feature keeps the appointments listed so you can have a record of your appointments.*

To delete an appointment, just use the Day, Week, or Agenda view to scroll to the appointment that you want to delete. Click the trackwheel to access the menu, and then click the Delete Appointment option. Click Yes in the confirmation message box that appears.

If you want to delete all of the appointments for any day (such as when you are sick or perhaps taking a vacation day), then use the Month view. Scroll to the date that has appointments you want to delete, click the trackwheel, and then click Delete Appointments. Click Yes in the confirmation message box that appears.

> TIP
>
> *Use caution when deleting appointments. Once you delete an appointment, you must manually reenter it if you want it back—there is no Undo option on the BlackBerry.*

Synchronizing the BlackBerry Calendar

The BlackBerry calendar is designed to synchronize with a desktop PIM. Using this feature, you can edit appointments both on the BlackBerry and on the desktop PIM, and with synchronization, the two can update each other. You can even have someone else update your desktop PIM for you so that your BlackBerry will be updated when you synchronize. The BlackBerry provides two different types of calendar synchronization, which are explored in the following two sections.

Manual Synchronization

As you learned in Chapter 5, you can synchronize data on your BlackBerry with a desktop PIM, such as Lotus Notes, Microsoft Outlook, ACT, GroupWise, and other personal information management applications. The calendar synchronization works in the same manner, using the RIM Desktop Manager software. I'll not repeat the information given in Chapter 5, but you can use the following text, "Synchronize the Calendar with a Desktop PIM," for a quick step-by-step reference for synchronizing calendar data with your PIM.

> TIP
>
> *Keep in mind that you can also create filters for calendar entries, depending on your PIM. See Chapters 5 and 8 to learn more about filter creation.*

Over-the-Air Synchronization

Consider this scenario: You use your BlackBerry in a corporate Lotus Notes or Microsoft Exchange environment. You, several assistants, and a department coordinator have access to your calendar so that updates and changes can be made. This calendar data is synchronized with your BlackBerry so that you can always know what is coming up. However, you travel several times a month, often for three or four days at a time, and in these instances you use only the BlackBerry. Although the calendar data resides on the BlackBerry, you are unaware of changes

10

Synchronize the Calendar with a Desktop PIM

To synchronize the BlackBerry calendar with a desktop PIM, follow these steps:

1. Open the Desktop Manager program on your PC and insert the BlackBerry into the cradle.

2. Double-click the Intellisync button, and then click the Configure PIM button in the Intellisync dialog box.

3. In the Configuration dialog box, select Calendar, and then click the Choose button.

4. In the Choose PIM dialog box, select the PIM that you want Tasks to synchronize with and click OK. Translators are available for various versions of Lotus Notes, Microsoft Outlook, Microsoft Schedule, ACT, GoldMine, and GroupWise.

5. Once you click OK, you see the Calendar is configured to synchronize with the PIM you selected, as shown in Figure 10-15. Click OK.

6. In the Intellisync dialog box, click the Synchronize Now button. The BlackBerry calendar and your PIM will be synchronized.

that are made to your desktop application while you are away. Sure, you can synchronize the data as soon as you arrive back at the office, but you are using stale calendar data when you are away. What if appointments are added or cancelled? You have no way to be aware of the changes unless a colleague gives you a call or sends you an e-mail. This takes time and energy and isn't that reliable. What can you do?

If you are using the BlackBerry Enterprise Edition, you don't have to do anything—in fact, you would likely never encounter the preceding scenario. The BlackBerry Enterprise Edition supports "over-the-air" calendar synchronization. Let's say that you are away on a business trip. An assistant adds a new appointment to your calendar on your desktop PIM. Because of the BlackBerry's wireless

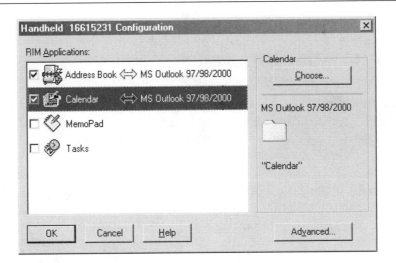

FIGURE 10-15   Calendar is configured to synchronize with the PIM

technology, this data is added to your calendar over the air with no synchronization or action from you at all. The next time you check your BlackBerry calendar, you will see the new additions. If you delete appointments, add them, or edit them, that same information is sent wirelessly back to your corporate network, where your desktop PIM is updated.

This may sound too good to be true, but if your corporate environment is configured for wireless calendar synchronization, it works like a charm. Since the configuration for wireless calendar synchronization is handled on the corporate servers, there is nothing for you to configure on your BlackBerry and nothing for you to do. More than likely, when you received your BlackBerry it was already setup for over-the-air calendar synchronization, so all you have to do is enjoy the benefits of being always connected and always synchronized!

10

Did you know?

Push Technology Makes the Difference

The BlackBerry is always connected, always on. You don't turn on your transmitter and check for e-mail. E-mail arrives to you automatically due to the BlackBerry's back-end server "push" architecture. This means messages are automatically pushed to your BlackBerry. The same technology is true for the calendar. Changes made to the calendar are automatically sent to your wired network, and changes made to your calendar on the wireless network are automatically pushed to your BlackBerry. The result is that your data is always up-to-date and you are always synchronized. And the good news: you don't have to do anything except enjoy the benefits of push technology.

Chapter 11

Organize Your Work and Time with BlackBerry Alarms and Tasks

How to…

- Configure and manage BlackBerry alarms

- Create and manage tasks

- Synchronize tasks with your desktop PIM

Picture this scenario: You travel to Atlanta for a convention. While you are there, you have a number of tasks that must be accomplished each day, and due to your hectic schedule, you must rise each morning at the bleary-eyed hour of 4:00 A.M. Sure, you can depend on notes jotted on a piece of scratch paper and a hotel wake-up call to keep you on track, but why not put your BlackBerry to work on these matters? Because the BlackBerry is such a great wireless communicator, it is easy to forget that the BlackBerry can help you in a number of other ways as well. In this chapter, I discuss two of those helper applications that allow you to have an "office on the run." You'll learn how to use the BlackBerry alarm and how to configure and manage tasks.

Configuring the BlackBerry Alarm

The BlackBerry alarm is just that—it is a simple utility that allows the BlackBerry to function like an alarm clock. Need to wake up earlier than usual? No problem, just easily and quickly set the BlackBerry alarm to wake you on time. Do you have an important meeting coming up at 1:30 in the afternoon? The BlackBerry alarm can give you a fifteen minutes "heads up" notice with a just a few keyboard strokes or trackwheel clicks. In fact, I find that the BlackBerry alarm can be configured in seconds and is much easier to set than a typical desktop clock alarm.

The BlackBerry alarm is available directly from the Home screen as an icon. On the 957 model the Alarm icon looks like an alarm clock, and on the 950 model the Alarm icon looks like a bell. Using your trackwheel to scroll and click the Alarm icon, you see the same interface on both the 957 and 950 models, as shown in Figure 11-1.

First of all, notice that the BlackBerry alarm is a daily alarm. Like most alarm clocks, you have the option of setting one alarm event per day—you can't set up multiple alarms during the same day. However, as you can see in Figure 11-1, the alarm interface is rather easy and can be changed quickly. For example, let's say you set the BlackBerry to wake you at 6:00 A.M. Once the alarm has sounded and you are up and at 'em, you also want the BlackBerry alarm to go off at 1:15 P.M.,

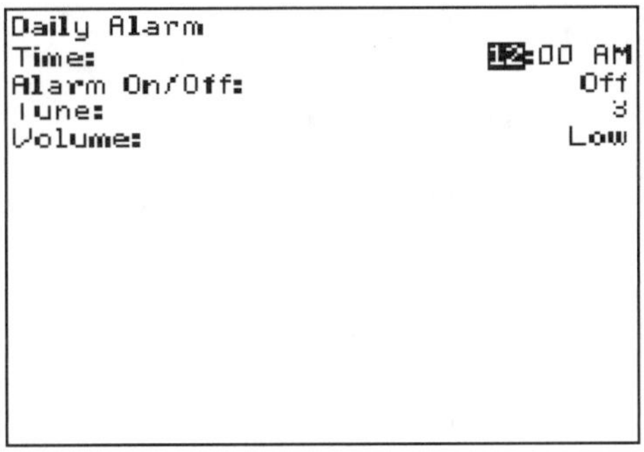

```
Daily Alarm
Time:                          12:00 AM
Alarm On/Off:                      Off
Tune:                                3
Volume:                            Low
```

FIGURE 11-1   BlackBerry Daily Alarm screen

which is fifteen minutes before the big meeting of the day. No problem—simply access the Daily Alarm screen and reset the alarm to 1:15 P.M. You can set the alarm in a matter of seconds, and the BlackBerry will give you a warning before your meeting.

Setting the alarm is easy. Use the trackwheel to scroll to and click the Alarm icon on the Home screen, or just press R on your keypad. Once you are in the Daily Alarm screen, as shown in Figure 11-1, you see the following configuration options:

- **Time**   Set the time you want the BlackBerry alarm to go off. Make sure the AM/PM setting is correct.

- **Alarm On/Off**   Turn the alarm on or off.

- **Tune**   Choose from six different alarm sounds, from simple beeps to various tunes.

- **Volume**   Set the alarm volume to high, medium, or low.

TIP   *Just like an alarm clock, the BlackBerry time must be set correctly in order for the alarm to actually sound at the correct hour of day. You can easily set the date and time using the BlackBerry Options, as explained in Chapter 4, or, if the BlackBerry is set to synchronize date and time with what appears on your PC, simply synchronize it (see Chapter 5), assuming the PC date and time are correct. Be careful, though—if the PC's date and time are not correct, your alarm's accuracy will be affected.*

11

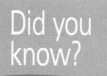

Don't Throw the BlackBerry out the Window!

You are probably familiar with the proverbial alarm clock that gets slapped, dropped to the floor, and thrown out the window because it will not stop ringing. Indeed, the clock alarm in my bedroom requires you to press two different keys simultaneously for the alarm to stop. It isn't the alarm that wakes me every morning—it is trying to make the blasted thing stop sounding in the dark morning hours.

Relax, the BlackBerry isn't going to make you press SHIFT-D3 or anything like that. To stop the BlackBerry from ringing, all you have to do is press any key on the keypad. The alarm will stop and the alarm settings remain untouched by your early morning key fumbling. That's great news for those of us who do not enjoy a challenge first thing in the morning.

Configuring the alarm is quick and easy. There are two different ways you can configure the alarm settings. First, use your trackwheel to scroll to the item you want to change. For example, if you are setting the time, scroll to the portion of the time you want to change, click the trackwheel to see the menu, and then click Change Option. The Change Option window appears, as shown in Figure 11-2. Scroll the trackwheel up or down to change the value to the one you desire, and then click the trackwheel. This returns you to the Daily Alarm screen.

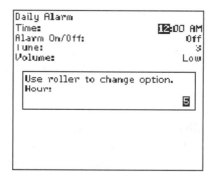

FIGURE 11-2   Change Option window for the Daily Alarm screen

An easier and much faster way to change the clock settings is to use the orange ALT key. After you highlight the item you want to change, if you hold down the ALT key and then roll your trackwheel, the value for the highlighted item will change. Release the ALT key to scroll to the next item you want to change. For example, let's say I want to configure an alarm for 5:00 A.M. I simply scroll to the first digit in the time, and then hold down ALT and roll the trackwheel to change the value to 5. Next, I release the ALT key and scroll to the next digits in the time. Essentially, this operation bypasses all of the menus and allows you set the alarm in a matter of seconds. Try it out!

When you are done making changes and the alarm is configured as you want, click the trackwheel to see the menu for the Daily Alarm screen and click Save Options. You are then returned to the Home screen.

Creating and Managing Tasks

The Tasks feature provided by the BlackBerry provides you a way to organize and keep track of tasks that you must complete or manage. Let's consider an example. You work for a firm that has sent you to a new office that is being established. While you are at the new office, you have fifteen different tasks that must be completed. These tasks were assigned to you, and they must be completed before you can come home. Using the BlackBerry, you can easily keep track of each task, assign the tasks different statuses, and even keep notes on the progress of the tasks. This can all be recorded on the BlackBerry, referred to time and time again, and the information even synchronized with your PC PIM application. Depending on your corporate use of the PIM application, your desktop PIM can even be synchronized with your manager's PIM at another office so he or she can keep track of your progress. The good news is that the BlackBerry Tasks feature is an easy tool to use and quite versatile. The following sections show you how to do everything with the Tasks feature.

Checking Out the Tasks Interface

The Tasks feature is available as an icon on your Home screen. On the 957 model, Tasks appears as a piece of paper with check marks and a pencil; on the 950 model, Tasks appears as a check box. On either model, you can use the trackwheel to scroll to and click Tasks, or just press t on the keypad.

The Tasks interface gives you a list of currently configured tasks (if there are any), as you can see in Figure 11-3.

FIGURE 11-3   The Tasks interface

You'll notice in Figure 11-3 that each task appears with a name and an icon beside it. Table 11-1 explains the meaning of the icons.

From this simple interface, you can examine the tasks you have created, manage those tasks, and create new tasks.

Configuring Task Options

Before getting into task creation and management, there are a couple of task options that you can configure. These two options simply determine how the list of tasks

Icon	Description
☐	The task has not been started.
☐	The task is in progress.
☑	The task has been completed.
🕒	The task is waiting.
🕒	The task has been deferred.

TABLE 11-1   Task Interface Icons

appear and whether or not you receive a confirmation message when deleting a task.

In the Tasks Options screen, click the trackwheel to access the menu for this screen, and then click Options. You see a simple window, shown in Figure 11-4, in which you can configure how tasks are sorted and specify that the deletion be confirmed.

Under the Sort By option, you can change how the lists of tasks are sorted by clicking the trackwheel and then clicking Change Option from the menu that appears, or just holding down the ALT key and rolling through the available options, which are as follows:

- **Status**   The task list is organized according to the status of each task, such as not started, in progress, waiting, etc.

- **Subject**   The tasks in the list are alphabetized by subject. This is the default option.

- **Priority**   You can assign different priority levels to tasks. This option organizes tasks according to priority.

- **Due Date**   This lists tasks according to due date.

11

```
Tasks Options
Sort By:                Subject
Confirm Task Delete:         Yes
```

FIGURE 11-4   Tasks Options screen

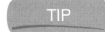
Keep in mind that there is no right or wrong way to configure the task list, and the way you organize the listing may vary from time to time. For example, you might typically use the subject option so that tasks are listed in alphabetical order, but if you are working on a highly time-sensitive project, you might consider listing the tasks in order by due date. You can change the way tasks are displayed at any time to meet your current needs.

The second option presented to you is Confirm Task Delete. This option, which enables delete confirmation, brings up a screen asking if you are sure you want to delete an item before it is actually deleted. This feature prevents you from accidentally deleting a task. You can turn this feature off so that you are not prompted before a task is deleted, but unless you are very sure of your keyboard strokes and trackwheel movements, I recommend that you leave this feature turned on. It's a great safety guard for you. Once you're done configuring the Sort By and Confirm Task Delete options, just click the trackwheel to bring up the menu for the Tasks Options screen and click Save Options.

Creating a New Task

You can easily create a new task at any time and it will be added to your task list. The process of creating a new task is rather easy—essentially, you complete the task fields as necessary for your needs. Once you create the task, you save it, and it appears in your task list according to the listing option you configured (such as by subject, due date, and so on). To learn how to create a new task, see "Create a New Task."

Any high-priority task appears with an exclamation point next to it in the task list. Any low-priority task appears with a down arrow next to it in the task list. Normal priority tasks have no indicator.

Editing a Task

Once you create a task, you can edit it at any time. For example, let's say that you have a task whose status is In Progress. You complete the task and now you want to change the status to Completed. You can simply edit the task, change the status, and even add more notes about the task completion if you like. As you are working, keep in mind that all of this information can be synchronized with your desktop

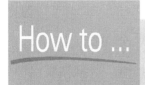 **Create a New Task**

When you need to create a new task, simply follow these steps:

1. On the Home screen, open the Tasks icon by scrolling to it and clicking or by pressing T on your keypad.

2. The Tasks screen appears. Click the trackwheel to access the menu for this screen, and then click New Task.

3. The New Task screen appears, as shown in Figure 11-5. Enter a descriptive name for the task. If you are creating a lot of tasks, make sure the name is descriptive enough to distinguish it from other tasks in your list. You should be able to glance at the task name and know exactly what it is. After you enter the name, roll your trackwheel to move to the Status option.

4. In the Status option field, click the trackwheel and then click Change Option from the menu that appears to select either Not Started, In Progress, Completed, Waiting, or Deferred. You can also scroll through the options by simply holding down the ALT key when the Status option field is highlighted instead of using the menu (which is faster). Make your selection, and then scroll to the Priority option.

5. You can assign a priority setting to your task, and, depending on your Options settings, you can have your tasks listed in order of priority. The priority options you can select are Low, Normal, and High. Click the trackwheel and use the menu that appears or hold down the ALT key and roll the trackwheel to make your selection, and then scroll to the Due option.

6. If you want to specify due dates for your tasks, click the trackwheel and use the menu that appears or hold down the ALT key and roll the trackwheel to choose the By Date option. This causes a day and date line to appear. Use the same methods to specify the day and date of the due date, as shown in Figure 11-6.

11

7. Finally, you see a Notes option. You can enter any notes about the task that are relevant here. You have plenty of typing room, so feel free to enter what you need.

8. When you're done, click the trackwheel and then click the Save Task option on the menu. The new task now appears on your Tasks screen.

PIM, so the Notes feature may be quite useful if your desktop PIM supports this feature. At any rate, you can make these editorial changes quickly and easily.

In the Tasks screen, use the trackwheel to scroll to the task that you want to edit. Click the trackwheel to see the menu for this screen, and then click Open Task. You see the same window as you do when you created the task. Just use the trackwheel to access menu options or hold down the ALT key and roll the trackwheel to change the items that you want. Click the trackwheel to see the menu and click Save Task when you're done.

Changing a Task's Status

In the previous section, I pointed out that you can easily change a task's status by editing the task. However, you can also change some status indicators more easily by accessing the Task screen's menu. When you use this option, you can change the status of a completed task back to In Progress, or you can change the status of

FIGURE 11-5   New Task screen

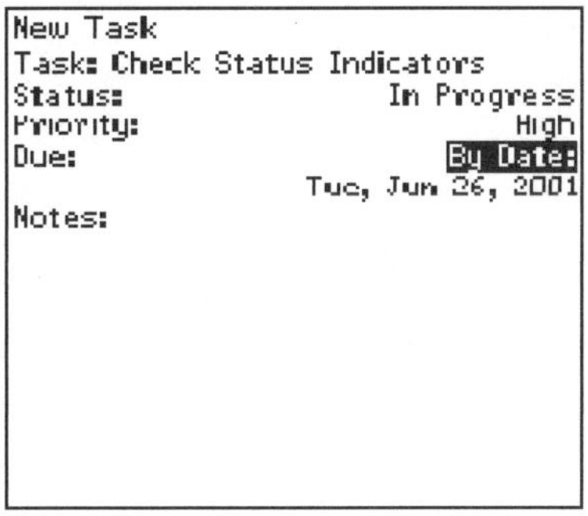

```
New Task
Task: Check Status Indicators
Status:                  In Progress
Priority:                      High
Due:                       By Date:
                 Tue, Jun 26, 2001
Notes:
```

FIGURE 11-6   Due Date option

a Deferred, Waiting, Not Started, or In Progress task to Completed. For all other indicator changes, you must use the task-editing feature explained in the previous section.

    To change a task's status, simply scroll to the task that you want to change in the Tasks screen, and then click the trackwheel to access the menu for the screen.

11

Did you know?

Swimming in the Task Sea

    The Tasks feature the BlackBerry provides is great. However, like all great things, too much can be a little overwhelming. As you are thinking about entering tasks, it is very important that the tasks you enter and the names for the tasks have real meaning to you. This is similar to setting alerts. Alerts are very helpful, but if you have too many, you to tend to start ignoring them. If you configure too many tasks, the list may become more confusing and a waste of time rather than helpful. You don't want to put every tiny detail of everything you need to do in a task, but you want to use tasks to outline goals and configure priorities and due dates to help you stay on track. Of course, in order for the Tasks feature to really help you, you have to get in the habit of checking it every day and keeping it updated. Like most things on the BlackBerry, keep your tasks to the point, keep them meaningful, and keep them organized so that the BlackBerry is a real help to you and your work.

Select either the Mark in Progress or Mark as Completed option, depending on which is available for the task you selected, as shown in Figure 11-7.

Deleting a Task

When a task is completed or no longer relevant to you, you can easily delete it from your task lists. You also have an additional option to delete all tasks that have been completed. For example, let's say that you complete five tasks in your task list. Instead of individually deleting each task, you can choose to delete all completed tasks. Of course, for this to work, you have to update the status of each task as it is completed so that it is marked as such.

> **TIP** *By default, you are given a delete confirmation message to make sure you want to delete the tasks you select. If you don't want to use this delete confirmation, access the Task Options screen to change it. See "Configuring Task Options" earlier in this chapter for more information.*

In order to delete a task, scroll to the task that you want to delete on the Tasks screen, click the trackwheel to access the menu, and then click Delete Task. Click Yes in the confirmation message box that appears, and the task is deleted. If you want to delete all completed tasks, click the trackwheel to access the menu, and then click Delete Completed. Click Yes in the confirmation message box that appears, and all completed tasks will be removed.

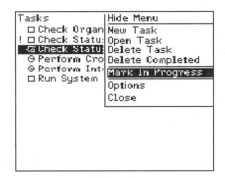

FIGURE 11-7   Task status

Helpful Keypad Shortcuts

As you are using the Tasks feature, you may find the following keypad shortcuts make your work faster and easier:

- ■ **DEL** Deletes a task

- ■ **T** Goes to the top of a task

- ■ **B** Goes to the bottom of a task

- ■ **C** Creates a new task

- ■ **M** Marks a task as In Progress or Completed, depending on the task's current status

- ■ **NUM** Allows you to highlight more than one task if held down as you scroll

- ■ **ALT** Allows you to scroll the task list more quickly if held down as you scroll

Synchronizing Tasks with Your Desktop PIM

As with other BlackBerry features, such as the address book and MemoPad, you can synchronize tasks with a desktop PIM that supports some kind of tasks function. This synchronization feature allows your BlackBerry tasks to appear in your desktop PIM and vice versa. RIM's Intellisync software makes the transfer of your BlackBerry Tasks feature files to your desktop PIM quick and easy.

For example, I use Microsoft Outlook as my desktop PIM. When I synchronize with my BlackBerry, any task files I have created are automatically converted to Outlook tasks, as you can see in Figure 11-8.

I can edit any task on my desktop PIM, and synchronize any changes with the BlackBerry as needed and vice versa. In an office setting, I can even have my assistant edit my task list, and then all I have to do is synchronize with the BlackBerry in order to update my tasks.

Chapter 5 tells you all about the Desktop Manager and synchronization software, so I'll not repeat that information here. For quick reference, however, the following text, "Synchronize Tasks with a Desktop PIM," shows you how to select a PIM for the BlackBerry and how to perform the synchronization.

11

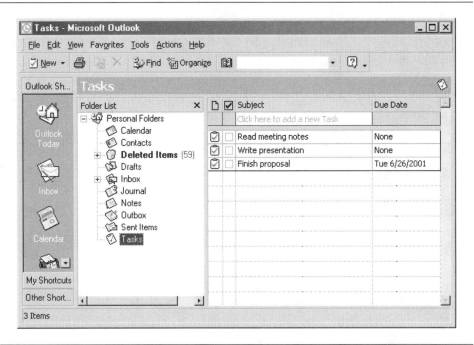

FIGURE 11-8   BlackBerry Tasks can synchronize with desktop PIM applications

TIP   *Keep in mind that you can also create filters for task entries, depending on your PIM. See Chapters 5 and 8 to learn more about filter creation.*

How to ... Synchronize Tasks with a Desktop PIM

To synchronize with a desktop PIM, follow these steps:

1. Open the Desktop Manager program on your PC and insert the BlackBerry into the cradle.

2. Double-click the Intellisync button, and then click the Configure PIM button in the Intellisync dialog box.

3. In the Configuration dialog box, select Tasks, and then click the Choose button.

4. In the Choose PIM dialog box, select the PIM that you want the Tasks feature to synchronize with and click OK. Translators are available for various versions of Lotus Notes, Microsoft Outlook, Microsoft Schedule, ACT!, GoldMine, and GroupWise.

5. Once you click OK, you see the MemoPad is configured to synchronize with the PIM you selected, as shown in Figure 11-9. Click OK.

6. In the Intellisync dialog box, click the Synchronize Now button. BlackBerry Tasks and your PIM will be synchronized.

11

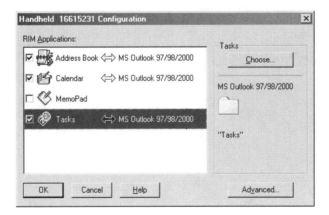

FIGURE 11-9   PIM configured to synchronize with BlackBerry Tasks

Chapter 12

Create Memos with MemoPad and Use the BlackBerry Calculator

How to...

- Create memos with MemoPad
- Synchronize MemoPad with a desktop PIM
- Use the BlackBerry's calculator features

Did you forget to write up that important document? Have you ever had a brainstorm in the air between New York and San Francisco? The possible needs are quite endless for short documents while you are on the go, and the BlackBerry is at your side to help you record information with MemoPad. MemoPad is a quick-and-easy tool that enables you to type information—notes, memos, outlines—and conveniently save them on the BlackBerry. You can then effortlessly synchronize with a desired desktop PIM and convert the information to new formats. In addition to MemoPad, you also have a calculator included on your BlackBerry, and in this chapter, you'll learn how to use both of these important, timesaving tools.

Recording Information with the BlackBerry MemoPad

MemoPad is a quick-and-easy BlackBerry application that enables you to record information in the form of memos. The BlackBerry MemoPad is commonly used to take down notes when you are away from your desk and to help you organize your thoughts, and it is a great tool to use during conferences and conventions where you are often sandblasted with information you need to remember and keep track of. Using MemoPad, you can easily enter and save information on your BlackBerry. You can return at any time and edit the information you have saved, and you can synchronize that information with your desktop PIM.

The BlackBerry MemoPad is found directly on your Home screen, shown in Figure 12-1, and appears as a piece of paper with a tack through it on the 957 model and as a text document on the 950 model.

> TIP *You can easily open MemoPad on either the 957 or 950 BlackBerry models by just pressing P on the keypad.*

The following sections show you how to use MemoPad.

FIGURE 12-1   MemoPad

Creating a New Memo File

When you first open MemoPad from your Home screen, you see a "No Memo" message because you have yet to create any memos. When you're ready to create a new memo, simply open MemoPad from the Home screen, and then click the trackwheel to see menu options. Click New Memo on the menu.

At this point, you see a Title prompt, and then a blank screen. Enter a title for the memo. Although not initially required, you will not be able to save the memo unless it has a title. Once you have typed a title, simply use the trackwheel to scroll to the memo body area. At this point, you can simply begin typing information as you would like, as shown in Figure 12-2. As you type, you'll notice that all keyboard features apply to MemoPad as well as AutoText, and MemoPad wraps your words automatically at the end of sentences so that your notations are easy to read and are not truncated at the end lines. For long memos, simply use your trackwheel to navigate from top to bottom.

As you type, MemoPad will continue to move down the page and will scroll to a new line once you have used the entire field. You can easily move through text that you have typed by using the trackwheel. As I mentioned, MemoPad will automatically wrap to the next line when one line ends, but you can force a hard return at any time by simply using the Enter key on the keyboard.

Additionally, if you make a number of mistakes or if you want to start over, you can click the trackwheel to bring up menu options and click Clear Field. This erases everything you have typed with the exception of the title. This information cannot be regained once it has been cleared unless you have previously saved the

12

FIGURE 12-2   Creating a memo via MemoPad

memo. When you are done typing your memo, just click the trackwheel and then click Save. Your memo is saved by the title you entered.

How to ... Create Effective Titles

MemoPad is like most other BlackBerry applications—once you use it for a while, you become hopelessly addicted and wonder how you ever survived without it. For the traveling professional or for those who simply like to write things down so they are not forgotten, MemoPad can be quite useful, and if you're like me, you will tend to generate a lot of memos.

The trick to effective memo usage is not in the actual text that you type, but in the titles. Since memos are saved according to the title that you enter, descriptive titles will be much more useful to you. In other words, the title "seminar" may be fine, but something more specific, such as "Aug 12 Seminar" or "8-12-01 Meeting" is better. In fact, an important item for you to remember is that memos are organized alphabetically by title, not by creation date. So, if you use memos a lot, you may want to include the date in the title, and if you want memos grouped by date, use a numeric representation of the date followed by additional title information as desired, such as "8-15-01 Luncheon Notes." This naming scheme will keep your memos organized by date and much easier to locate if you use this feature regularly.

Viewing Memos

Once you have created memos, you can easily view them at any time. To view a memo, just click the MemoPad icon on your Home screen, and you'll see a list of the memos that you have created and saved, as shown in Figure 12-3.

To view a memo, simply roll the trackwheel to the memo you want to view. Click the trackwheel and from the menu that appears click View Memo.

 When you're viewing a memo, you can't make any editorial changes to it. If you want to make changes to the memo, see the following section, "Editing Memos."

Editing Memos

Once you create a memo and save it, you can return to that memo at any time and make editorial changes to it. For example, let's say that you have entered some notes from a meeting you attended. While you're on the plane ride home, you realize that you forgot to enter some key information. To make sure that information is not forgotten, you pull out your BlackBerry and make the addition to the memo. Or, what if you have saved a memo, but you need to rename it with phrasing that is more descriptive? No problem. You can use the BlackBerry's editing feature to make changes to any memo that you have previously created. See "Edit a Saved Memo" for instructions.

12

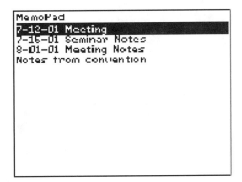

FIGURE 12-3   List of created memos

Edit a Saved Memo

To edit a saved memo, follow these steps:

1. On the BlackBerry Home screen, click the MemoPad icon.

2. In the list of memos that appears, scroll to select the one that you want.

3. Click the trackwheel and from the menu that appears click Edit Memo.

4. The memo now appears. You can change both the body text and the title as desired. If you want to use the Clear Field feature, place the trackwheel in either the title field or the memo field, and then click the trackwheel to see menu options. Click Clear Field.

5. Once you are done editing the memo, click the trackwheel and then click Save.

Why Is There a View and Edit Mode?

At first glance, the view mode may seem sort of ridiculous. After all, why not just use edit mode when looking at memos, and then you can make changes at any time if necessary? Although you can always check out memos using the Edit Memo feature and simply not save changes, the view mode is a safety feature that allows you to easily peruse your memos without fear of accidentally changing something in one of them. This simple concept can quickly become important on a bumpy plane or bus ride. If you need to edit a menu you are viewing, then just click the trackwheel and click Edit Menu. This way, you can view menus without fear of accidental changes, but you can easily edit them if you find something that needs changing.

 *If you change the title of the memo, it will be moved in your list of memos according to how the titles are organized.*

If you are viewing a memo and want to edit it, you don't have to back out of View, and then move to Edit. While in view mode, simply click the trackwheel to see the menu and click Edit Memo.

Deleting Memos

When you no longer want to keep a memo, you can easily delete it. In order to delete a memo, click the MemoPad icon on the Home screen to access your list of memos. Use the trackwheel to scroll to the memo that you want to delete, and then click the trackwheel to access menu options. Click Delete. A delete confirmation message appears. Click Yes, and the memo is deleted.

 *Remember, there is no fail-safe for the Delete functions. Once you delete a memo, it is removed from the BlackBerry and cannot be recovered later.*

Quick MemoPad Keyboard Shortcuts

As you work with MemoPad, you can avoid using the trackwheel on a number of operations by simply using keyboard shortcuts. These shortcuts will save you time and make your work with the MemoPad easier. Try them out:

- Press T to go to the top of the memo in the memo list.
- Press B to go to the bottom of the memo in the memo list.
- Press ESC to exit the MemoPad screen and return to the Home screen.
- Press DEL to delete a memo.
- Press ENTER to view a memo.

Synchronizing Memos with a Desktop PIM

Without the synchronization feature, MemoPad wouldn't be that helpful. After all, your notes, information, and other text that you enter in MemoPad will need to be transferred to a desktop application in order for it to be useful in other ways. Fortunately, RIM's Intellisync software makes the transfer of MemoPad files to your desktop PIM quick and easy.

12

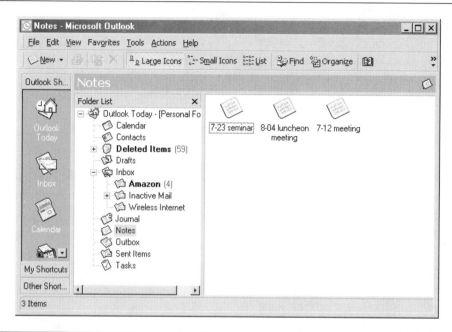

FIGURE 12-4   BlackBerry MemoPad files are converted to Notes in Outlook

For example, I use Microsoft Outlook as my desktop PIM. When I synchronize with my BlackBerry, any MemoPad files I have created are automatically converted to Outlook Notes, as you can see in Figure 12-4.

At this point, I can open any of these notes and add content to them, or I can cut and paste the information into another program, such as Word. Let's consider a quick application. Let's say I need to give a business presentation a few weeks down the road. While traveling home on a three-hour plane ride, I decide to use the BlackBerry's MemoPad feature to begin working on my presentation. I create an outline, and then use the BlackBerry to record notes about each portion of the presentation. When I return home, I synchronize the BlackBerry with Outlook, which places my presentation notes into Outlook Notes. At this point, I cut the text from my Outlook Notes and paste it into a Word document, in which I finish my presentation and polish it up. I can then convert my Word document to a PowerPoint presentation and I'm all set. As you can see, there is no typing and retyping—what began on the BlackBerry ends as the final presentation that I present to my colleagues. Because I can so easily create notes in MemoPad and then synchronize with my desktop PIM, the BlackBerry is always with me so I can store information whenever I want.

I should note here that Chapter 5 tells you all about the Desktop Manager and synchronization software, so I'll not repeat that information here. For quick reference, however, the following text, "Synchronize with a PIM," shows you how to select a PIM for the BlackBerry to synchronize with and how to perform the synchronization. Most PIMs have some type of memo or note feature you can configure to synchronize with the BlackBerry.

Keep in mind that you can also create filters for MemoPad entries, depending on your PIM. See Chapters 5 and 8 to learn more about filter creation.

Using the BlackBerry Calculator

At first glance, the idea of a calculator, let alone reading a chapter section about using a calculator, may not seem too exciting. After all, who *doesn't* know how

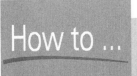 **Synchronize with a PIM**

To synchronize with a PIM, follow these steps:

1. Open the Desktop Manager program on your PC and insert the BlackBerry into the cradle.

2. Double-click the Intellisync button, and then click the Configure PIM button in the Intellisync dialog box.

3. In the Configuration dialog box, select MemoPad, and then click the Choose button.

4. In the Choose PIM dialog box, select the PIM that you want MemoPad to synchronize with and click OK. Translators are available for various versions of Lotus Notes and Microsoft Outlook.

5. Once you click OK, you see the MemoPad is configured to synchronize with the PIM you selected, as shown in Figure 12-5. Click OK.

6. In the Intellisync dialog box, click the Synchronize Now button. MemoPad and your PIM will be synchronized.

12

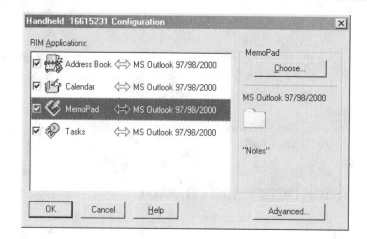

FIGURE 12-5   MemoPad PIM selection

to use a basic calculator. That's true enough, but what you will soon see is that the BlackBerry calculator is far more than a simple onscreen calculator. It is a powerful tool capable of many different types of calculations, and there is even a recording feature so you can keep calculations that you make. Depending on your occupational needs, the calculator may be something that you use on an irregular basis or something you use every day. Regardless, this section is your companion so you can learn to use all of the BlackBerry's calculator features.

Getting to Know the BlackBerry Calculator

The BlackBerry calculator is available directly from your Home screen by clicking the Calculator icon, or by simply pressing U on the keypad. Let me say up front that the calculator found on the 957 handheld model is much better than the one found on the 950 pager model. The 950 calculator performs only basic calculator functions, so I'll distinguish the two models as necessary throughout this section.

When you open the calculator on the 957 model, you see three different sections on your screen, as shown in Figure 12-6. The top portion of the screen functions as a display area. Calculations that you are currently working with appear in the display area for you to review. The middle portion is the entry dialog box. As you press keys on the keyboard, the numbers you enter appear here. Finally, you see a function section that lists the available functions you can select with your trackwheel.

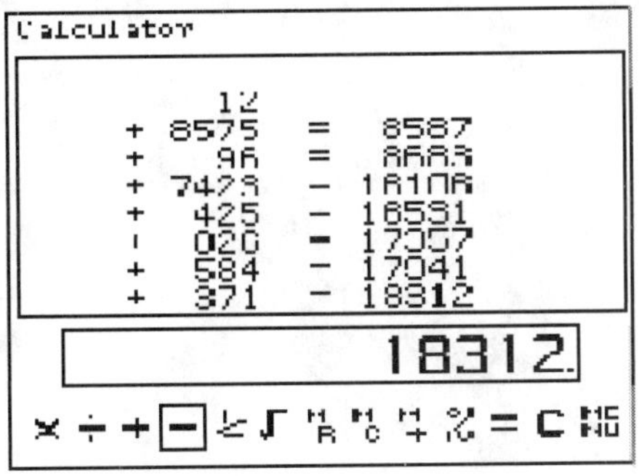

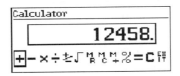

FIGURE 12-6   957 Handheld calculator

TIP

When you use the Calculator, the BlackBerry knows that you need numbers only, so you don't have to use the ALT key on the keypad to enter numbers.

On the 950 pager model, you see two screen areas. First, you see the entry dialog box. As you press keys on the keyboard, the numbers you enter appear here. Also, you see a function section that lists the available functions you can select with your trackwheel, as shown in Figure 12-7.

For both the 957 and 950 models, the function keys are essentially the same, and are demonstrated in Table 12-1.

12

Using the Calculator

To perform basic calculations, just use your keypad to enter the first set of numbers for the calculation. The numbers you enter appear in the entry dialog box. When you have entered the first set of numbers, use the trackwheel to select the function that you want to use, and then click the trackwheel. Repeat this process as necessary.

FIGURE 12-7   950 pager calculator

Icon	Operation
✕	Multiply
÷	Divide
+	Add
−	Subtract
±	Change sign
√	Square root
MR	Memory recall
MC	Memory clear
M+	Add to memory
%	Figure percentage
=	Equals
C	Clear all
EXIT	Exit calculator (available only on the 950 model)
MENU	Access the menu (available only on the 957 model)

TABLE 12-1   BlackBerry Calculator Functions

For example, to add 12 and 2, enter 12 with the keypad, scroll to and click the
+ sign, enter 2 again, and then scroll to and click the = sign. Aside from having
to use the trackwheel to select the function you want, the calculator functions like
any other desktop calculator.

Now I'll contradict what I just said. You have to use the trackwheel in order to
select functions, true enough, since those functions do not reside on your keypad.
However, the BlackBerry provides you with keyboard shortcuts for each function
available. You'll have to memorize these, but if you use the calculator a lot, you'll

Function	Keyboard Shortcut
Add	Press D
Subtract	Press F
Multiply	Press X or A
Divide	Press S
Change sign	Press Z or SPACE
Square root	Press V
Memory recall	Press J
Memory clear	Press K
Add to memory	Press L
Equals	Press G
Clear screen	Press C

TABLE 12-2 Calendar Keyboard Shortcuts

be a pro in no time, and skipping the trackwheel movements will speed up your calculator usage. The keyboard shortcuts in Table 12-2 can be used to replace trackwheel selections for calculator functions.

Using Calculator Memory

The BlackBerry calculator provides basic memory functions that are found on most calculators. Use the MR, MC, and M+ function selections to manage memory. To add a figure into memory, simply scroll to and click M+. Whatever number is found in the entry dialog box will be placed into memory. You'll notice that the memory figure appears at the top of your screen as M=*figure*. If you want to recall the figure, scroll to and click MR. The figure once again appears in the entry dialog box. To remove the figure from memory, just scroll to and click MC.

The calculator only remembers one figure at a time. If you enter another number and press the M+ function when another figure is currently in memory, then the new figure is added to the old figure.

Using the Tape Feature

The RIM 957 model contains a "tape" feature, which essentially records calculations so you can make changes to them if necessary. This feature is not available on the 950 model. The great aspect of the tape feature is that you can edit, insert, or delete

12

entries in a series of calculations that you are working on. For example, consider Figure 12-8.

Let's say that after entering all of these calculations, the 425 number should have been 431. Sure, you can add in the difference, but on complex calculations, this can be difficult. With the tape feature, you don't need to worry about manually compensating for errors because you can simply edit the entry to make the change. In the same manner, you can insert lines and delete lines from figures as well.

To use the tape feature, just follow the steps in "Use the Calculator Tape Feature."

Performing Conversions

The 957 model has the capability to convert to and from metric as well as perform several other metric conversions, as listed here:

- Centimeters to inches
- Meters to feet
- Meters to yards
- Kilometers to miles
- Kilograms to pounds
- Celsius to Fahrenheit

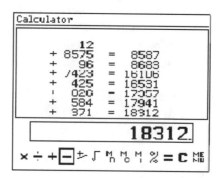

FIGURE 12-8   Calculations

How to ... Use the Calculator Tape Feature

To use the Calculator tape feature, follow these steps:

1. Use the calculator for functions as desired. When you need to switch to the tape feature in order to make changes to those calculations, use the trackwheel to scroll to and click the Menu option.

2. On the menu, click Switch to Tape with your trackwheel. You see that switching to tape now puts your trackwheel in the display portion of the screen, as shown in Figure 12-9.

3. Use the trackwheel to select the figure that you want to change, and then click the trackwheel to access menu options. You can choose to edit an entry, delete an entry, or insert an entry by simply clicking the appropriate option on the menu. For example, if you want to edit an entry, a dialog box appears around the entry and you can make changes using your keypad, as shown in Figure 12-10.

4. When you're done, just click the trackwheel and click Return to Calculator.

12

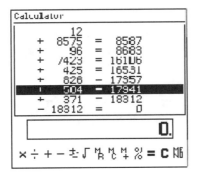

FIGURE 12-9   Tape

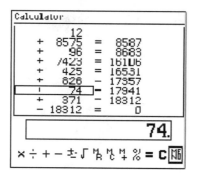

FIGURE 12-10   Edit feature

The metric and conversion features are only available on the 957 model calculator; they are not available on the 950 pager model. To use the metric conversion feature, follow the steps in "Perform Conversions."

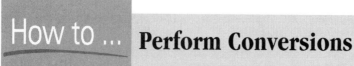

How to ... **Perform Conversions**

To use the metric conversion feature, follow these steps:

1. Using the calculator, type the number that you want to convert.

2. Scroll to and click the Menu option, and then click either From Metric or To Metric.

3. An additional menu appears, as shown in Figure 12-11. Select the type of conversion that you want to perform and click it.

4. The conversion appears in the calculator entry dialog box.

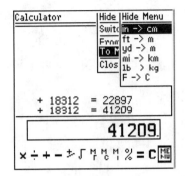

FIGURE 12-11   Conversion options

Chapter 13

Extending the BlackBerry

How to...

■ Extend your BlackBerry with additional Internet solutions

■ Extend your BlackBerry with business solutions

The BlackBerry is not island—and that's good news for all of us. After all, your business and the management of your life is not isolated either, and it is due to the software integration needs of BlackBerry users that you can synchronize and transfer files using desktop PIM software with the BlackBerry. After all, the BlackBerry alone would be rather limiting.

Following this same line of thought, the BlackBerry provides additional services and features that are available through third-party vendors and associates. The term *third-party*, which is often thrown around in the computer world, simply means that a company outside of RIM developed the solution for the BlackBerry. That company is responsible for creating the solution and supporting that solution for users. With that said, this chapter explores some third-party solutions that are available for you and your BlackBerry.

Why Use Third-Party Solutions?

As you get started in this chapter, let's first consider your needs. After all, do you really need to think about using some kind of third-party solution on your BlackBerry, most of which are fee based? That's a big question, and one you should consider seriously. It is always tempting to take any kind of electronic device, such as a computer or PDA, to the ultimate limit. After all, if the device can do it, why not?

Although this approach may be interesting, the end result will typically be a BlackBerry full of services and features that have no usefulness to you. For this reason, you should carefully evaluate your needs before extending your BlackBerry with a third-party solution. In the following sections, you'll learn about five third-party solutions that are currently available with the BlackBerry. Of course, the world is always turning, so be sure to check out http://www.blackberry.net for more information about new third-party solutions as they become available. Also, you can learn more about navigating BlackBerry.net in Chapter 15.

So, should you use one of the third-party solutions that are available and described in the following sections? As you read about the solutions that are available, be sure to ask yourself these questions:

■ Will the service assist me in my business or the management of my personal life?

■ Even if the service will assist me, is this something I think I will actually use?

■ If I will use the service and it is needed, is the service cost effective (if there is a fee)?

It is important to point out that some of the third-party solutions are implemented at the corporate level. Your BlackBerry may already be equipped with one or more of these, depending on your company. If you are an individual user, some of these may be helpful to you, whereas others will not be. So, check out the following sections to learn more about the third-party solutions that are available for your BlackBerry.

Ask@OracleMobile

How would you like some free information? Need to know something quickly, without hassles, and without parting with your hard-earned money? No problem, just use the cool Ask@OracleMobile feature that is supported by your BlackBerry.

The Lean and Mean BlackBerry

Since I'm talking about extensions in this chapter, and the next chapter explores applications and fun stuff, now is a good time to mention the "lean and mean BlackBerry." Your BlackBerry, which ships to you with default applications, is designed to hold the third-party services described in this chapter as well as the applications described in Chapter 14. However, that does not mean that you should install everything you can get your hands on. Keep in mind that the BlackBerry, although powerful, does have a limited amount of storage space. The more room left on your BlackBerry, the more availability it provides when you really need to install something new. So, my point here is simply this: install whatever you need—but don't install a bunch of items just for the heck of it and don't keep applications that you are no longer using. When you're not using it—lose it! Remove any services or applications that are not needed and keep your BlackBerry lean and mean!

13

Ask@OracleMobile is a free service provided by OracleMobile (a division of Oracle Corporation), and this service allows you to gather information from the Internet without actually using the Internet. Based on specific categories, you can send a short e-mail message to ask@oraclemobile.com, and you will quickly receive information back from the web site. However, before you test out this nifty tool, make sure you read the rest of the section and all of the instructions at the end. Also, there's a tutorial you should try at the OracleMobile web site, so read on.

Oracle Corporation is a leading wireless solutions provider, including hosting, consulting, and even applications. You can visit the primary site at http://www.oraclemobile.com, as shown in Figure 13-1, and learn more about the company and other wireless services it offers.

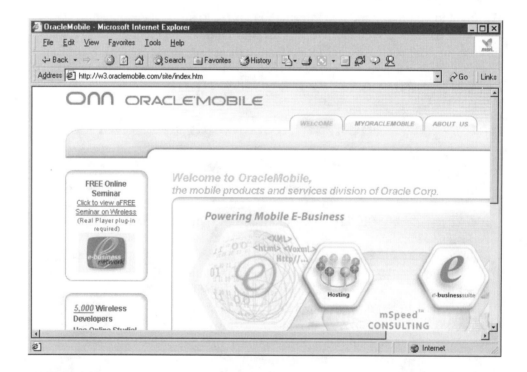

FIGURE 13-1   OracleMobile web site

TIP *Check out the wireless seminar on the home page by clicking the link. You'll need Real Player, freely downloadable at http://www.real.com, in order to view the seminar.*

What Ask@OracleMobile Provides

As I mentioned, Ask@OracleMobile is a free service that lets you e-mail the web site and get information about a specific topic returned to you. It's like finding web content, but using e-mail to do so. The Ask@OracleMobile service provides several distinct services you can use in order to gather the content that you need. Specifically, you can find information about the following:

- **Stocks** If you are away from your computer and playing the stock market, you might miss something important. Don't worry—with OracleMobile, you can get live stock quotes delivered to your BlackBerry. You can view your entire portfolio, access market news, and even set up an alert that is delivered to your BlackBerry when a stock reaches an important high. If stocks are your game, then this free service can keep you in touch while you are on the move.

- **Directions** Consider this scenario: you are in an unfamiliar city meeting with a client. Your next task of the day, as shown in your BlackBerry calendar, is to meet a potential new client at a restaurant. You have rented your own car, and you are now faced with driving to the restaurant— without a lot of time to spare. Ask@OracleMobile and your BlackBerry can quickly come to your rescue. Just request information about driving directions from one location to another, and Ask@OracleMobile can pull that information from MapQuest and deliver it to you on your BlackBerry. It's simple, easy, and can get you going in the right direction.

- **Flights** If you are a frequent airline traveler, you know this scenario: You dash out of your hotel room and grab a cab to the airport. You are running late, and by the time you arrive at the airport, you are gripping your briefcase tightly, hoping you will make the flight. You run through the airport to the terminal, only to discover that the flight has been delayed for two hours. Just think, you could have spent that time sleeping.... Ask@OracleMobile can give you up-to-the-minute flight status information. Find out easily and quickly if your flight has been delayed or cancelled, or if any other status has changed.

13

■ **Weather**   You can use this service to find out current weather conditions and forecasts in virtually any city. This service is great if you live in an area where the weather is always changing, or if you are traveling and need to keep up with the weather while you are on the move.

■ **Dining**   Using OpenTable.com, this service allows you to find a restaurant and make reservations over the Internet. Let's say you are at a client site and you forgot to make those dinner reservations. No problem—during a meeting break, just use your BlackBerry to make the reservations. It's fast and easy.

■ **Traffic**   Ah, traffic—the never-ending fight to get from one place to the other. If you live in a major city, the fight can be grueling. However, the BlackBerry can help you fight the fight with traffic reports. Find out about construction and bottlenecks, and then locate alternative routes so you can get to your destination quickly and without twiddling your thumbs.

■ **Movies**   Want to know what is playing, but you don't have access to a newspaper? Once again, Ask@OracleMobile can give you information about movies that are currently playing, including start times and ratings. You can even get reviews and use your ZIP code to find a theater near you. Using this feature, you can also link to driving directions and weather.

■ **Horoscope**   If you are a horoscope addict, you can use Ask@OracleMobile to view your daily horoscope. Find out your daily predictions and have fun!

■ **Dictionary**   Can't find the right word or need a precise definition? Just use the Dictionary feature so you can get the words right. You can even use the Thesaurus feature to find related words. This service can be very helpful if you are using your BlackBerry to create memos (or even when composing long e-mail messages).

■ **Lottery**   If you are a lottery player, use this service to find up-to-date information about lottery numbers and winners.

■ **Translation**   Need help translating words and phrases into other languages? No problem—Ask@OracleMobile can provide you with the translation you need. Just enter the word, select a language, and you'll get the result you need. It's fast, easy, and effective.

Once you register for the Ask@OracleMobile service, you can even personalize content that you specifically want to see on the OracleMobile web site. The next section shows you how to get set up and start using Ask@OracleMobile.

Using Ask@OracleMobile

In order to use the Ask@OracleMobile feature, you need to register at the OracleMobile web site. Remember that this service is totally free—you will not be asked for any money during registration or for using the service. To register for the service, just follow the steps outlined in "Register with Ask@OracleMobile."

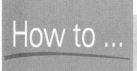 **Register with Ask@OracleMobile**

To register with Ask@OracleMobile, follow these steps:

1. From an Internet browser, access http://www2.oraclemobile.com/ myomobile/register1.jsp, which takes you to the Registration page shown in Figure 13-2.

2. Complete the information that you see on this page, and then click the Next button. Note that the password must be numeric, such as 956789, and the e-mail address you provide you should be your usual e-mail address.

3. The second page asks if you will access the site using only your computer browser, or your computer and a wireless device. Select the radio button option Computer and wireless device, and then click the Next button.

The registration process completes, and you can now use the service or customize the kind of content that you want to receive.

13

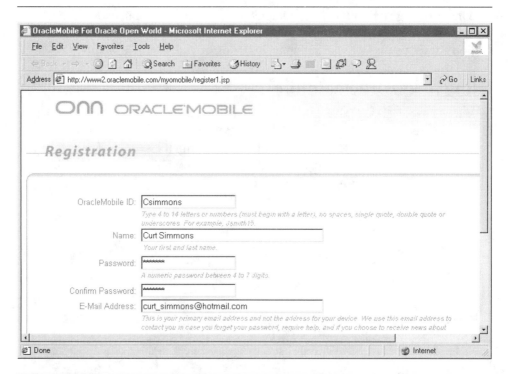

FIGURE 13-2   OracleMobile registration page

Once you have registered with the service, you can then send e-mail messages to the service at ask@oraclemobile.com, requesting the information that you want. Keep the request short, such as "Driving directions from Dallas, TX to Tyler, TX" or whatever information you want to find.

Also, check out the OracleMobile web site and customize the content you want to view. Go to http://www.oraclemobile.com and click the My OracleMobile tab. This takes you to the main customization page, where you can log in using the username and password you created during registration. You are then taken to the My Portal page, as shown in Figure 13-3.

You see boxes for flights, messaging, weather, news, and so on. Once you first log in, the basic presets are configured, but you can edit the content you see on this page by clicking the Edit Content link, which appears in the upper-right portion of the window. On the Edit Content page, shown in Figure 13-4, select the check boxes next to the services that you want to use and click the Save Changes button at the bottom of the page. Remember that you can return to this page and add or remove content at any time.

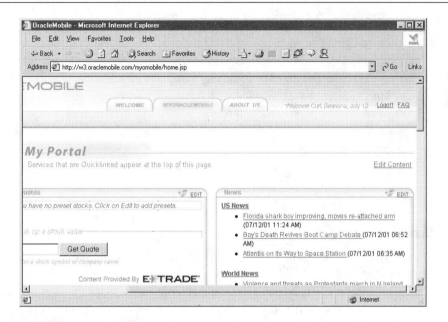

FIGURE 13-3 My Portal page

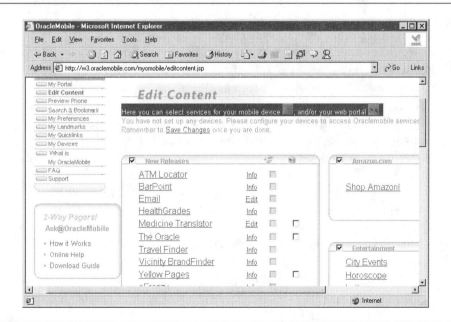

FIGURE 13-4 Edit Content page

As you can see, Ask@OracleMobile provides a wealth of information and quick access to that information. If it's information you need, then check out this free service for the BlackBerry.

Using the Ask@OracleMobile service can be really helpful, but as with any kind of information service, you have to be wary of information overload. It is very easy to sign up for too many services that give you too much information. After all, important information is great, but too much information tends to undermine its importance because you can't manage it. So, from my point of view, and I think you will agree, less is sometimes more.

PocketGenie

In Chapter 9, you learned about accessing the Internet through the Go.Web browser and related services. The BlackBerry also supports the PocketGenie web browser and service, provided by WolfeTech. You can customize content for this browser and easily collect information that you want. Although the Go.Web browser is the most popular for the BlackBerry, you should check out PocketGenie and see what it has to offer you. For starters, you can learn more about WolfeTech by visiting http://www.wolfetech.com and clicking the Products link to bring up the page shown in Figure 13-5.

As you can see in Figure 13-5, you can click the appropriate BlackBerry device graphic to find out what is available to you. Clicking the graphic or the BlackBerry 957 takes you to the page shown in Figure 13-6. Here, you can learn more about WolfeTech's consulting services as well as access the PocketGenie product for your device.

Clicking the PocketGenie icon takes you to the PocketGenie page where you can learn more about the PocketGenie and download a free trial version (U.S. residents only) as well as several documents in PDF form so you can learn more about the PocketGenie. If you try the PocketGenie service and decide you want to use it on a regular basis, then you must pay a monthly fee. At the time of this writing, 50 uses per month will cost you $4.95, with $0.25 per use overage fee. If you want unlimited access, it will cost you $9.95 a month, which is actually a good deal as far as web access goes. For either service, you must pay a $9.95 setup fee. If you decide that the PocketGenie is right for you (or if you decide to check out the trial version), then the following sections show you how the PocketGenie works.

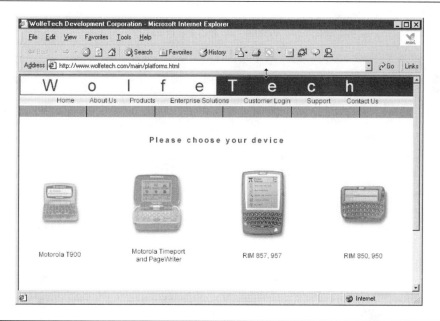

FIGURE 13-5   WolfeTech site Products page

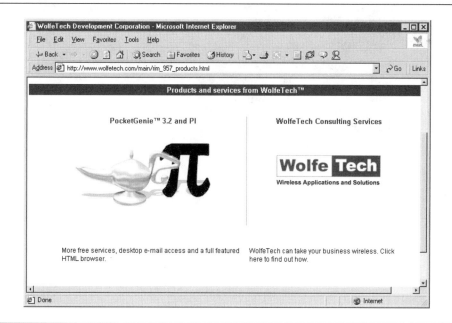

13

FIGURE 13-6   PocketGenie link

Did you know?

From WAP to HTML

An interesting thing about the PocketGenie web browser for the BlackBerry is its use of HTML instead of WAP. Now, those two acronyms may not mean anything to you at all, so I'll explain them a bit. When the Internet first came onto the scene, computers used *Hypertext Transfer Protocol* (HTTP) to access *Hypertext Markup Language* (HTML) documents on the Internet. All Internet sites are written using the HTML language, and HTTP is a communications protocol your computer uses to contact and access HTML documents on the Internet.

Wireless Internet access, however, uses a different protocol, called *Wireless Access Protocol* (WAP). PDAs, Web-enabled phones, pagers, and other types of Internet-ready mobile devices use WAP to access web sites on the Internet. If a web site doesn't support WAP, then your wireless device cannot access the site. Currently, somewhere between 5 and 10 percent of the sites on the Internet support WAP, so wireless Internet surfing is rather limited at this time.

The PocketGenie is breaking these rules by providing an HTML-based mobile browser. Since the browser is HTML based, it can access any site on the Internet, because all sites support HTML. The PocketGenie supports frames, forms, cookies, 128-bit Secure Sockets Layer (SSL), and even e-mail links. Basically, anything you want on the Internet you can access with the PocketGenie. The problem, of course, is download time. The PocketGenie compresses information to make download over the wireless network faster, but you will have to spend some time playing with this cool tool to see if it is right for you and your business.

Installing the PocketGenie

Once you download the PocketGenie from the WolfeTech web site, you can install it on your BlackBerry using the installer program and your BlackBerry Desktop Manager. The installation process works basically like any other application installation. Check out the following text, "Install PocketGenie," for specific steps.

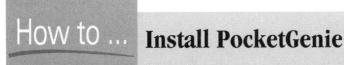

Install PocketGenie

Follow these steps to install the PocketGenie on your BlackBerry device:

1. Double-click the PocketGenie package that you downloaded from the Internet. An installation window appears, as shown in Figure 13-7. Click Next to continue.

2. The user license agreement appears. Read the agreement and click Next.

3. The program copies files to your computer and a message appears telling you that the Desktop Manager must be run to install the software. Click Next.

4. The Desktop Manager program automatically opens. At this time you need to perform a backup before installing the PocketGenie software. Double-click the Backup/Restore icon in Desktop Manager and perform a complete backup of your unit.

5. Once the backup is completed, you are now ready to install the PocketGenie on the BlackBerry. Double-click Application Loader and click Next on the Welcome screen.

6. In the selection window that appears, place a check next to WolfeTech PocketGenie, as shown in Figure 13-8. Click Next.

7. In the next window, choose the radio button option Keep the current handheld settings, and click Next.

8. Click Finish.

The PocketGenie is installed and now appears on your BlackBerry as indicated by the PocketGenie icon on your Home screen (see Figure 13-9).

13

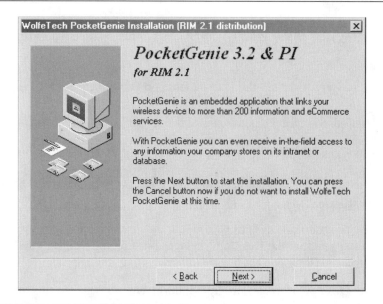

FIGURE 13-7   Installation screen

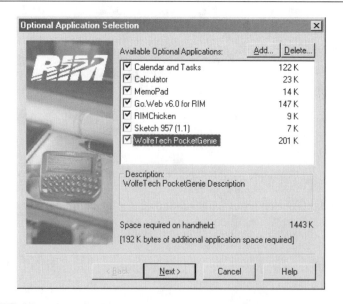

FIGURE 13-8   Select the PocketGenie option

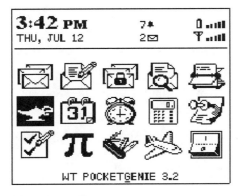

FIGURE 13-9   PocketGenie Home screen icon

Setting Up the Browser

Once you have the PocketGenie installed, you must register the application before you can begin using the browser. The registration process is quick and easy—just follow the steps in "Register the PocketGenie."

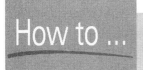 **Register the PocketGenie**

1. On the Home screen, click the PocketGenie icon.

2. A message appears, as shown in Figure 13-10, telling you about WolfeTech and where to find the license agreement. To move forward, click the trackwheel and click Next on the menu that appears.

3. In the Country screen, scroll to and click either Canada or the United States, click the trackwheel, and then click Next.

4. In the Welcome to the PocketGenie screen, enter your first name and middle initial, and your last name on the lines provided, as shown in Figure 13-11. Click the trackwheel and click Next when you're done.

5. In the Business contact information screen, shown in Figure 13-12, enter the company and contact information as requested (and required), click the trackwheel, and click Next.

6. The Residential information window appears. You can enter the information here if you like, but you can also skip it by clicking the trackwheel and clicking Next.

7. A message appears asking if WolfeTech can notify you of upgrades. You should choose Yes so you'll be aware of new products and upgrades as they become available.

8. A message appears asking if you accept the WolfeTech licensing agreement. You must click Yes in order to continue. At this time, your information is sent over the Internet and PocketGenie is now ready to use. The PocketGenie Home screen appears, as shown in Figure 13-13.

FIGURE 13-10   Registering with WolfeTech

```
┌────────────────────────────────┐
│Welcome to PocketGenie!         │
│Please take a few moments to    │
│register your product.          │
│First, MI: Curt, N              │
│Last name: Simmons█             │
│                                │
│                                │
│                                │
│                                │
│                                │
│                                │
│                                │
└────────────────────────────────┘
```

FIGURE 13-11   User information

```
┌────────────────────────────────┐
│Welcome to PocketGenie!         │
│Business contact information    │
│(required)                      │
│Company: Simmons Technical      │
│Address: P.O. Box 056450        │
│                                │
│City, State: Dallas, TX         │
│ZIP: 000076                     │
│Phone: 2145551212               │
│Fax: 2146661818                 │
│Email: curtsimmons@usrcr.com█   │
│                                │
│                                │
└────────────────────────────────┘
```

FIGURE 13-12   Business contact information

13

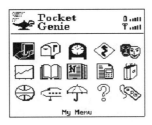

FIGURE 13-13   PocketGenie Home screen

What's Available on the PocketGenie Home Screen

The PocketGenie Home screen provides you with a number of icons, organized in the same manner as the BlackBerry's Home screen. Using the PocketGenie's Home screen, you can access a number of different PocketGenie features, all of which you will probably find helpful. The following sections review these features and give you quick steps and pointers to get you started.

My Menu

Let's face it. Using the BlackBerry for Internet surfing is not as easy as using a computer. The keyboard is small, and moving around the Internet can be cumbersome. The PocketGenie does not live in the wireless clouds, so a feature called My Menu is included so that you can maneuver around the Internet more easily.

The My Menu icon, found on the Home screen (sorry, there are no keyboard shortcuts for any of these icons), gives you access to the My Menu interface, which at first glance doesn't provide you with anything since you haven't created any menu items yet. You can add items to the My Menu area for quick access. For example, let's say that you frequently use the News and Travel features of PocketGenie (explored later in the sections "News" and "Travel"). You can simply add those items to My Menu so that they reside in one easy-to-access place. To add an item within PocketGenie, just click the trackwheel to access the screen menu, and then click Add to My Menu.

As you add items to My Menu, you'll find that you can access this single page and get to the items you want quickly and easily without having to wade through a bunch of different screens.

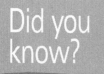

Once a Browser, Always a Browser

The PocketGenie's menu works a lot like a typical web browser, such as Netscape and Internet Explorer. If you've played around with the PocketGenie, you see that by clicking the trackwheel, a menu appears. However, this menu acts more like a web browser by giving you Next, Back, Info, and Main options. Other options will appear on the menu as well, depending on what you are doing at the moment, but it is helpful to get into the familiar "back and forward" navigation mode when using the PocketGenie, just like you do when using a computer-based web browser.

PG Inbox

The PG Inbox stores all Internet queries that you make. For example, let's say you use the Pocket Internet tool on your Home screen (explored later in this chapter in the section "Using the Pocket Internet") to make a URL request, such as www. osborne.com. This URL request is treated as a query, and the information returned is stored in the PG Inbox. These query answers are considered to be messages and are stored here. I like to think of the PG Inbox as the Favorites folder you typically see in web browsers. That's not completely accurate from a technical point of view, but the PG Inbox gives you a quick-and-easy way to see what you have requested. The PG Inbox can hold about 30 messages at any given time, and you can read and delete them using the inbox menu.

Alerts

The next icon is for the Alerts feature, but you need to know a little about the other categories before using Alerts, so I'll return to it a little later in the chapter in the section "Revisiting Alerts."

Driving

Getting lost is never a fun proposition, but fortunately, PocketGenie can help you find your way using Internet maps. This tool works by gathering a starting and destination address from you so it can provide driving directions. The tool is easy to use, and the following text, "Get Driving Directions," shows you the steps.

13

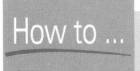 **Get Driving Directions**

1. Click the Driving icon, the fourth icon in the top row on the PocketGenie Home screen, and click Next.

2. Enter a starting address, as shown in Figure 13-14. This address is where directions will start from (in other words, where you are currently). Click Next.

3. Enter the city and state or ZIP code for the starting address. Click Next.

4. Enter the ending address street location and click Next.

5. Enter the city and state or ZIP code for the ending address. Click Next.

6. In the Route screen, you can choose from a major highway route or you can avoid major highways. You can also choose fastest route or shortest route. Make your selection and click Next.

PocketGenie will locate driving directions on the Internet and return them to you.

Entertainment

The Entertainment icon provides you access to a listing of entertainment features—basically information that can be pulled from the Internet and returned to your BlackBerry, as shown in Figure 13-15.

To use the Entertainment features, just scroll to and click the item that you want. Next, enter or select the information that is necessary for that particular section. For example, to find out information about restaurants, you would first select the Restaurants option from the Entertainment Services screen. You would then have to select the kind of restaurant you want, as shown in Figure 13-16, and enter a city, state, or ZIP code to find all restaurants of the type you specified in that area. The tools here are fun and easy, so check them out and enjoy.

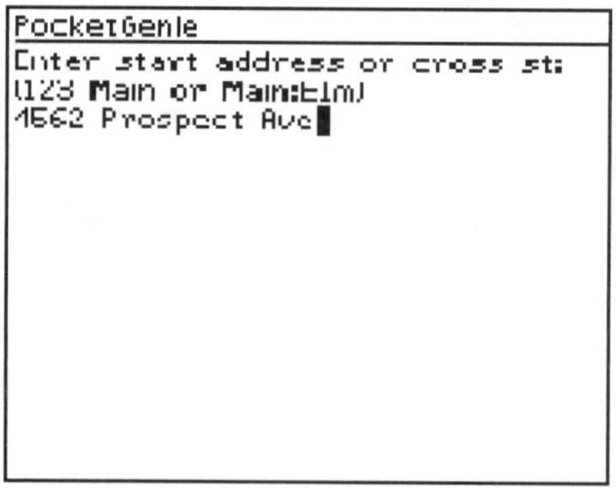

FIGURE 13-14   Starting address

FIGURE 13-15   Entertainment listings

Financial

The Financial Services area of the PocketGenie, shown in Figure 13-17, gives you a place to view your online portfolio and gather all kinds of financial information and news. If you are watching the stock market and keeping up with events in the financial world, this feature of the PocketGenie should prove useful. Here you can also find information about different companies, use a handy currency converter, and access a number of related financial news and services.

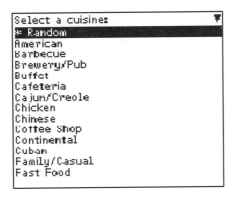

FIGURE 13-16   Find a restaurant

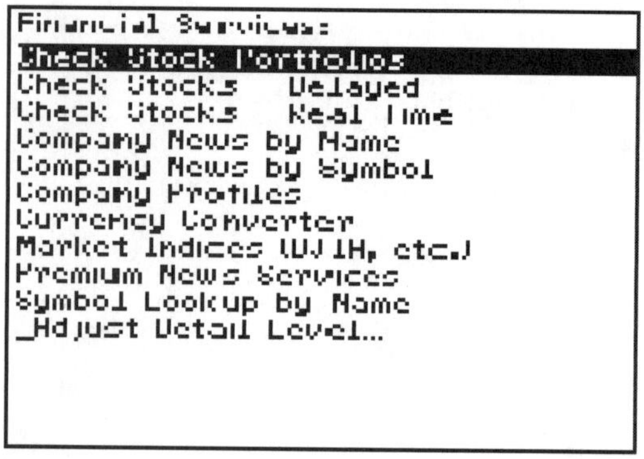

```
Financial Services:
Check Stock Portfolios
Check Stocks    Delayed
Check Stocks    Real Time
Company News by Name
Company News by Symbol
Company Profiles
Currency Converter
Market Indices (DJIA, etc.)
Premium News Services
Symbol Lookup by Name
_Adjust Detail Level...
```

FIGURE 13-17   Financial options

Lookup

The Lookup feature of the PocketGenie is a handy tool that finds different kinds of information on the Internet for you. For example, do you need to find an area code for a certain city? No problem—let Lookup find it for you. How about a phone number or e-mail address? How about the Yellow Pages? The Lookup options screen, shown in Figure 13-18, gives you a quick way to find the information you need. Note that not all of these services are free, but the Lookup screen lets you know what's free and what's not.

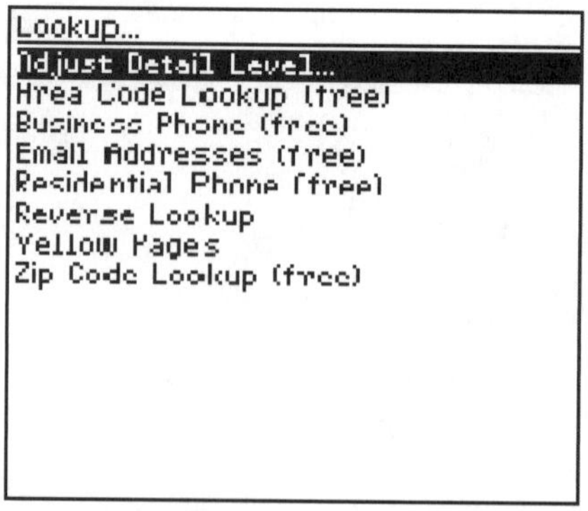

```
Lookup...
Adjust Detail Level...
Area Code Lookup (free)
Business Phone (free)
Email Addresses (free)
Residential Phone (free)
Reverse Lookup
Yellow Pages
Zip Code Lookup (free)
```

FIGURE 13-18   Lookup feature

News

You can use the PocketGenie to easily keep up with what is going on in the world around you. The News area of the browser gives you access to all kinds of news items, including top stories, business headlines, entertainment headlines, and a host of others, as shown in Figure 13-19. Just click the item you want, and the PocketGenie will pull the information from the Internet for you.

Office

The Office feature of the PocketGenie, which I find very helpful, gives you access to several quick tools that use the Internet in order to find the information you need. For example, do you need to find the spelling of a word, or do you need to create a document you can fax? You can do these things and much more using the PocketGenie's Office tools. The available tools, which are shown in Figure 13-20, all function in the same basic manner—you input some information, and the PocketGenie uses the Internet to retrieve the answers for you. In the case of faxing, you simply enter a phone number or e-mail address and type the fax you want to send. You can even check on packages that are currently in the shipment process at major providers such as Airborne Express, DHL, FedEx, and others.

```
Select a news category:
* Top Stories
Business Headlines
Company News by Name
Company News by Symbol
Entertainment Headlines
Finance Headlines
Nation Headlines
Premium Finance News
Premium Sports News
ShowBiz News
Sports Headlines
Technology Headlines
World Headlines
_Accessing News Help...
```

FIGURE 13-19   News screen

FIGURE 13-20   Office tools

PG Store

The PG Store provides you with access to a few shopping sites, such as Flowershop.com, Movie Tickets, online auctions, and related shopping options. You can also browse other online stores by simply requesting a URL, which you'll explore a little later in this chapter in "Using the Pocket Internet."

Sports

The Sports section of the PocketGenie works just like Entertainment and News. After clicking the Sports icon on the PocketGenie Home screen (the first icon in the bottom row), you are given a list of categories, as shown in Figure 13-21. To

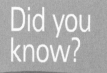

The Mobile Office

Once of the reasons I like the Office feature of the PocketGenie so much is that it provides you with many of the tools and accessories you would use if you were sitting at a desk. These tools enable you to get information you need and continue working, even when you are away. And the best news is the tools are all located on the BlackBerry, so they are easy to carry, yet they access the power of the Internet. For the mobile professional, that's a great combination.

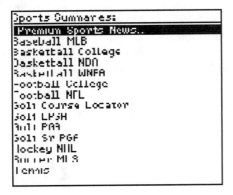

FIGURE 13-21   Sports screen

view a category, just click the category you want to see, and the sports information
will be downloaded to your BlackBerry from the Internet.

Travel

Use the power of the Internet to check flight listings and flight status with the
Travel option. You can also get directions to the airport and use the currency
converter and translator tools here as well.

Weather

Using the Internet, the PocketGenie can find the weather for your area or for any
city and state (or ZIP code). Just enter the information, and you'll get a weather
report back in seconds.

Support

And finally, if you are having problems with PocketGenie, the Support section
gives you quick tips and instructions, or you can ask for help using WolfeTech
support. The options provided here are self-explanatory.

Revisiting Alerts

I mentioned the Alerts feature earlier in this section, and now that you have taken
a look at the other items available, let's back up and examine the Alerts feature.
The Alerts feature enables you to configure information from one of the content
categories, such as News, Sports, Entertainment, and so on, to automatically

13

appear on your BlackBerry at a desired time. For example, let's say that you get up every morning at 7:00 A.M. While you are having coffee, you want to use your BlackBerry to read stock quotes. Sure, you can manually access that information each morning, but why not have it arrive automatically—just like a morning paper delivery? You can do this by setting up alerts, an easy process. Check out "Configure an Alert" for instructions.

Configure an Alert

To configure a PocketGenie alert, follow these steps:

1. On the PocketGenie Home screen, select the Alert icon (the third icon in the top row) and click Next.

2. In the Schedule Alerts screen, shown in Figure 13-22, select a category for which you want to configure an alert and click Next.

3. In the screen that appears, like the one shown in Figure 13-23 that appears after the Financial category is selected, choose the item you want to configure an alert for, and then click Next. Additional screens may appear for further information clarification or restriction. Just complete the requested information and click Next.

4. In the Select the day(s) screen, select the days that you want the alert to run. To select a day, click the trackwheel and click Toggle Item in order to place a check next to it. As you can see in Figure 13-24, I am configuring this alert for Monday, Tuesday, and Wednesday. Click Next when you're done.

5. In the Time screen, select the times at which you want the alert to run. Use the Toggle item feature on the menu to make your selections. You can select as many times as you want. When you're done, click Next.

6. Enter the number of minutes past the hour to run the service. For example, if you selected 7:00 A.M. on the previous window, but you want the alert run at 7:15 A.M., just enter 15. Click next.

7. You can choose to send a copy of the information to your e-mail or not. Make a selection, and click Next.

At this time, the item is configured and you will begin receiving the alerts at the next time interval.

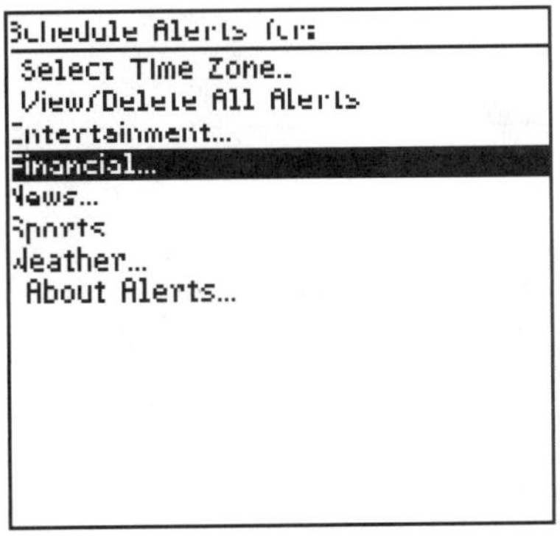

FIGURE 13-22   Select category

FIGURE 13-23   Select item

13

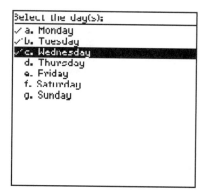

FIGURE 13-24 Select day

> **TIP** *If you no longer want to use an alert, just access the Alerts screen and choose the View/Delete All Alerts option. You can then select and remove any alert that you no longer want to use.*

Using the Pocket Internet

The PocketGenie gives you a great way to access all kinds of information using the Internet. However, this tool may restrict you because you can't really surf the Internet. No fear, the PocketGenie automatically installs with the Pocket Internet (represented by a pi symbol on your BlackBerry Home screen). The Pocket Internet gives you the power to surf and find information you need without categories. The Pocket Internet Home screen is shown in Figure 13-25.

FIGURE 13-25 Pocket Internet Home screen

As you can see in Figure 13-25, Pocket Internet basically functions like a computer browser. In order to open a web page, simply click the Open a new web page option, and then enter the URL. The information will be retrieved from the Internet. You can then bookmark the page using the trackwheel menu options.

If you are having problems finding what you want, you can use the Google search engine, which will help you find Internet items. You can also use several Internet utilities that allow you to test for connectivity. Overall, the Pocket Internet is very streamlined and easy to use, and if you spend about ten minutes working with it, you'll be a pro.

> **TIP**   *Save typing time—be sure to bookmark any Internet sites that you want to visit on a regular basis.*

Business Solutions

As you have learned throughout this book, the BlackBerry is great for both the business user and the individual user. The BlackBerry, however, has always been geared to the corporate professional, and the following three third-party solutions were developed for corporations. In a nutshell, these services extend the BlackBerry by making corporate information easier to access or providing some other type of BlackBerry-corporate link. Your company may already be using these services, and if not, you should definitely read the following sections and find out about these options which are available for your company.

WebFOCUS Mobile Solutions

WebFOCUS Mobile Solutions constitute a set of wireless tools that enable you to get reports and other types of corporate information over the national wireless network via the BlackBerry. In short, it's a way to stay intimately connected to your corporate network and receive information about your business when you are not in the office.

WebFOCUS was developed by Information Builders, an e-business company focused on e-business solutions. More than 9,000 companies, including most of the Fortune 100 companies, use WebFOCUS, and since the BlackBerry is geared to Fortune 100 companies, it's no surprise that the BlackBerry works well with this solution. You can access the Information Builders web site at http://www. informationbuilders.com, and you can learn specifically about WebFOCUS at http://www.informationbuilders.com/products/webfocus/mobile.html, as shown in Figure 13-26.

13

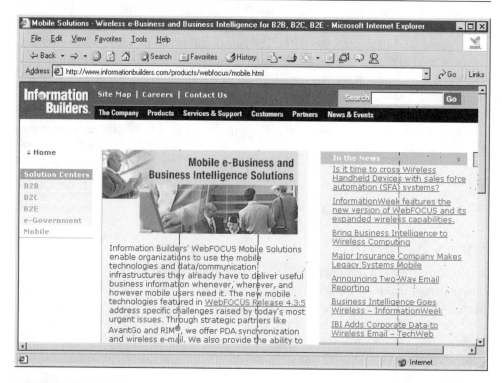

FIGURE 13-26 WebFOCUS site

So, what exactly does WebFOCUS provide? The software solution allows your business to keep its current network infrastructure and deliver timely, necessary information to users on mobile devices, namely the BlackBerry. For example, one of the features of WebFOCUS is TellMe By Email, which delivers preconfigured reports via e-mail to the BlackBerry at timed intervals. This allows mobile users to maintain contact with their business when they are not at their desks. In lay terms, you can query servers on your company network using e-mail and receive reports that you desire, assuming they are allowed by network administrators. This automated system uses a push/pull approach to deliver content. Alerts and report notifications can be pushed to the BlackBerry via e-mail, and users can respond to those e-mails in order to receive business reports. In the same manner, users can send an e-mail to the WebFOCUS system in order to pull report information that may be available. All of this is configured on your company's servers, and security restrictions can be invoked to protect critical data.

Obviously, you can't use the WebFOCUS solution unless it is deployed on your network. If you think this solution might be right for your business, begin by reading the documentation at http://www.informationbuilders.com/products/webfocus/mobile.html.

Brience Framework

Brience, a mobile technology company, provides a solution that allows your network to extend corporate applications to the BlackBerry using JAVA and XML. The idea is to extend the local network to the wireless network and provide network applications to the mobile user via the BlackBerry without changing the existing architecture of the network. This works with a server-side solution that can extend applications over the wireless network to your BlackBerry.

The Brience Framework provides a number of server software products that process network data directly and channel it in a way that will be meaningful to BlackBerry users. The end result is more information from your corporate network comes to your BlackBerry—information that you can use and manipulate in much the same way as if you were sitting at your desk.

You can learn more about the Brience Framework at http://www.brience.com, which is shown in Figure 13-27.

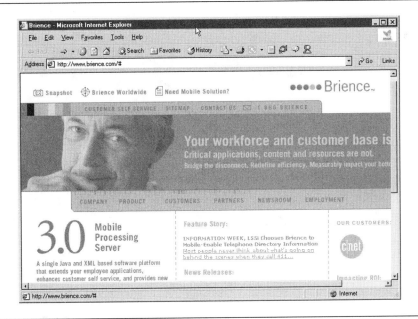

FIGURE 13-27

13

Afaria

Afaria provides systems management software that enables corporations to track and manage BlackBerry operating systems and units. As a BlackBerry user, you won't see any advantage if your company is using Afaria, but the Afaria software enables your administrators to manage system software, BlackBerry updates, licensing, and other issues. This may not seem that important, but systems management can be very costly and very timely, and Afaria can help control those costs for the BlackBerry. You can learn more about Afaria and the solutions it provides at http://www.afaria.com, as shown in Figure 13-28.

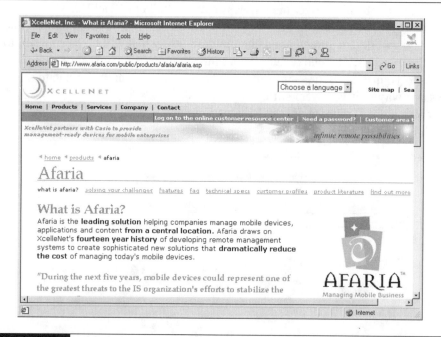

FIGURE 13-28   Afaria.com

Chapter 14

BlackBerry Applications and Fun Stuff

How to...

■   Download BlackBerry software

■   Install software

■   Check out available software from the Internet

The BlackBerry is a full-featured wireless communication device that also acts like a PDA—it contains the most common applications, functions, and features you are likely to need while you are mobile. However, we all have different needs, and certainly different tastes, and in that spirit there are a number of additional applications, utilities, and games that you can download and install, if you desire, on your BlackBerry. These programs are not created by RIM, but rather they come from third parties, and many from individuals who know how to do a little programming. Some of the available applications are marginally helpful, some are very helpful, and some are just great fun. So in this chapter, I'll explore every application, utility, and game available for the BlackBerry at the time of this book's publication. You'll see where to download them from and how to install and use them, as well as pricing information (some are even free).

The Basics of Software Download and Installation

Before you get into the fun of checking out the available downloads, let's first take a minute and review software download and installation. The BlackBerry alone is not capable of downloading and installing software—even if you are using the wireless Internet with one of the browsers discussed in Chapters 9 and 13. The BlackBerry, although powerful, does not have the disk space or processing ability to download an application and run the installation program itself; for this action, it will need some help from your PC and the Desktop Manager software.

Because the BlackBerry cannot download and install software itself, your trusty PC and the BlackBerry Desktop Manager software must help. As you learned in Chapter 5, all applications and software updates or deletions are performed on the BlackBerry using the Desktop Manager. This includes all of the applications, utilities, and games that I discuss in this chapter. For the most part, downloading and installing these items requires three steps:

1. Download the item.

2. Unzip or uncompress it.

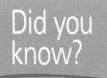
Did you know?

Understanding Downloads

When you download an item from the Internet, you are taking a copy of that item from some web server and placing a copy of that item on your PC—it's that simple. The term *download* simply means that your computer is copying something from a web server—that copy can be a document, a picture, an application, and essentially anything else.

In the case of BlackBerry downloads, you are downloading an application. That application will almost always be downloaded to your PC in compressed or zipped format that enables the application to download more quickly. When the download is complete, the zipped or compressed file may appear as a filing cabinet in vice grips or it may appear as some kind of installation icon; both types of icons are shown in Figure 14-1. Either way, the end result is the same. The application is downloaded to your PC, ready for installation to the BlackBerry.

3. Use the Desktop Manager to install the software on the BlackBerry.

The following sections show you how to do each of these tasks.

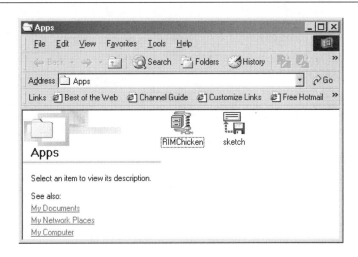

FIGURE 14-1   Zipped/compressed applications

Downloading an Application

In order to download an application, you need a web browser, such as Internet Explorer or Netscape. Downloading BlackBerry applications works just like downloading any other item on the Internet. However, if you are not a typical Internet surfer, just follow the steps in "Download an Application."

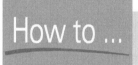 **Download an Application**

1. In order to download a BlackBerry application, use your web browser to access a web site that contains downloadable applications. For this example, I am using http://www.rimroad.com. You can also try http://www.tucows.com (see "Where to Download Applications" later in this chapter for further exploration of these two sites).

2. At the desired web site, locate the downloads section and choose RIM or BlackBerry downloads as necessary. The end result is you will see a page, similar to the one in Figure 14-2, where you select different download categories.

3. Click the desired category, and when you see the application that you want to download, click the application. An additional window may appear that gives you more information about the download. You may then see a Download Now link. Click this link as prompted by the web site.

4. Momentarily, you'll see a Windows file download box, as shown in Figure 14-3. Select the Save this file to disk radio button option and click OK.

5. A Save As dialog box appears, as shown in Figure 14-4. Select a location on your computer to save the file (your desktop is fine), and then click Save.

6. When the download completes, click the Close button. The application's icon now appears in the location you selected in Step 5.

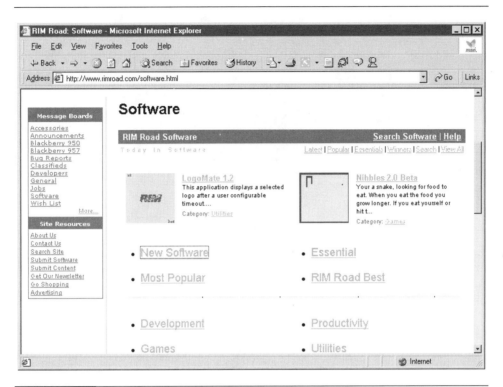

FIGURE 14-2 Download categories

NOTE

Are you concerned about downloading viruses that could affect your BlackBerry? Don't worry about it. Although there is always a potential to download a PDA virus and install it, the odds are extremely small from the trusted sites explored in this chapter. In fact, PDA viruses are almost unheard of, so you can relax. You should, however, always perform a complete backup of your PDA before installing any applications, and you should only download files from trusted web sites, such as those discussed in this chapter and Appendix C.

14

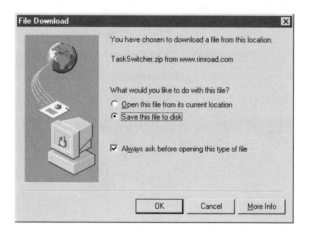

FIGURE 14-3   Windows File Download box

Unzipping an Application

Zipped files are compressed files that are essentially "shrunk" using the WinZip technology (http://www.winzip.com). WinZip is a common compression software application and is even natively available in Windows Me and Windows XP.

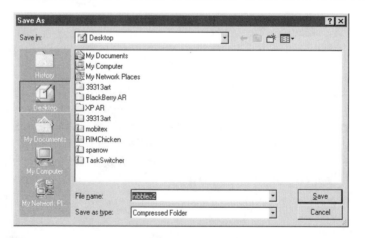

FIGURE 14-4   Save As dialog box

Using WinZip, files are often shrunk to half of their normal size, thus reducing download times. When you receive the file, it will normally appear as a filing cabinet with vice grip squeezing it. In order to use the contents of the zip file, you have to uncompress the files. See "Unzip an Application" to learn how.

TIP   *PDA application download sizes are usually small—often under 15 kilobytes, which is about the size of a long e-mail message. Even using a 56K modem, you can download BlackBerry application files in only a matter of seconds.*

Unzip an Application

1. Before unzipping a file, you'll need a folder to save the file to. You can save the application files to a single folder (I created one called Apps for this purpose), or you can save the application into its own folder so that it can be installed on the BlackBerry. Make a decision and create a folder if necessary.

2. When you download a zipped application, the icon for that application will typically appear on your Windows desktop or in some other folder that you specified during installation. Double-click the icon.

3. The WinZip window appears, as shown in Figure 14-5. Click the I Agree button to continue.

4. The unzipped application files appear in the WinZip window, as shown in Figure 14-6. Click the Extract icon (your icon may read Unzip or Unzip Now).

5. In the selection window that appears, select the folder that you want the files to be extracted to, and then click the Extract button. The files are extracted to that folder and are ready for installation using the Desktop Manager.

6. Click the Close button on the WinZip window.

14

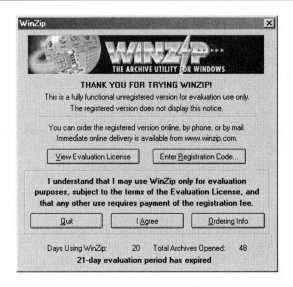

FIGURE 14-5   WinZip window

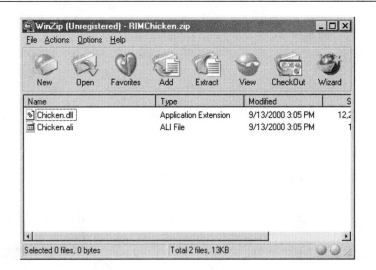

FIGURE 14-6   Zipped files

Using Installer Applications

Some applications that you download will appear as a custom icon instead of a WinZip icon. Although these applications are also compressed, they contain an installer program that gets the files ready for installation on your BlackBerry. Essentially, these types of applications walk you through a little setup routine before you use the Desktop Manager to install the application. The setup routine is somewhat different for each application (depending on the programmer who wrote it), but they all essentially work in the same way. To learn how to go through a typical Installer application setup, see "Run an Installer Application."

NOTE   *What is the difference between an installer application and a zip file? Nothing really—both of them simply extract files and place the files in a folder where they are kept until you install them on the BlackBerry using the Desktop Manager. Using WinZip, this process happens automatically, and the installer application helps you by walking you through a stepped process. There is no advantage of one over the other.*

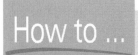 **Run an Installer Application**

1. Locate the item you downloaded and double-click its icon.

2. A licensing window may appear. Click the I Agree button to continue.

3. A destination window may appear, such as the one shown in Figure 14-7. Select a folder where you want to save the installation files (or create a new folder). Make your selection and click OK.

4. Additional screens may appear, asking you for the model of your BlackBerry (950 or 957). Answer these screens as prompted, and then click Finish.

14

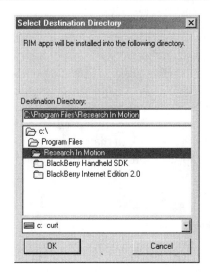

FIGURE 14-7   Destination window

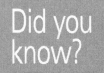

J2ME and the BlackBerry

You may have heard some buzz about J2ME in BlackBerry circles. J2ME, which stands for Java 2 Platform, Micro Edition, came onto the scene in June of 2001 when BlackBerry and Sun Microsystems produced the first BlackBerries built on the Java programming language, which is one of the most popular programming languages in the world. By embracing Java, the BlackBerry becomes more integrated with Internet applications, and a new world of potential programs and applications can be easily developed for the BlackBerry. Indeed, corporations can even write their own custom applications for corporate BlackBerry users with the J2ME platform. The end result—the BlackBerry is becoming more and more versatile all of the time and easier for corporations to customize.

Installing Applications on the BlackBerry

You install applications on the BlackBerry using the Desktop Manager, and any applications you download from the Internet, whether they are utilities, games, or whatever, are all installed in the same way. You explored application installation in Chapter 5, but the following text, "Install Software on the BlackBerry," reviews the process for you here for quick reference.

TIP

For the most part, all applications have an .ali file and an associated .dll (dynamic link library) file. The .ali file installs the application on the unit and the .dll file allows the BlackBerry to load and run the application. Both are important and both are needed for the application to function correctly.

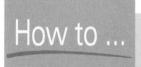 **Install Software on the BlackBerry**

1. Connect your BlackBerry to the cradle, and then open the Desktop Manager software on your PC.

2. Double-click the Backup and Restore icon and perform a complete backup of your BlackBerry.

3. Once the backup is complete, double-click the Application Loader icon.

4. Click Next on the Welcome screen.

5. In the Optional Application Selection dialog box, shown in Figure 14-8, click the check box by the application that you want to install. If the application does not appear in this window, click the Add button and then browse for the application you downloaded. The Application Loader will look for an .ali file, and you'll need to select the .ali file for the application you want to install. Click Next.

6. Click Next on the following screens. The application is installed on your BlackBerry and now ready for use.

14

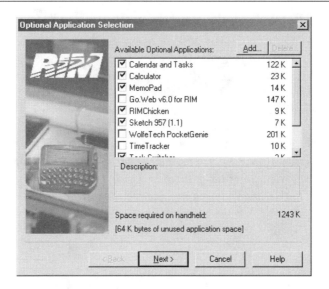

Choose an application

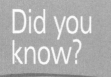

"Perform a Backup—or Deserve the Consequences!"

Don't worry, I haven't become complacent and downright mean—I would never want you to lose data when installing applications. However, the importance of performing a full backup each time you install a new application cannot be overstated because you never know what problem may arise. When I was teaching some computer courses, a fellow instructor often stood on his soapbox when it came to backups. "Perform a backup, or deserve the consequences!" he would say. True enough, and the BlackBerry is no exception. Always perform a full backup before installing or removing applications from your BlackBerry.

Where to Download Applications

Keep in mind that the applications explored in this chapter are all third-party applications. This means that the applications were developed by companies or individuals outside of RIM. Therefore, you will not find any of these at the RIM or BlackBerry sites, but you will find them at two primary gadget and application sites, discussed in the next two sections.

> **TIP** *The web sites explored in this chapter are the easiest to use at the time of this book's writing. By the time you read this, there may be another site available. Just search the Internet for BlackBerry applications to see if you come up with anything else.*

RIM Road web site

RIM Road (http://www.rimroad.com) is a division PDAStreet.com. This site contains a number of useful items about the BlackBerry (see Appendix C to learn more) as well as a number of helpful downloads. When you access RIM Road, you see a link for free downloads, as shown in Figure 14-9. Click the Free Downloads link to access the selection page where you can choose the download that you want. You may need to navigate through a few additional screens, but you'll see that the site is well constructed and easy to navigate.

Tucows web site

Tucows (located at http://www.tucows.com and pronounced "two cows") is a general application and information site devoted to PC and PDA applications, as shown in Figure 14-10. Under the PDA section on the Home Page, you see a link for RIM. Click this link and follow the prompts. You will be asked to select your country and state or province in order to select a download site nearest you. From there, you can browse content categories and download the applications that you want.

Curt's Catalog of Applications, Utilities, and Games for the BlackBerry

The time has finally come—you get to download and use some of these very helpful and very fun software products. In the following sections, I'll review the major software downloads that are available, most of which can be found at the RIM Road and/or Tucows sites. If an application is found elsewhere, I'll give you the URL. For each application, I'll tell you where you can download it, show you

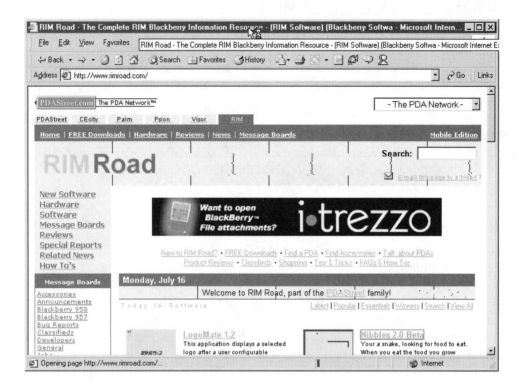

FIGURE 14-9   RIM Road web site

what it's all about, and give you any configuration information that you may need.
I'll also provide a rating for each item based on its functionality and usefulness. Use
the rating to help you determine if the software product is right for you. Five stars
is the top rating while 1 star is the lowest. Please do note that I have no relatives
who have developed any of these applications, so my evaluations are objective—
not the final word, just something to help you out.

Applications

An application is loosely defined as a software product that can help you with
some task. They are developed to help you work, and you'll see that the following
items are designed to give your BlackBerry additional functionality that can help
you with your job.

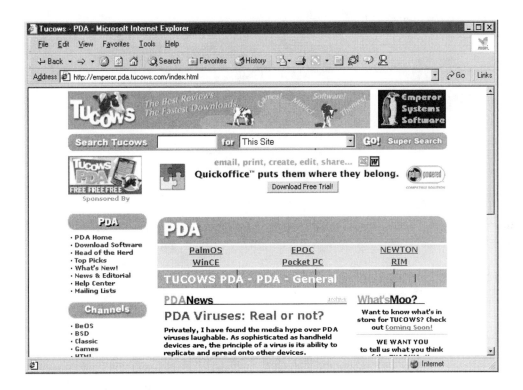

Onramp Ticker

Rating: ****

Available from: RIM Road

Price: Demo available for download—full price is $49.95

The Onramp Ticker provides you a tickertape that runs on your BlackBerry. You can configure the tickertape to report live stock quotes on your unit so that you never miss a moment in the stock market world.

Once you have the Onramp Ticker installed on the BlackBerry, you'll see a new icon on your Home screen that looks like a ticker tape. Click the icon to bring up the Onramp Ticker Options screen, shown in Figure 14-11, through which you set up the ticker. You can enter your e-mail address and determine what stock quotes you want reported on the tape. Once the ticker is configured, it appears on your

14

Onramp Ticker Options

Not Activated
Scroll Speed   Medium
Email Address: csimmons@myblackbe
rry.net
Registration Key:
          STOCKS TO REPORT ON:
1 ^DJI (DOW IND.)
2 ^IXIC (NASDAQ)
3

FIGURE 14-11   Onramp Ticker

Home screen. You can watch the reports from your Home screen as desired. It's simple, easy, and a great way to keep in real-time contact with your stocks.

ExpenseMinder

Rating: ****

Available from: Tucows

Price: Demo available for download—full price is $20.00

ExpenseMinder is a great utility that allows you to keep up with expenses when you travel. Once installed on your BlackBerry, a new icon appears on the Home screen. If you click the icon, you see the Reports section. Before doing anything, click the trackwheel to bring up menu options and click Configure. Here, you can enter your name and company name so that it appears on all reports.

To create an expense report, just click the trackwheel and then click New Report on the screen that appears; enter the expense information and toggle the check boxes as needed, as shown in Figure 14-12. You can then save the report to your report list. From the report list, you can edit or delete any report, and you can also send the report via e-mail, which essentially places the report text into the e-mail. This is a nice feature, of course. Overall, ExpenseMinder is a simple tool, but one you may find helpful if you are constantly trying to track expenses and recover your money.

BBSafe

Rating: ***

Available from: RIM Road

Price: Demo available for download—full price is $19.99

FIGURE 14-12   ExpenseMinder report

BBSafe locks your unit when you are away and encrypts the data on the unit using 128-bit encryption. As you may recall, your BlackBerry has a password-protect feature that locks the unit after a time period has elapsed. To access the unit, you enter the required password. The BBSafe tool works the same way, but it also encrypts the data while it is locked so that essentially the data cannot be stolen. If you are really worried about security, then you may find this tool helpful, but it really doesn't do anything else that is particularly helpful except encrypt your system.

TimeTracker

Rating: *

Available from: Tucows
Price: Free
TimeTracker is a simple utility that enables you to keep time while working on a task. You can then create a simple report, which you can e-mail, listing the amount of time required for the task. If you are billing clients by the hour, this utility can help you. It doesn't do much more than this, but it's free and you may find it useful, depending on your type of work.

Calculator

Rating: **

Available from: Tucows
Price: Free
If you are using an older BlackBerry model that does not have a built-in calculator, you can download this free version from Tucows. It essentially works

14

the same and provides the same features as the one included with the BlackBerry, but this one is here for the taking if you need it.

Forms2Go

Rating: ****

Available from: RIM Road

Price: Free demo available for download—full price is $50.00

Forms2Go enables you to create forms on your BlackBerry and even have form fields submitted to you via e-mail. Fields can include the date, text, time, and any numeric values. The tool works well, so if you need forms on your BlackBerry in order to safely and accurately store data, then be sure to check this one out.

StockBoss

Rating: ****

Available from: RIM Road

Price: Free trial

If you need to keep up with your stocks and stock news, this is a great utility—and it's free. The StockBoss is able to get portfolio updates for you and gather stock quotes and market data, as you can see in Figure 14-13. You can even see charts, set alerts, and gather other data. To take full use of its services, you need to subscribe to StockBoss and upgrade your account, but the trial version does give you a lot of functionality. If you need to keep up with the stock market, you'll like this application.

FIGURE 14-13   StockBoss

RIM Reader

Rating: ***

Available from: RIM Road

Price: Downloadable trial version—full version is $15.00

If you like to read (and my guess is that you do), then the RIM Reader is the perfect utility for you. You can cut and paste basically any document into the RIM Reader so it can be viewed when you are away from your desk. You can even cut and paste the entire text of an electronic book into the reader so it is available in the palm of your hand. The RIM Reader is very easy to use and enables you to carry as much information as your BlackBerry can handle (which is a quite a lot).

The RIM Reader provides you with a PC application that allows you to cut and paste text, give it a name, and then transfer that text to the BlackBerry, as you can see in Figure 14-14.

Then, using the BlackBerry, you access the Reader's menu and click Receive. The text is transferred to the BlackBerry, and you can then read the text using the Reader at your leisure.

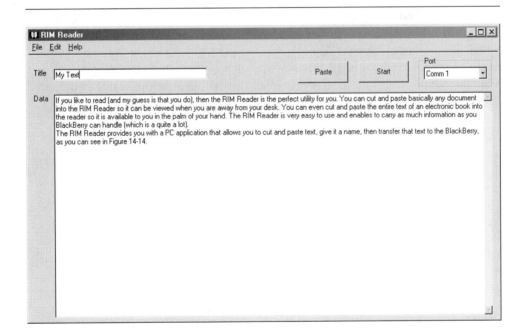

14

FIGURE 14-14   RIM Reader

Sparrow Mail

Rating: ****

Available from: RIM Road and Tucows

Price: Free

Sparrow is a free e-mail application for the BlackBerry. You may be thinking, "Wait a minute, the BlackBerry already has e-mail." True enough, and the BlackBerry's e-mail tools are quite good. Sparrow mail was developed by an individual to address some shortcomings of BlackBerry's mail applications. Probably the most compelling item that Sparrow provides is a folder view of e-mail that looks more like a desktop PIM, as you can see in Figure 14-15.

You can set rules for folders, alerts, and similar e-mail features found in the BlackBerry. Like I said, this one is simply optional, but it is free, so you may want to check it out.

WordWave Desktop

Rating: *****

Available from: RIM Road and Tucows

Price: Downloadable trial version—full version is $25.00

The major problem with wireless e-mail these days is attachments. After all, the BlackBerry (or any other PDA for that matter) lacks the capability to handle e-mail attachments. The units do not have the RAM, disk space, or the applications required to read typical e-mail attachments, such as documents and pictures. So what do you do when you receive an e-mail that has an attachment that you need to send to someone else or manage in a different way when you are thousands of miles from the office?

FIGURE 14-15   Sparrow mail

WordWave Desktop is just the solution you need. Using a variety of commands issued through e-mail, WordWave runs on your PC or even a corporate server. You can send e-mail to WordWave that gives the system instructions about your inbox and specific e-mail messages. But you can also use WordWave to actually view attachments on your BlackBerry. Using the WordWave engine, e-mail attachments can be converted to a generic form that is readable through e-mail instead of via a specific application. As you can see in Figure 14-16, you are given an Explorer-based pane on your PC so you can select which folders and files are managed by WordWave. Using this interface and the commands you issue from your handheld, you can even manage your inbox, read unopened mail, and forward attachments to other people. Despite a slight learning curve, WordWave is fairly easy to use, yet gives you a world of new e-mail management possibilities.

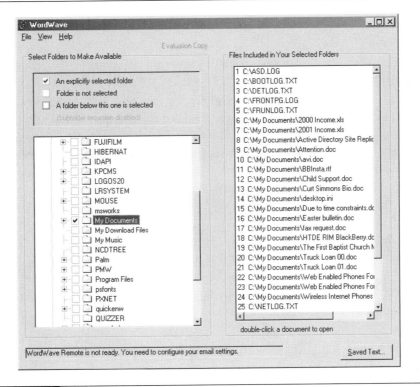

FIGURE 14-16   WordWave Desktop

 *There is also a white paper at the RIM Road site that you might want to download and read in order to learn more.*

PageMe

Rating: ***

Available from:Tucows

Price: Downloadable beta version

At the time of this writing, PageMe is in beta development, but you can download it for free and check it out. The PageMe service is designed to run on your BlackBerry so that you can send pages to yourself as reminder notices. The pages will work with any e-mail address, alpha pager, or Inter@ctive pager. My initial pass of this product didn't impress me too much, as the BlackBerry calendar has the same basic features. However, PageMe is in beta at the time of this writing, so you should certainly check it out and see what new developments have been made and if the software might be right for you.

Itrezzo

Rating: *****

Available from: Itrezzo

Price: To be determined

Itrezzo is a mobile solutions company that offers some interesting services and features for the BlackBerry. You can find out more about Itrezzo at http://www.itrezzo.com, as shown in Figure 14-17. Itrezzo is geared to the corporate BlackBerry user with solutions that are helpful in a corporate setting, although home users may find some of the features intriguing as well. You can choose to purchase different Itrezzo plans that have a variety of services, such as those listed here:

- **File Attachment Conversion** This tool converts over 30 different kinds of file attachments to plain text so that they can be viewed on your BlackBerry. You can try out this service for free. Simply forward messages that have attachments to agent@itrezzo.com. The server will convert the attachment to plain text and send it back to you in an e-mail message—very cool and very fast!

- **Global Address Book** In corporate settings, Itrezzo can look up names in the corporate address book and return the address book information to you in an e-mail message on the BlackBerry. This makes retrieving contact information from your corporate network while you are away a snap.

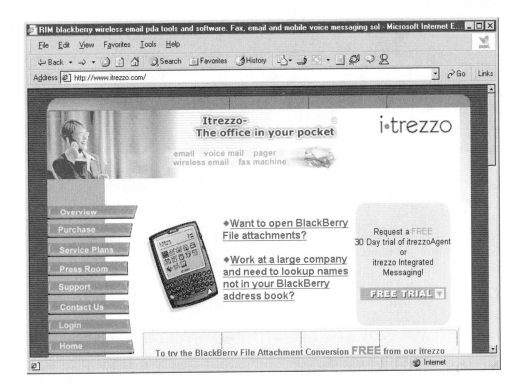

FIGURE 14-17   Itrezzo home page

■ **URL Lookup**   If you are not using a browser on the BlackBerry, you can still retrieve the text from any URL using Itrezzo. Simply make a URL request, and the text from the page will be copied into an e-mail message and sent to you. You must use the exact URL for the page that you want, but this is a great way to get information from the Internet quickly and easily.

■ **Print to Fax**   You can print items from your BlackBerry by sending them to a fax machine. This tool is very helpful when you need to share information with someone in printed form. Just send the text to them via fax. It's simple and easy.

As you can see, each of these tools can be very helpful. You can try the File Attachment Conversion utility for free—just go to the Itrezzo site to download it. The other items are available for free trial download, but you have to call a number to get access to the download, which is not so much fun. Still, I think these tools are great and quite helpful, so I'm giving them a five-star rating.

Mobile TimeBilling

Rating: ****

Available from: Wireless Verticals

Price: Fee trial download—full version is $99.00 per BlackBerry

Time billing is a constant source of headaches and time consumption for the mobile professional who must bill clients based on time. Mobile TimeBilling is a software product that helps you manage and control time billing tasks. You can use the TimeBilling "slip" feature to record time, expenses, mileage, and so on, and then you can easily e-mail that slip to the appropriate person. The slip can then be run through the PC-based program for further manipulation. The application includes a timer that runs on the BlackBerry, and you can even use different rates and generate reports. This is a full-featured program that works well. If you or your corporation are in need of time management software for the BlackBerry, then certainly review this one. You can visit the site at http://www.wirelessverticals.com, as shown in Figure 14-18, and download the BlackBerry trial software from the site.

Handango Financial Calculator

Rating: ****

Available from: Handango

Price: $39.95

The Handango Financial Calculator (available at http://www.handango.com) performs all of the advanced calculating functions you would expect from such a calculator, but all on the BlackBerry. With the financial calculator, your work becomes mobile and always at the touch of your fingertips.

Attachmate

Rating: *****

Available from: Handango

Price: $10.00

The Attachmate program, available from Handango (http://www.handango.com) is very beneficial to the mobile professional because it allows you to attach memos, task lists, and calendar entries as e-mail text. For example, let's say you use

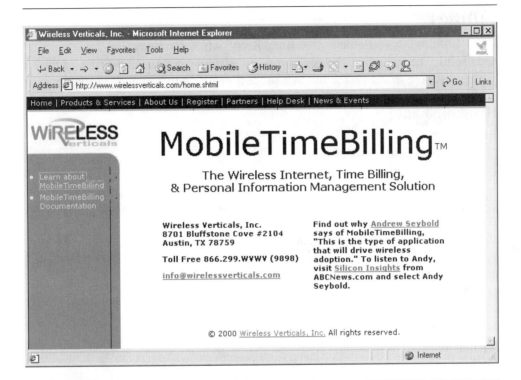

| FIGURE 14-18 | Wireless Verticals home page |

MemoPad to create a memo. Once you are done, you can simply attach that memo to an e-mail message and send it—no waiting until you get to the office, and no keying in every piece of information directly into an e-mail. This one is well worth the money and is easy to use.

Scholarus Wireless

Rating: ****

Available from: Scholarus Wireless

Price: $29.99

Scholarus Wireless (http://www.scholarus.com) provides educational materials for a variety of college tracks, such as engineering, education, science, and so on. Using the service, your BlackBerry can tap into a wide variety of information offered by Scholarus.

14

Utilities

A few utilities are available for the BlackBerry, which you may find interesting and useful. The following sections show you what is available at the time of this writing. Be sure to search the Internet for new products that may be available.

Handango Safe

Rating: ****

Available from: Handango

Price: Free trail version—full price is $19.99

The Handango Safe (available at http://www.handango.com) gives you a secure place to store information on your BlackBerry. The information in the safe is encrypted so that even if someone else gains access to your BlackBerry, he or she cannot gain access to information in the safe. As you can see in Figure 14-19, you can easily create groups of information, e-mail addresses, passwords, URLs, notes—you name it. Overall, this is a great utility to have if you need to keep private and sensitive data on your BlackBerry.

RIM Walker

Rating: ***

Available from: Tucows and RIM Road

Price: Free trail version—full price is $15.00

Let's say you install a new application, and then later remove that application. How do you know if all of the application's files are really gone? In truth, you don't. That is where the RIM Walker comes in. Using this tool, you can see every

FIGURE 14-19   Handango Safe

file that is on your BlackBerry, and you can even choose to delete any file that should not be there. Essentially, this utility gives you more control over the data found on your BlackBerry, but be warned: incorrect use of the RIM Walker or deleting files can cause your BlackBerry to crash. So, proceed with caution. You can see the RIM Walker in Figure 14-20.

Task Switcher

Rating: *****
    Available from: RIM Road and Tucows
    Price: Free
    Task Switcher sets up a hot key so you can switch between BlackBerry applications quickly and easily. Now that may not sound like much, but once you start using the Task Switcher, you will wonder how you ever managed without it. For example, let's say you are using the Tasks feature but you want to switch to MemoPad. Instead of returning to the Home screen, you can simply press ALT-ESCAPE and see a menu of options, as shown in Figure 14-21. Then, you just select the next application you want on the menu. Very simple, very easy, and a great time-saver!

Character Viewer

Rating: ***
    Available from: RIM Road and Tucows
    Price: Free

14

FIGURE 14-20 RIM Walker

FIGURE 14-21   Task Switcher

Character Viewer is a simple utility that allows you to see all of the characters
that are available on your BlackBerry, as shown in Figure 14-22. Beyond viewing
all of the available characters, there isn't anything else you can do with this utility.

LogoMate

Rating: ****

Available from: RIM Road and Tucows

Price: Free

LogoMate is a free utility that essentially gives you a screen saver on the
BlackBerry. This utility is for fun rather than any practical purpose and it's easy
to use. Once you install LogoMate, access the LogoMate option from the Options
screen. As you can see in Figure 14-23, this utility lets you configure a desired

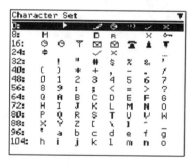

FIGURE 14-22   Character Viewer

FIGURE 14-23   LogoMate

logo, determine when the screen saver comes on (after one minute, two minutes, and so on), positioning, and whether or not to show date and time, e-mail message icons, and battery status on the logo.

Piano Simulator

Rating: ***

Available from: Tucows

Price: Free

The Piano Simulator is more of a pastime than a useful utility. The Piano Simulator appears as an onscreen piano, as shown in Figure 14-24. You simply use the keyboard to simulate the piano. The piano is capable of only two octaves— you have to press the CAP LOCK key to get the second one.

14

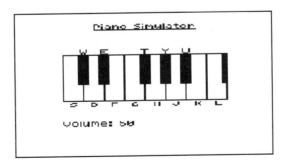

FIGURE 14-24   Piano Simulator

InStep Printing

Rating: ****

Available from: RIM Road
Price: Free trial—full product is $29.99

InStep Printing is a utility that allows you to easily print e-mail messages on your BlackBerry, even when you are not connected to a computer. Various types of documents are supported. You can even adjust printer setup directly from the BlackBerry. Download the trial version and check it out!

RIM Wallet

Rating: *****

Available from: RIM Road and Tucows
Price: Free trial—full product is $25.00

The RIM Wallet gives you a safe-and-easy way to store sensitive data on your BlackBerry in an encrypted format. You can also easily manage that information using a desktop component that is installed too, as shown in Figure 14-25. You can even use the RIM Wallet to access private information on your PC from the BlackBerry. Download the trial version and see what the RIM Wallet can offer you.

Games

Although not the mainstay of the BlackBerry, games are a great pastime for the mobile user. After all, how many newspapers can you read while sitting on a plane? The games listed here are all easy to use and fun. You'll find that downloading and installing them is a real snap, so pick a few of them and try them the next time you stranded in a cab, at the airport, or just about anywhere else.

Sketch

Rating: ****

Available from: RIM Road and Tucows
Price: Free

Okay, this one may show your age. Can you remember Etch-a-Sketch, the little box with the knobs you turned to draw pictures? I thought so. The Sketch game for the BlackBerry is the same thing, as you can see in Figure 14-26. You simply roll the trackwheel to draw vertical lines and roll the trackwheel while holding down the ALT key to draw horizontal lines. It's that simple.

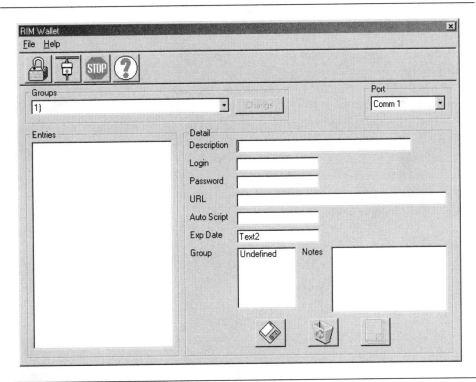

FIGURE 14-25   RIM Wallet

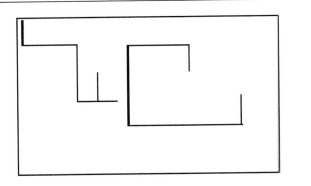

FIGURE 14-26   Sketch

14

RIM Chicken

Rating: *****

Available from: RIM Road and Tucows
Price: Free
Question: How did the chicken cross the road?
Answer: With the BlackBerry trackwheel.

Corny, I know, and this game is rather corny too—but the funny thing is that it is quite addictive and amusing. The object, as you can see in Figure 14-27, is to get the chicken, which you control with the trackwheel, across the road. With each screen you finish successfully, you get a new screen that is a little harder. Believe me, you can easily let an hour slip by doing this, and it is a good pastime when you're stuck at the airport.

Black Dice

Rating: ****

Available from: RIM Road and Tucows
Price: Free

If you are up for a little gambling, then you can play the Black Dice game, as shown in Figure 14-28. This typical dice game has several menu options that give you a full spectrum of play, and the game even includes an informative Help file to make sure you are playing accurately (and fairly, of course!).

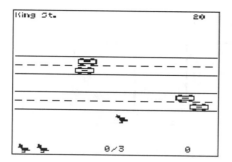

FIGURE 14-27   RIM Chicken

```
BlackDice: Untitled
              6
Q            1D4
W            1D6
E            1D8
R            1D10
T            1D12
V            1D20
U           1D100
I            2D4
D            2D6
P            2D8
          (menu)
```

Black Dice

Mines

Rating: **

   Available from: RIM Road and Tucows
   Price: Free
   The popular Mines game is also available for the BlackBerry, and you can
see what the BlackBerry version looks like in Figure 14-29. Just install the game,
choose a grid size, and use the trackwheel to maneuver around the mine field.
The game is simple and fun.

Hockey Pong

Rating: ***

   Available from: RIM Road and Tucows
   Price: Free

14

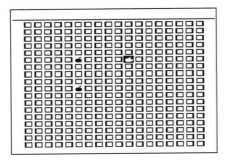

Mines

BlackBerry's Hockey Pong is an easy, fun game that allows you to compete with the BlackBerry, as shown in Figure 14-30. The BlackBerry keeps score and you can even compete against imaginary teams. Overall, this one is a lot of fun, so be sure to check it out.

Nibbles

Rating: ****

Available from: RIM Road and Tucows
Price: Free
Nibbles is an entertaining game that allows you to chase a series of black dots around the screen. It is similar to other worm or snake games, is easy to play, and provides a bit of fun.

Maximum Card Games

Rating: *****

Available from: RIM Road and Tucows
Price: Free trial—full version is $5.88
If you love card games, then this is it. With Maximum Card Games, you can play your favorite games, including poker and black jack. Maximum Card Games gives you an easy-to-understand display of card drawings, as shown in Figure 14-31.

RIM Cell

Rating: *****

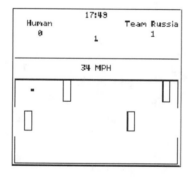

FIGURE 14-30   Hockey Pong

FIGURE 14-31   Maximum Card Games

Available from: RIM Road and Tucows
Price: Free
The RIM Cell provides you with a full-featured cell game, as shown in Figure
14-32. Just use the trackwheel to manage the game, and access the menu to pause
the game when you need to step away. This one is good—and easy to play.

RIM Tetris
Rating: ****
Available from: RIM Road and Tucows
Price: Free

14

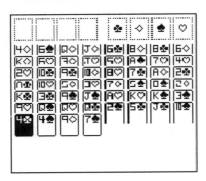

FIGURE 14-32   RIM Cell

If you enjoy Tetris, the BlackBerry version is just as fun. You'll find the download includes not only an interactive game, but also help files to get you started. It's quick and easy, so download it and check it out.

Robot Arena

Rating: **

Available from: RIM Road and Tucows
Price: Free

Robot Arena traps you in an area with a bunch of robots that explode when touched. The object of the game is to simply stay away from them. You have an EMP (energy module) with one charge, but after that, you are on the run, as you can see in Figure 14-33. This is a quick game that you will enjoy (don't cheer during your meeting, however).

Solitaire

Rating: ***

Available from: RIM Road and Tucows
Price: Free

Last but not least is Solitaire, the famous card game you play when you are alone. The BlackBerry version works just like the card version of the game, as you can see in Figure 14-34. This one is a great way to pass the time, and if you like this game, you should certainly get it for your BlackBerry.

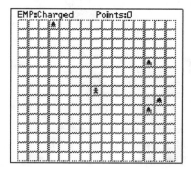

FIGURE 14-33   Robot Arena

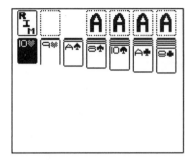

Solitaire

14

Chapter 15

Surfing
BlackBerry.net

How to…

■ Check out BlackBerry.net

■ Find information you need

■ Visit RIM.net

■ Find other BlackBerry information online

Are you a web site addict? You are if you're anything like me—I always visit the web site of any product or service I am interested in or am currently using, and BlackBerry.net is no exception. BlackBerry.net is your single source for finding out the latest news and information about BlackBerry developments. As a BlackBerry user, you should get in the habit of checking out BlackBerry.net on a regular basis so you can keep up with what is new and available from RIM. BlackBerry.net is an easy-to-use, friendly web site where you can pick up all kinds of information. In this chapter, I'll take you on tour of BlackBerry.net, show you where some goodies are located, and get you ready to use the web site on a regular basis. Before doing that, however, let me offer a big disclaimer. Web sites change often and without notice, so it is possible that some information referenced in this chapter may not be in the actual location listed. That's okay—if you can't find something I mention here, BlackBerry.net has a handy search feature so you can track it down. So, without further introduction or disclaimer, let's surf BlackBerry.net.

Accessing BlackBerry.net

In order to get the most out of BlackBerry.net, you need to put aside your BlackBerry unit for the moment and access the BlackBerry web site via a PC that is connected to the Internet. The wired version of BlackBerry.net will give you all the features and benefits the web site has to offer. When you're ready, just point your web browser to http://www.blackberry.net. This will open the BlackBerry.net home page, as you can see in Figure 15-1.

Once you have found your way to the BlackBerry.net home page, spend a few minutes getting your bearings. This will help you familiarize yourself with all the BlackBerry.net site has to offer.

Let's begin with the top title bar of the BlackBerry.net home page. You'll notice that there are links to the four major divisions of the web site—Solutions, Support, Purchasing, and News. Since these links make up the bulk of the web

FIGURE 15-1 BlackBerry.net home page

site's content, I'll explore them individually later in the chapter. For now, just realize that access to the major sections of the BlackBerry web site is available via links at the top of the home page.

To the far right of the home page, you also see a few more links. First, you see a Buy Now link, which takes you directly to the BlackBerry.net storefront. Here, you can purchase actual BlackBerry units and other products. Since this falls under the Purchasing category, I'll explore this feature in more detail later in the chapter.

You also see a Search box. You can enter keywords and phrases you want to search for in the Search box, and then click the Go button. BlackBerry.net will scan its database and return all records to you that match your inquiry. I've played around with the Search feature and have had good luck finding the items that I have searched for, so when you're having trouble finding something, be sure to use this feature.

15

 *You can just press the Enter key on your keyboard after you've entered a keyword instead of clicking the Go link in order to perform a search.*

Directly above the Search box, you see a Home | Contact link. The Home link appears in the upper right-hand corner of each BlackBerry.net page that you access. At any time and in any location, you can click the Home link in order to return directly to the home page. The Contact link gives you easy access to a number of RIM contacts, such as support, information, feedback, and so forth. You can easily find both e-mail addresses and phone numbers by clicking this link.

In the right side of the home page, you see press releases. You can read summaries of the most recent press releases and click any of the date links in order to access the full press release. All of these are also available in the News section of the web site.

In the main part of the home page, you see a brief introduction to the BlackBerry product and, once again, options to access the main divisions of the web site, such as Solutions, Support, and Purchasing. Beneath each of these categories, you also see additional links that you can directly access, such as those that take you to information for software upgrades, documentation, and credit applications.

In the left pane of the window, you see a few additional links that you may find helpful. First, you see the Developer Zone. The Developer Zone is for software

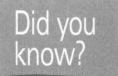 ## Making Searches Count

If you have ever used Internet search engines, you know what a real pain they can be. You can search for "chicken soup" and come up with information about mud wrestling. The BlackBerry site, however, does a good job of returning successful keyword matches. The trick is to enter search information that the BlackBerry can use. As the old saying goes, "Garbage in, garbage out." To find what you need, be as succinct as possible and try to find the correct keyword. In other words, let's say you want to find out information about BlackBerry downloads. To find this information, just enter the keyword "downloads." Do not muddle the search up by entering a lot of other words, such as "how can I download stuff." These extra words only cause more problems in the search, so try to stick to one or two descriptive words.

developers who want to write applications for the BlackBerry. Unless you are a developer, you don't have any use for the Developer Zone section, but if you are into software development or want to learn more about how applications are written for the BlackBerry, you can find all kinds of information here, including the BlackBerry Software Developers Kit, which includes a PC BlackBerry simulator program. The Developer Zone is also directly accessible at http://developers.rim.net, as shown in Figure 15-2.

The second link option in the left pane of the home page brings up the BlackBerry Partner site. The Partner site provides all kinds of information about BlackBerry partners, such as business retailers and the like. You can't access much information here unless you are a partner, in which case you are given a login ID and password.

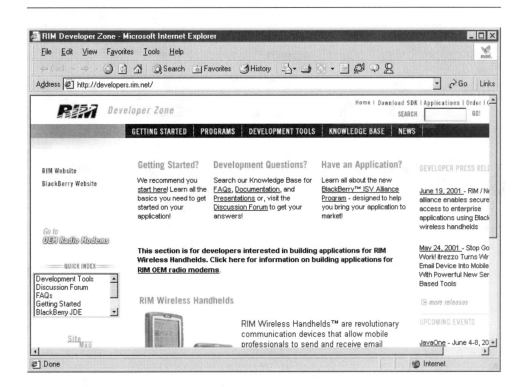

FIGURE 15-2   BlackBerry Developer Zone

The next link goes to the *BlackBerry Connection*. The *BlackBerry Connection* is a newsletter that Research In Motion creates and disseminates to subscribers. The newsletter contains information about current developments and other newsworthy items. If you are interested in keeping track of what is going on the BlackBerry world, I recommend that you click the link and enter the information requested in order to receive the newsletter.

Next is the Send a Page link. For subscribers to BlackBerry's Paging service (see Chapter 9), you can easily and quickly send a page to a particular subscriber using the BlackBerry.net site. If you click the link, you can enter the subscriber's PIN number and type a short text message to send to the subscriber, as shown in Figure 15-3. If you are using paging, this feature is great to keep in mind.

Finally, the home page gives you access to a site map, shown in Figure 15-4. I use the site map frequently because it lists the major categories of the site, and

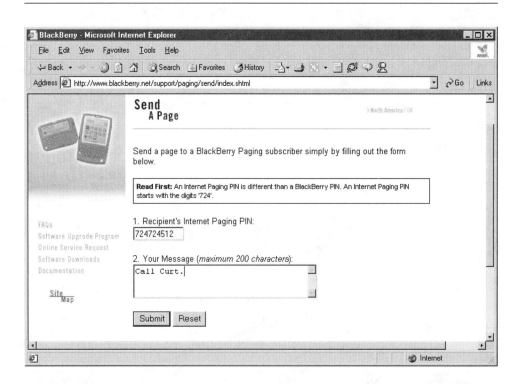

FIGURE 15-3   Sending a page

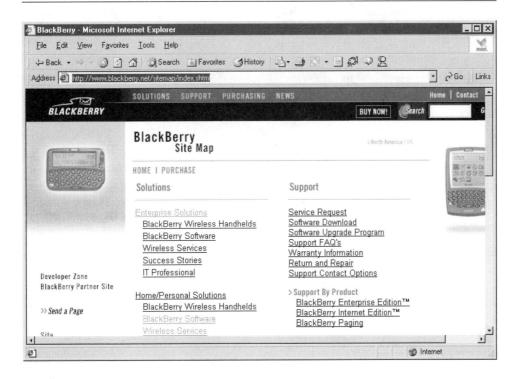

FIGURE 15-4   Site map

then gives you relevant links within each category. For example, if you are looking for a certain item, the site map can help you easily find that item and go directly to it.

Checking Out Major Site Sections

As I mentioned in the previous section, BlackBerry.net has four major site divisions, which are Solutions, Support, Purchasing, and News. The following sections examine each of these.

Solutions

The Solutions area of BlackBerry.net contains information about the BlackBerry product. This is essentially an information area that is designed to help businesses and individuals make decisions about which BlackBerry product is right for them.

When you first click the Solutions link on the home page, you see a link for an interactive demo on the resulting page, as shown in Figure 15-5. If you want to learn more about BlackBerry, you should click this link and walk though the demo. In the main part of the window, you see that the Solutions section has three divisions—Enterprise Solutions, Home/Personal Solutions, and Third Party Solutions. Each of these divisions tells you about the solutions available for particular environments, as described here:

■ **Enterprise Solutions**   The BlackBerry unit and the BlackBerry Server software can function in Microsoft Exchange and Lotus Domino environments for total wireless e-mail and calendar connectivity. This section tells you about these features and gives you the option to download an Adobe Acrobat document that contains more information.

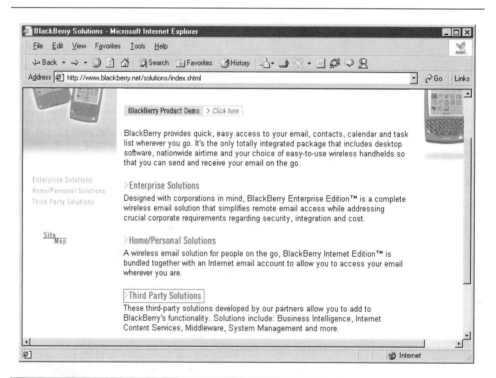

FIGURE 15-5   Solutions page

- ◾ **Home/Personal**   The Home/Personal solution provides you with access to Internet mail. This section gives you a quick summary of the features.

- ◾ **Third Party Solutions**   A number of solutions supported by other companies are explored in this section. You can also learn more about these solutions in Chapters 9 and 13 of this book.

Support

The BlackBerry Support section of BlackBerry.net gives you access to information that may help you solve problems. If you click the Support link, you then see that there are three basic divisions of support available to you—online support, support by product, and online documentation.

The Online Support section gives you access to a variety of information, including Frequently Asked Questions (FAQ) pages where common answers and solutions are posted. You can get information about your warranty and invoice from this section as well.

Before contacting Customer Care, you should read the online documentation and the FAQs. Often, you can correct problems on your own without filling out an online request by simply referring to these documents.

In addition, you can enter a service request from this location by filling out a form (you'll need your BlackBerry's serial and PIN numbers), which is then sent to Customer Care. A Customer Care representative will then get in touch with you to help you solve the problem you may be experiencing with your BlackBerry.

SHORTCUT   *You can use the online form to contact Customer Care, but you can also send an e-mail to help@blackberry.net that will reach the same group. However, you should always talk to your local provider first—this is your first line of support, and RIM may even bounce you back to your provider.*

Support is provided for both the BlackBerry Enterprise and Internet editions. The link option provides you with additional FAQs and troubleshooting information for both editions. If you are a paging customer, you can also access support for paging from this category (a login is required). All of the support here is documentation only.

The last type of support available is in the form of online documentation. The Online Documentation feature provides you with downloadable PDF documents.

You can access the entire user manual for the BlackBerry product, and you can access technical documents and white papers for the BlackBerry Enterprise products. I'll warn you here that some of the documents are rather heavy technical reading, but this can be a great resource area to gather all kinds of information. Of course, all of the information here is free to download.

Finally, you see a link for coverage maps, as shown in Figure 15-6, and support contact information, which is essentially the same contact information seen in other areas of the Support site. The coverage map gives you a look at the entire United States and Canada coverage areas, or you can drill down based on states or provinces. If you are having problems connecting while you are traveling, the maps should be the first troubleshooting step so you can find out if you are currently in a coverage area or not.

Purchasing

The BlackBerry Enterprise and Internet Editions are available directly from the BlackBerry web site as well as from a number of resellers. Since you are reading this book, my guess is that you already own a BlackBerry. If not, you may find this section of the web site very helpful, and if you already own a BlackBerry model, you can find additional products that you might need. When you click the Purchasing link from the BlackBerry.net home page, you see a page five other link options, as shown in Figure 15-7.

The Buy Now link takes you to the BlackBerry StoreFront, where you can purchase a BlackBerry unit and service plan online. This includes package deals for the Enterprise BlackBerry and the Internet BlackBerry. For businesses

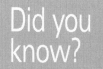

Technical Advisories

The Online Documentation Section contains an option called Technical Advisory. This link allows you to access advisories that alert you to some kind of known problem and the solution to that problem. Again, some of the information you will find here is rather technical, and much of it is focused on Enterprise server configuration and management, but this is one section that you should keep an eye on. If there is some problem you are experiencing, definitely check this part of the web site out for possible information that may help you.

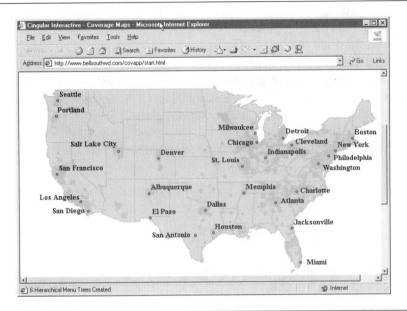

FIGURE 15-6   Coverage map

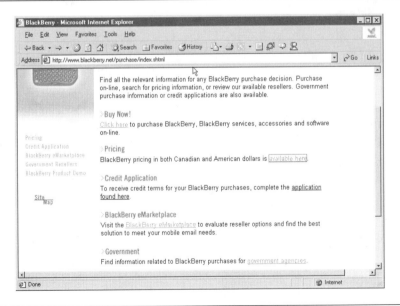

FIGURE 15-7   BlackBerry Purchasing page

15

purchasing the Enterprise BlackBerry, server software and client licenses are included in various packages and configured for Microsoft Exchange or Lotus Domino environments.

If you are interested in purchasing a BlackBerry Internet Edition unit, you are given a list of resellers in both the United States and Canada, as shown in Figure 15-8. If you click one of these links, you are taken to the reseller's web site where you can find the price of the unit and the service plan.

 Use this page for easy comparison shopping between different providers!

At the bottom of the Buy Now window, you can add or remove services (such as paging) and upgrade software. These two options are available only for Enterprise

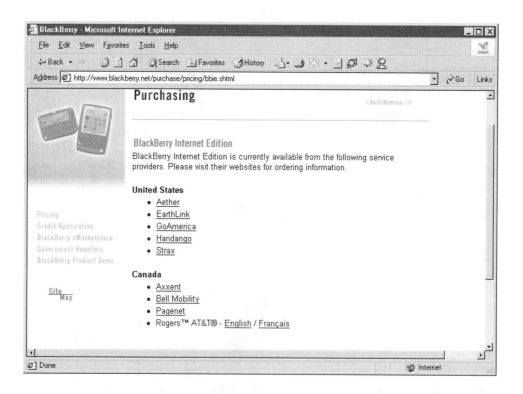

FIGURE 15-8   Internet Edition providers

customers. You can also access the BlackBerry Accessories page, where you can find replacement parts or items that will make your work with the BlackBerry much easier, as shown in Figure 15-9.

The next section is Pricing. The Pricing section gives you the same information you can find in the Buy Now section, but the information is laid out in a single page, which is easier to view. Check out this page for quick-and-easy price comparisons.

Next, you see a Credit Application link. The credit application is for businesses that want to open a credit line for a bulk BlackBerry unit/software purchase.

The next link is to the BlackBerry e-MarketPlace. The BlackBerry e-MarketPlace provides more information about service providers and cobranded products, such as the Compaq BlackBerry solution and Cingular Interactive solution. Check out this page for more details on these deals and services.

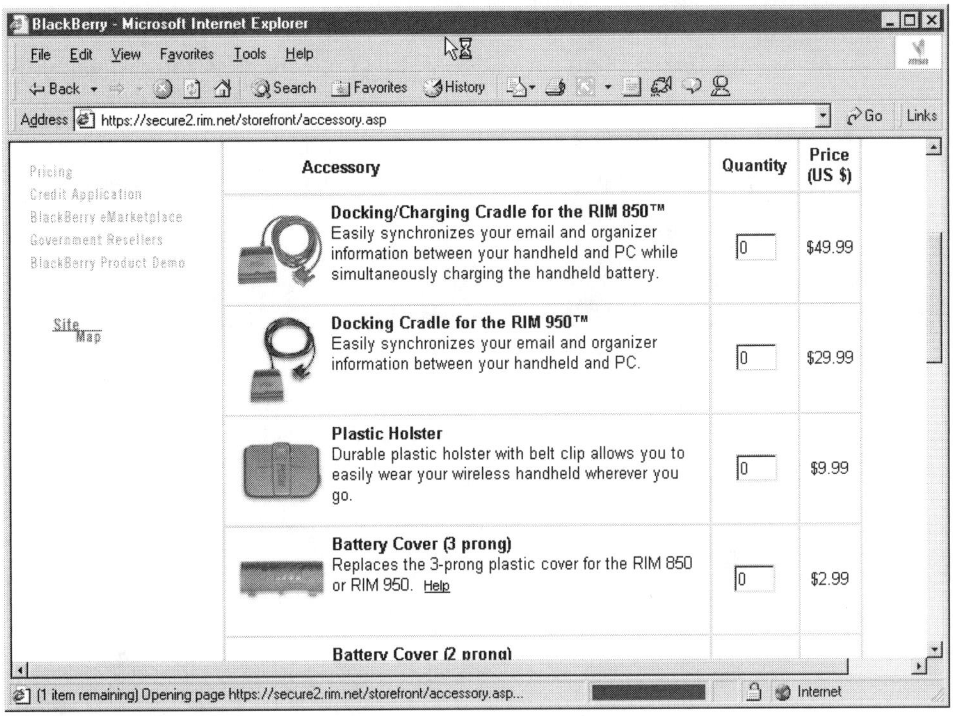

FIGURE 15-9   BlackBerry Accessories page

Finally, the Government link allows government agencies that want to purchase the BlackBerry solution to access information about government resellers.

News

The final section of the BlackBerry site is News. The News section, as shown in Figure 15-10, gives you access to press releases, current news topics, public relations contacts, and the BlackBerry newsletter, BlackBerry Connection. Obviously, this is the place to go in order to stay up to date on BlackBerry news and information, and the sections presented here are self-explanatory.

Visiting Research In Motion

Research In Motion, the creators of the BlackBerry, also have a corporate site located at http://www.rim.net. The corporate site, shown in Figure 15-11, provides you with information about the company and products (of which the BlackBerry is mainly it). You can also access some software downloads from this page by simply following the links. There isn't a lot of direct information you can gather

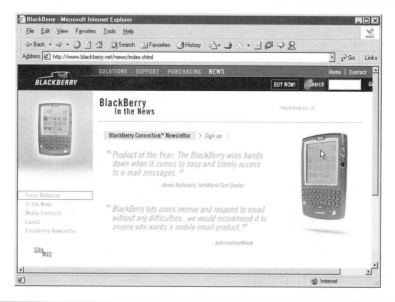

FIGURE 15-10   News section

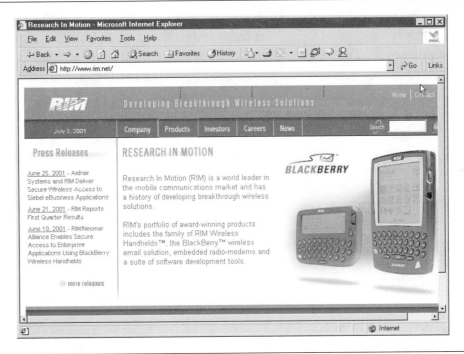

FIGURE 15-11   RIM.net

from this site about using your BlackBerry, but if you want to find out more about RIM or access some additional contact information, you might want to check it out.

Quick URL List

Now that you have made your way around the BlackBerry and RIM web sites, the links in Table 15-1 will put you in direct contact with key web site features. Remember, link addresses change from time to time, so if you have problems accessing one of these, be sure to use the Search feature, available at both BlackBerry.net and RIM.net.

15

Site or Site Section	URL
BlackBerry home page	http://www.blackberry.net
Developer Zone	http://developers.rim.net
BlackBerry Connection sign-up form	http://www.blackberry.net/news/connection/index.shtml
Send a Page feature	http://www.blackberry.net/support/paging/send/index.shtml
BlackBerry.net site map	http://www.blackberry.net/sitemap/index.shtml
BlackBerry demo	http://www.blackberry.net/solutions/demo/index.shtml
Solutions page	http://www.blackberry.net/solutions/enterprise/index.shtml
Support page	http://www.blackberry.net/support/index.shtml
Purchase page	http://www.blackberry.net/purchase/index.shtml
Accessory page	https://secure2.rim.net/storefront/accessory.asp
News page	http://www.blackberry.net/news/index.shtml
RIM corporate page	http://www.rim.net

TABLE 15-1 Quick URL List

Chapter 16

Solving Problems with Your BlackBerry

How to...

- Troubleshoot problems
- Get help
- Find solutions

Imagine a perfect world where no problems exist…yeah, right, you might say. I'd be the first to tell you that nothing is foolproof. No matter how good the design and no matter how great the product, there is always the potential for problems, and the BlackBerry is no exception. In some cases, the unit is the problem, and in other cases, the user is the problem, but no matter who is to blame, you need fast solutions. Don't worry, this chapter is here to help, and in it I've tried to cover most every problem you are likely to have with the BlackBerry. Sure, you might experience something that isn't discussed here, but I've searched high and low for BlackBerry problems and their solutions. So use this chapter as a quick reference to solve problems you might be experiencing with your BlackBerry, or if you really want to be a BlackBerry troubleshooter, study this entire chapter.

Troubleshooting 101

Whenever I talk about troubleshooting, I always like to start out with a basic section that gives a few general pointers about solving problems. At one time during my PC career, I worked as a lead trainer for a technical support center. My experience in this line of business tells me that problems will occur—they are unavoidable—and sometimes people make those problems much worse! This is when users start working in either "panic mode" or "frustration mode." In panic mode, a problem occurs with an electronic device, such as the BlackBerry. The user panics and begins pressing buttons and trying all kinds of things without first taking the time to logically work out the problem. This often causes more problems that also must be solved. In frustration mode, the user becomes frustrated with the device and begins doing all sorts of things to the unit that will not help the problem (such as banging it against a table or thumping the screen). This, too, causes more problems.

So when a problem does occur with your BlackBerry, it is important that you follow my list of do's and do not's. First of all, the do not's:

- Do not randomly press keys or haphazardly try different possible solutions. You need to keep track of what you are doing if the unit is not working.

Should you end up on the phone with technical support, they will need to know what you have and haven't done.

■ Do not tap the BlackBerry against a desk, slap it, poke it, thump it, or stomp on it. This may make you feel better at the moment, but these actions will only damage your unit.

■ Do not call technical support first. Use this chapter instead to try and resolve the problem yourself. In the end, you will save time and learn a few things if you do.

And for the list of do's:

■ Do relax. The BlackBerry will not explode or disintegrate when something happens. Take your time and be calm.

■ Do note what you were doing when the problem occurred. When we experience problems, we often become so enamored with the problem itself that we forget about what might have caused the problem. For the BlackBerry, your clues to the solutions are often right under you nose because the activity you were performing may be the culprit. When a problem occurs, stop and think about what you were doing when the problem appeared. In fact, it doesn't hurt to write this information down because technical support will likely ask you this question.

■ Do identify the problem. Instead of randomly pressing keys or trying solutions, note what might be the problem. Next, use this chapter to explore possible solutions.

Your Technical Support Line

The BlackBerry is such a stable device that you will most likely never need technical support. That's great news because you can spend time using the BlackBerry instead of trying to solve problems. However, it is possible that you may experience a problem that you can't solve. In this case, you need to get some help, and here's what you should do:

■ Identify the problem you are having, and then consult this chapter. The odds are very good that this chapter will offer you a solution or least tell

16

you what the next step is in solving the problem. Your first line of defense against problems is this book!

■ If you are a corporate user, contact your local technical support. Administrators in your environment may be able to help you resolve the problem, depending on your environment's support structure.

■ If you are an Internet Edition user, contact your Internet service provider for the BlackBerry. They are responsible for helping you with all kinds of issues, and if they cannot resolve the problem, they will often act as a liaison with RIM technical support.

■ Your final, top of the ladder support option is RIM technical support, which you can access on the Internet (see Chapter 15).

Solving Problems

So, you have experienced some problem with the BlackBerry. Don't worry, the odds are very good that you can resolve the problem quickly yourself using this

Is It a Problem... or a Mistake?

Okay, no one wants to hear this, but here are the cold, hard facts: products, such as the BlackBerry and other electronic devices, experience problems because they are made by humans, who by nature make mistakes. That much is obvious, but one item users often overlook is the "mistake factor." When something on the BlackBerry does not seem to be working correctly, we often assume the BlackBerry is at fault and not us. In fact, "problems" with the BlackBerry often originate through user mistakes more than operating system glitches. These problems occur when a user believes the BlackBerry should work in a particular way, when in fact, it works in a different way. Regardless, when a problem occurs you should ask yourself, "Did I cause the problem, or do I just think there is a problem?" Next, use this book to review information on the BlackBerry that might help you resolve the issue yourself. I know, I know, one never wants to admit to mistakes, but solving your own "problems" can avoid a call to technical support.

chapter. To make the solution to your problem easier to find, I have divided the possible problems into several different categories. This way, you can first locate the category and then find the problem you are experiencing. I know that problems need to be solved quickly, so I provide you with a quick explanation of each problem and its solution. Where it is helpful, I have provided step-by-step explanations to make the solution easier.

Operating System Problems

Operating system problems are rare on the BlackBerry, unlike with the PC computer operating systems we are all familiar with. An operating system problem typically occurs when Dynamic Link Library (DLL) files within the system conflict with each other. Like I said, this is rare, but if it does happen, there are some easy fixes. Check out the following sections.

My BlackBerry Has Locked Up

If the BlackBerry locks up, a DLL conflict has likely occurred. This basically halts the system so you have little to no control. Your Home screen may be visible, but the trackwheel doesn't do anything.

First things first, don't worry. You won't lose any information on the unit. The only exception is if you are typing a message, a memo, a task, or whatever—the information will be lost. This is because the current information you are typing is stored in RAM, and in order to get control of your BlackBerry, you'll need to perform a reset, which is the equivalent of a reboot in PC terms. All information on the BlackBerry is saved on the disk, but current information you are creating lives in RAM and therefore will be lost.

To reset the BlackBerry, try pressing ALT-SHIFT-BACKSPACE. If this does not reset the unit, you can manually reset the unit by pressing the reset button on the back of the unit. You'll need to use a paper clip to press the button, which can be found in the tiny hole on the lower portion of the back of the unit. Simply insert a paperclip end into the hole and gently press the button. The BlackBerry will switch off and you will see the initializing message.

My BlackBerry Is Telling Me to Press R

If the BlackBerry detects a problem, a message may appear on the screen telling you to press R in order to perform a reset. In other words, the problem was caught by the system before a lockup occurred. Simply press the R key to reset the system. You will not lose any information on your BlackBerry except any unsaved information you were creating at the time (such as an e-mail message).

16

 *Sometimes, you can type **info** when you see this screen and the BlackBerry will give you information about what device is causing the problem. However, this may not work all of the time, but it is worth a try.*

Resetting My BlackBerry Doesn't Do Anything

If you have tried resetting your BlackBerry and nothing happens, there may be some internal problems with the unit. Now is the time to seek help from your network administrators or from your ISP. Consult your BlackBerry service agreement paperwork for the correct phone numbers.

My BlackBerry Locks Up All the Time

System lockups should be rare. If they are not, then there is some internal problem that is causing the lockup. You have three courses of action:

- Review applications. If you have installed several applications from the Internet, one of them may not be working correctly and is causing the system to lock up. Remove them one at a time and see if this corrects the problem.

- If the application issue doesn't solve the problem, it's time to get help from your network administrator or ISP support line. Consult your documentation for specific contact information.

- You can use the Desktop Manager to remove all of the BlackBerry's applications, and then reinstall them. This will destroy all of your data, however, so you'll need to perform a full backup first. This is sort of a last ditch effort, so I would try to get help from support personnel first.

An Application Keeps Crashing

If an application or game that you have installed keeps locking up, then you need to remove the application. There is some problem or some corrupt DLL causing the conflict. If you downloaded the application, you can redownload and reinstall it if you want to try using it again.

Connectivity Problems

The most common problems you are likely to have with the BlackBerry will be those that involve connectivity. After all, wireless communication is the whole purpose of the unit, and the wireless network is less than perfect. As a general rule, there are only a few solutions you can try before you'll need to get help if you are having a lot of connectivity problems, but this section can help you identify the current problem you are experiencing.

I Can't Connect

If you are simply having problems connecting to the wireless network, there are three simple items that you need to check. First, check your BlackBerry and make sure that the wireless radio modem is turned on. The wireless network indicator appears in the upper right-hand corner of the Home screen. This may seem ridiculously simple, but if you keep your modem on all of the time and it is inadvertently turned off, it may not occur to you to check the modem first. Begin with the simplest item, and make sure the wireless modem is turned on. The icon on your Home screen will appear as an airplane if the wireless modem is turned on.

Second, you may be out of the network area. If wireless connectivity seems to be going on and off and you are traveling, then you are probably just moving in and out of coverage. There's nothing to be done except to get back in the coverage area.

> TIP
>
> *Remember, you can always type e-mail when you are out of the network coverage area. When you are back in the network, your messages will be automatically sent.*

Finally, you should check the network settings on your BlackBerry just to make sure everything is correct. To learn how to do so, see "Check Network Settings."

My Network Status Is Listed as Inactive

Your BlackBerry must be activated with the network in order to be operational. You'll need to check your provider's instructions for specifics, but as a general rule, you need to access the Network Settings screen (seen in Figure 16-1), click the trackwheel, and then click Register Now on the menu that appears. If your unit registers with the wireless network, you will receive a confirmation e-mail message.

If you are an Internet Edition user, you may need to access an Internet page and choose an activation option in order to get your BlackBerry up and running. Check your provider's documentation for details.

Connectivity Is Intermittent

If you are in a coverage area and connectivity is intermittent, there may be some problems with the wireless network, or there could be problems with your unit's

16

 **Check Network Settings**

1. On the Home screen, click the Options icon.

2. In the Options screen, scroll to and click Network Settings.

3. In the Network Settings screen, shown in Figure 16-1, ensure that Roaming is set correctly to your country, that Radio is set to On, and that Status is set to Active.

wireless modem. When you can't get connected, stop and take note. Are you in a parking garage or some other structure that might prevent wireless communications? Do you lose connectivity in the same places? If so, there is no problem with your unit—you are simply in a blackout area. If connectivity seems sporadic at different locations with no apparent pattern, you need to contact your tech support so that someone can troubleshoot your unit—there may be a hardware problem that needs to be fixed.

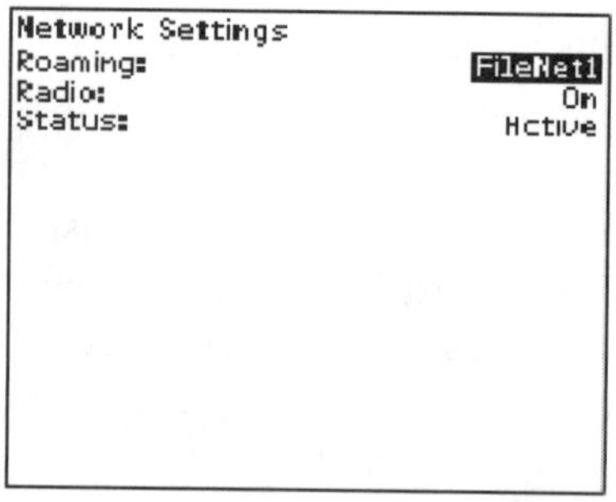

```
Network Settings
Roaming:                    FileNet1
Radio:                           On
Status:                      Active
```

FIGURE 16-1   Network Settings screen

Messaging Problems

The BlackBerry's messaging software is easy to use and works very well. If you have general usability questions, be sure to read Chapters 6 and 7, where you can learn how to use all of the BlackBerry's e-mail features.

Messages Are Not Sent

If your messages are not being sent, you are either not connected to the wireless network (the modem is not turned on), your network settings list you as inactive or pending, or you are out of the coverage area. Check these three items. If these settings are as they should be for allowing messages to be sent, try sending yourself a message and see if it comes back to you. Remember that a copy of sent messages is stored in your Messages folder. Messages that have been sent appear with a check mark beside them, and messages that you receive appear with a message icon beside them.

Message Delivery Has Failed

If the delivery of a message has failed, once again ensure that you are connected and active on the network. A returned message appears with an X beside it in the Messages folder. You can try resending the message once you are sure that your unit is in the network coverage area and active on the network.

I Have Accidentally Deleted a Message

Once a message is deleted from the BlackBerry, it cannot be recovered. The BlackBerry does not maintain a trash or deleted items folder like some desktop PIMs. Depending on your provider, there may be copies of messages stored on the server, so you'll need to check your provider's documentation. In Exchange and Lotus Domino environments, this may also be the case, so check your network documentation or ask your administrators.

In order to avoid this problem, you want to make sure that the delete confirmation option is enabled. This feature gives you a warning prompt before something is actually deleted. This feature is enabled by default, but if it has been inadvertently turned off, you can easily turn it back on. In the Messages folder, click the trackwheel to see the menu, and then click Options. In the Options screen, shown in Figure 16-2, make sure that Confirm Delete is set to Yes.

16

Confirm Delete settings

I Am Not Notified When New E-mail Arrives

The BlackBerry's "always on, always connected" state allows e-mail to arrive to you automatically—you don't ever have to check for e-mail, it just shows up on the BlackBerry. Because e-mail automatically arrives, you have some notification features to alert you when e-mail is received. If you are not being alerted when new e-mail arrives, then you need to check some settings to ensure that you are. To learn how to review and change these settings, see "Check Notification Configuration."

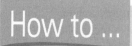 **Check Notification Configuration**

1. On the Home screen, click the Options icon.

2. In the Options screen, scroll to and click Notify.

3. Review the settings on this screen, as shown in Figure 16-3. Make sure that the Volume setting is not turned off and that the In Holster, Out of Holster, and Tune settings are not turned off unless you specifically do not want to use one of them. Also, make sure that the Level 1 Notify Only option is not turned on if you want to be notified of all messages that arrive.

```
Notify
In Holster:                Vibrate+Tone
Out of Holster:                    Tone
Tune:                                 1
Volume:                             Low
Number of Beeps:                      4
Repeat Notification:                Off
Level 1 Notify Only:                 No
Consider PIN Level 1:               Yes
```

FIGURE 16-3   Notify configuration

I'm Very Slow at Typing Messages

This isn't a problem, per se, but it is a sentiment expressed by new BlackBerry
users. The trick to typing on the BlackBerry is practice. The QWERTY keyboard
is designed for thumb typing, and that takes some getting used to. You can greatly
speed the rate at which you type by using AutoText, which can complete words
and phrases for you automatically. To learn more about AutoText, see Chapter 4,
which discusses using and configuring AutoText.

I Can't CC Several People at One Time

In a typical desktop PIM, you can enter several e-mail addresses using the CC line.
On the BlackBerry, you can only enter one e-mail address per CC field, but you
can add multiple CC fields so that everyone that you want to receive the message
is copied. When in the message window, simply click the trackwheel to see the
menu and click Add CC. Select the desired address book entry, and then repeat
this process to add other CC recipients. You can perform these same actions for
the To and BCC fields.

How Can I Send Attachments?

With wireless devices like the BlackBerry, you are pretty limited with attachment
sending. The BlackBerry allows you to attach an address book entry to an e-mail
address, but that is all you can natively do. Other third-party products provide
additional functionality, such as Attachmate, which enables you to attach calendar
entries, memos, and so on (see Chapter 14). There are also utilities available that
you can use to read attachments that are sent to you—see Chapter 14 for details.

16

My BlackBerry Will Only Let Me Use PINs Instead of E-mail Addresses

If your BlackBerry only allows the use of a PIN instead of an e-mail address, then the unit is not activated on the network. Open Network Settings from the Options screen and re-register the BlackBerry on the network. You may also need to visit a Web site and activate your unit if you are an Internet Edition customer.

Application Problems

The BlackBerry comes to you with a standard set of applications, such as an address book, MemoPad, and so on. This section explores the problems you are likely to have with these items. Note that you can install a number of additional applications developed by third parties, including Web browsers. Since these are developed by third parties, problems and solutions for each of them are not discussed here, but you may be able to access help for these items by visiting the vendor's Web site. For some third-party utilities and games developed by individuals, what you see is what you get, so if you are having problems with such an application, you may just have to live with the problem or try reinstalling it in order to correct the problem.

I Need to Change How My Address Book Lists Names

The address book enables you to organize entries by first name, last name, or company name in alphabetical order, depending on which option you choose. You can easily change the option by opening the address book and choosing Options from the menu. In the Address Book Options screen, change the Sort By field to the desired option, as shown in Figure 16-4.

My Address Book Doesn't Allow Duplicate Names

In case you need to use duplicate names, your BlackBerry address book can further sort your entries by e-mail address. To enable this option, simple open your address book, click the trackwheel to see the menu, and return to the Options screen. In the Address Book Options screen, change the Allow Duplicate Names field to Yes.

I Can't Edit an Address in My Address Book

The address book provides View and Edit options. Use the View option on the menu to view an address and prevent accidental changes to the address. If you need to

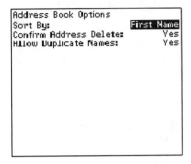

FIGURE 16-4   Address Book Options screen

change the address, select it in the address book, then click the trackwheel to see
the menu, and then click Edit Address.

Calendar Doesn't Display the Hours I Need

The default calendar view displays the hours of 9:00 A.M. to 5:00 P.M., which is
a typical workday. You can easily change this default setting so that the calendar
shows the hours that are required for you. Simply open the calendar from the home
screen, and then on the menu, click Options. This opens the Calendar Options screen,
shown in Figure 16-5. Edit the Start of day and End of day values as necessary,
and then save the changes.

FIGURE 16-5   Calendar Options screen

16

Calendar Doesn't Remind Me of Appointments When I Need It To

When you create an appointment, you must set the reminder for that appointment. The calendar does not have a global reminder setting—each appointment must be set individually. When you create a new appointment, as shown in Figure 16-6, simply set a value for the reminder and save the changes. By default, the value is 15 minutes for each appointment, but you can change the setting to whatever you want.

How Can I Easily Delete All Appointments for a Single Day?

When using the calendar, keep in mind that there is a month, week, day, and agenda view. When using the day, week, and agenda views, you can delete appointments individually. If you want to delete appointments for an entire day, switch month view. Select the desired date and choose Delete Appointments from the menu, as shown in Figure 16-7.

My Alarm Doesn't Work

If you have configured the alarm to sound at a certain time and it does not, one of two problems might be possible. First, you may have simply configured the alarm to sound at the wrong time. Open the alarm from the Home screen and check your settings (check the AM/PM setting). The second possibility is the volume is set too low. If you are not hearing the alarm, try a higher volume setting.

FIGURE 16-6   New appointment reminder

| FIGURE 16-7 | Delete appointments |

BlackBerry Unit Problems

The BlackBerry unit itself is well designed and unlikely to give you any problems. Problems that you might experience, however, are most often generated through various configurations on the BlackBerry Options screen. I've pointed out the ones in the following sections that you might have troubles with.

My BlackBerry Turns Itself Off During the Day

The BlackBerry has an Auto On/Off feature that enables you to tell the BlackBerry when to turn itself on and off each day of the week and on weekends. If your BlackBerry is taking naps when you don't want it to, incorrect settings are the likely culprit. To change the setting, open Options from the Home screen, and then click Auto On/Off. On the configuration screen, shown in Figure 16-8, adjust the settings as desired, or disable them altogether.

The Date and Time Keep Changing on My BlackBerry

You can set the date and time for the BlackBerry by choosing the Date/Time option on the Options screen and making changes. However, if you synchronize your BlackBerry with a desktop PIM, the date and time will be synchronized as well. So if the date and time are wrong on the PC, they will be wrong on the BlackBerry as well.

My Screen Is Hard to See

You can easily change the resolution settings of your BlackBerry LCD screen by opening Screen/Keyboard on the Options screen. Change the font and screen

16

FIGURE 16-8   Auto On/Off

contrast settings as desired, as shown in Figure 16-9. You may need to play around with these settings a bit to find the ones that are right for you.

My Keypad Beeps, and It's Driving Me Crazy!

If your keypad beeps every time you press a key, then the Key Tone feature is turned on. This setting is found on the Screen/Keyboard screen, accessible through the Options screen (shown in Figure 16-9). Access this setting and turn it off.

What Is the Best Way to Store My BlackBerry?

If you are not going to be using your BlackBerry for an extended period of time, you should remove the AA cell from the 950 model and simply store it. For the

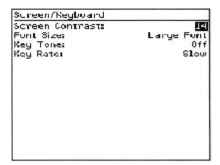

FIGURE 16-9   Screen/Keyboard settings

957 model, you need to put the unit into storage mode. See Chapter 4 to learn how to use storage mode.

Desktop Software Problems

The Desktop Manager provided with your BlackBerry is easy-to-use software that runs on any modern version of Windows (95 and later). Software for the Macintosh is also available. Typically, the Desktop Manager is easy to use, and you are unlikely to have any problems. If you do, check out the following sections, which review the problems typically experienced with the desktop software.

When I Put My BlackBerry in the Cradle, I Am Prompted for a Password on My Computer

This option occurs if your BlackBerry is password protected. Simply enter your password and continue. If you do not want to continue using password protection, you can change the setting using the Security screen, accessible through the Options screen. If you do not have password protection and you still have the problem, remove the handheld from the cradle and press ALT-SHIFT-BACKSPACE to reset the unit.

Desktop Manager Doesn't Detect My BlackBerry

If the Desktop Manager does not detect the BlackBerry once you insert the BlackBerry into the cradle, then there are a couple of things you need to try:

1. First, ensure that the cradle is properly connected to your computer.

2. Remove any other device that is currently connected to the serial port.

3. Use the Serial Settings dialog box (choose Options | Serial Settings) to manually select the COM port, as shown in Figure 16-10. Use the Detect button and try different ports if you are still having problems.

I Want the Desktop Manager to Automatically Back Up My Handheld

You can easily configure Desktop Manager to automatically back up your handheld. Simply open the Backup/Restore icon, and then click the Options button. You see an Automatic Backup option with a number of features that you can configure, as seen in Figure 16-11.

16

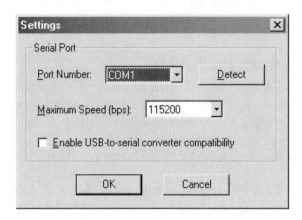

FIGURE 16-10   Serial Settings dialog box

TIP   *You can learn all about the Desktop Manager's features in Chapter 5.*

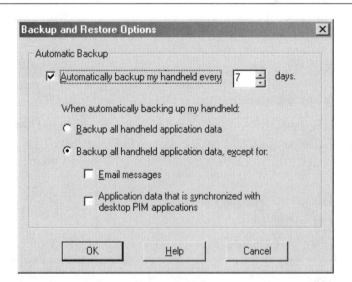

FIGURE 16-11   Automatic Backup options

Did you know?

Getting Help at RIM Road

One additional place you might be able to find some help is on the Internet, particularly at RIM Road (http://www.rimroad.com), which hosts a RIM discussion board. You'll find a lot of posts there and a number of discussions about specific products, such as the AOL- and Yahoo-branded BlackBerry products. You'll also find more information about Go America there as well. You can post a question, and the odds are quite good that someone will get in touch with you and try to help you solve the problem. So, aside from this book and technical support, you might find the discussion board a great place to hang out, learn more, and solve problems!

16

Part 5 Appendixes

Appendix A

Keyboard Shortcut Quick Reference

How to...

■ Use keyboard shortcuts

Throughout the book, I have pointed out the relevant keyboard shortcuts that are available for each BlackBerry application. These shortcuts save you time by reducing the number of trackwheel scrolls and clicks you must perform. Keyboard shortcuts are not always easy to remember, however, so I have compiled them in this quick reference you can use time and time again.

Basic Commands

Check out the basic BlackBerry commands in Table A-1, which can be used in any menu or pop-up dialog box. Also, be sure to check out the inside back cover for a table of Home screen icon keyboard shortcuts.

Sending and Composing Mail Messages

The keyboard shortcuts in Table A-2 save you time and energy when you are sending and composing new mail messages.

 Any autotext entries that you have created also apply here.

Reading Messages

The keyboard shortcuts in Table A-3 are helpful when receiving or reading messages.

Action	Keyboard Shortcut
Jump directly to any item in a menu or list of choices	Press the first letter of the item you want
Select Yes in a pop-up dialog box	Y
Select No in a pop-up dialog box	N
Cancel a dialog box	ESC or C

TABLE A-1   Basic Command Shortcuts

Action	Keyboard Shortcut
Create a new message (must be in the Messages screen)	C
Insert the @ (at sign) and . (period) characters in an e-mail message	SPACE key (957 model) or SYMBOL key (950 model)
Automatically insert a period when typing an e-mail	SPACE key (957 model) or SYMBOL (950 model) key twice
Find a specific contact	Press the first letter or two of the name
Turn on CAP LOCK	ALT-CAP
Turn on NUM LOCK	ALT-NUM
Capitalize a letter	Press and hold down the letter key if Key Rate is turned on (you need to be in the Messages or Home screen for this to work)

TABLE A-2   Shortcuts for Sending and Composing Messages

Message Inbox and Outbox Shortcuts

The shortcuts in Table A-4 can help you manage your inbox.

Action	Keyboard Shortcut
Go to the Messages screen	M
Go to the Saved Messages screen	V
Go to the top of a message	T
Go to the bottom of a message	B
Page up in an open message	ALT-ENTER
Return the cursor to the last position in a message	G
Go to the next message	N
Go to the previous message	P
Go to the next unread message	U
Reply without text (replies to the sender only)	R
Forward a message	F

TABLE A-3   Shortcuts for Reading Messages

A

Action	Keyboard Shortcut
View all inbox messages	ALT-I
View all outbox messages	ALT-O
Search for messages in both the Messages or Saved Messages screens	ALT-hotkey
Go to the Saved Messages screen	V
Toggle between marking a message as read or unread	ALT-U
Delete all messages prior to a certain date	Highlight the date filed and press DEL

TABLE A-4   Shortcuts for Managing the Inbox

Address Book

Use the keyboard shortcuts in Table A-5 to manage your address book.

Tasks

Use the keyboard shortcuts in Table A-6 to manage tasks.

Calendar

The calendar keyboard shortcuts in Table A-7 may be helpful to you.

Action	Keyboard Shortcut
Insert @ (at sign) and . (period) in an e-mail address	SPACE key (957 model) or SYMBOL key (950 model)
Find an address book entry	Press the first letter or two of the name
Capitalize a letter	Press and hold down the letter key (if Key Rate is turned on)

TABLE A-5   Shortcuts for Managing the Address Book

Action	Keyboard Shortcut
Delete a task	DEL
Go to the top of a task	T
Go to the bottom of a task	B
Create a new task	C
Mark a task as In Progress or Completed	M

TABLE A-6 Shortcuts for Managing the Address Book

MemoPad

Check out the MemoPad keyboard shortcuts in Table A-8.

Action	Keyboard Shortcut
Delete an appointment	DEL
Go to the top of an appointment	T
Go to the bottom of an appointment	B
Create a new appointment	C
Switch to Day view	D
Switch to Week view	W
Switch to Month view	M
Switch to Agenda view	A
Scroll through calendar views	S
Go to Today in the calendar screen	T
Go to the previous day, week, or month	P
Go to the next day, week, or month	N
Go to a specific date	G

TABLE A-7 Calendar Shortcuts

A

Action	Keyboard Shortcut
Go to the top of the menu list	T
Go to the bottom of the menu list	B
Delete a memo	DEL
View a memo	ENTER
Exit MemoPad	ESC

TABLE A-8   MemoPad Shortcuts

Calculator

Try the keyboard shortcuts in Table A-9 when using the BlackBerry calculator.

Action	Keyboard Shortcut
Add	D
Subtract	F
Multiply	X or A
Divide	S
Change the sign	Z or SPACE key (957 model) or SYMBOL key (950 model)
Find the square root	V
Recall memory	J
Clear memory	K
Add the number into memory	L
Result of a calculation	G
Clear the calculator screen	C

TABLE A-9   Calculator Shortcuts

Appendix B

Curt's Top Ten Application Picks

How to...

■ Select Applications

In Chapter 14, you learned all about BlackBerry applications that are available for download. These applications, developed by third parties, are either free or inexpensive. There are quite a few of these applications, and new applications are being developed all of the time, so be sure to search the Internet or RIM Road (http://www.rimroad.com) or Tucows (http://www.tucows.com) for new applications as they become available.

So, to help you out as you get started with applications, I've listed my ten favorites here. This is not to say that the other applications are not good—I just happen to find the following the most useful or the most fun. I've included a mix of applications and games here, so as you start downloading and using BlackBerry programs, be sure to check these out! I've ranked my favorites from 1 to 10, with 1 being the best! Most of the applications listed here are available at either the RIM Road or Tucows sites, and if not, I tell you where to go to find the application.

10. RIM Reader

This one may not seem all that exciting, but it is a great way to take information with you. In fact, the RIM Reader can hold the entire text of most electronic books. Just paste the text into the RIM Reader PC application, as shown in Figure B-1, and then transfer it to your BlackBerry. No matter where you go, the information can travel with you. This one is a real snap, and I use it all of the time.

9. Mobile TimeBilling

If you are someone who needs to keep track of time and expenses, then this application is for you. This full-featured application enables you to track time and related hourly issues and even e-mail that information to the necessary individuals. Check it out at the Wireless Verticals site (http://www.wirelessverticals.com).

8. Sparrow Mail

Sparrow mail, shown in Figure B-2, gives you an e-mail application with an easier-to-use folder view. This is a full-featured e-mail program that you can use in lieu of the BlackBerry's e-mail tools. Overall, there are not a lot of differences between the two applications, but you may find this one slightly more intuitive.

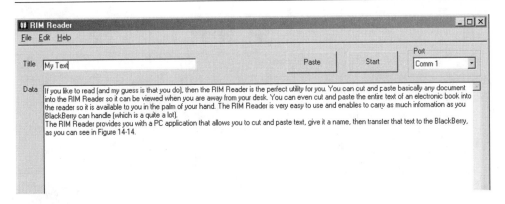

FIGURE B-2   RIM Reader

7. Handango Safe

If you need to encrypt information on your BlackBerry so that it is not readable by someone else even if your BlackBerry is stolen, then you should definitely check out the Handango Safe. You can store all kinds of information in the safe, such as e-mail addresses, passwords, URLS, and even text. Overall, it is easy to use and is a great way to protect sensitive data.

6. Solitaire

If you need a good pastime, then a simple game of solitaire might do it for you. As you can see in Figure B-3, this electronic version for the BlackBerry is fun, easy, and

B

FIGURE B-1   Sparrow mail

FIGURE B-3   Solitaire

works just like the desktop game. If you like to play Solitaire, you should definitely keep this on your BlackBerry.

5. StockBoss

If you are into the stock market, then this tool is one you are sure to want. StockBoss, shown in Figure B-4, enables you to mind your portfolio, get stock news, view charts, set alerts, and perform a number of other useful tasks. It's your full-featured mobile connection to the stock market.

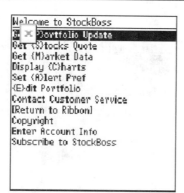

FIGURE B-4   StockBoss

4. RIM Chicken

I know, I know, RIM Chicken seems like a poor choice for a Top Ten list, but I'm telling you this game is great fun and a great way to pass the time (see Figure B-5). When I first showed the game to my wife, she said, "That seems kinda silly." Now, she is a Chicken fanatic and plays it all the time. Enough said!

3. WordWave Desktop

This application enables you to use your BlackBerry to manage your desktop-based e-mail. You can issue commands using your BlackBerry and manage e-mail attachments. You can even directly convert e-mail attachments so that they are readable. This application takes some getting used to, but it provides a lot of great e-mail management features.

2. Task Switcher

Task Switcher is a simple, free utility that makes moving around the BlackBerry easier. From any location, you can access Task Switcher and move to a different BlackBerry application—no fumbling around to get back to the Home screen. You should definitely download and use this one—it will save you time.

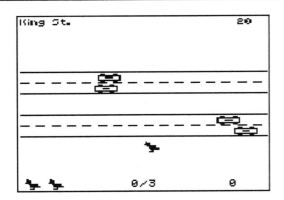

FIGURE B-5   RIM Chicken

B

1. Attachmate

And in the Number One spot, in my humble opinion, is a little utility called Attachmate. The problem with wireless e-mail tends to be attachments, and this utility brings you one step closer to attachment freedom by enabling you to include a number of BlackBerry application pages as text attachments to your e-mail. You can include attachments from memos, task lists, and calendar entries instead of just address book entries provided by the BlackBerry. As you can imagine, this gives you a number of new attachment options, and it can help save you a lot of time and headaches. Try it!

Appendix C Helpful Web Sites

How to...

 Locate helpful Web sites

The Internet is a great place to keep up with the latest developments in technology, and BlackBerry and related PDA information is certainly no exception. You can find a wealth of information on the Internet about the BlackBerry as well as the latest on handhelds and PDAs. In this appendix, I've listed some of the most helpful Web sites that you should check out often.

> **TIP** *Of course, you should keep a watch at www.blackberry.net and www.rim.net for new BlackBerry information. I haven't mentioned them here because Chapter 15 is devoted to these sites.*

PDAStreet.com

PDAStreet.com is a full-featured Web site strictly devoted to all kinds of PDAs. On the home page, shown in Figure C-1, you can access a BlackBerry subsection

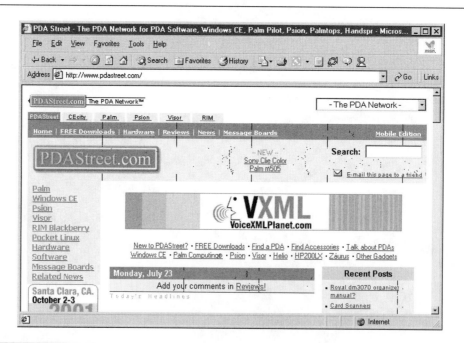

FIGURE C-1   PDAStreet.com

of the site. From this location, you can download all kinds of applications (see Chapter 14) and you can even check out discussion boards and other news. This is a great site for BlackBerry enthusiasts, and you should keep a watch here for up-to-the-minute news and information.

Tucows

Tucows is primarily a download site where you can get all kinds of applications for a number of different products, including the BlackBerry, as shown in Figure C-2. (See Chapter 14 to learn more about downloading applications from Tucows.) Note that you can subscribe to the Tucows newsletter through the home page, which will keep you abreast of all kinds of new applications and developments. You should consider subscribing to the free newsletter for PDA information as well as several others that are available.

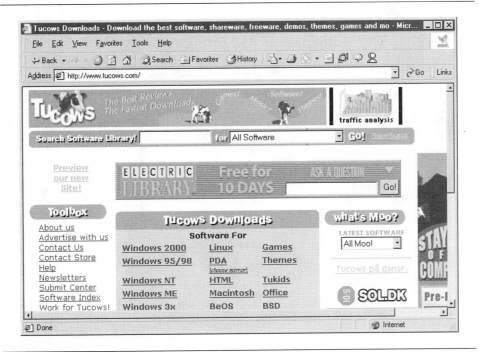

FIGURE C-2   Tucows

C

Thinkmobile.com

Thinkmobile.com is a diverse Web site that brings you all kinds of news and information about the mobile market, as shown in Figure C-3. You can find current information about various PDA devices, cellular phones, laptops, and essentially anything else that comes along. This is a general usage site, but it is a good one to visit for the latest news and information.

ZDNet

ZDNet is an extensive news site that can provide you with late-breaking news about the BlackBerry, and essentially anything else in the handheld/computing world as well. From the home page, shown in Figure C-4, you can search for any topic of interest. If you search for the BlackBerry here, you will find news and related site links. This is a great site to watch for the latest developments in the handheld world, and in computing in general.

FIGURE C-3   Thinkmobile.com

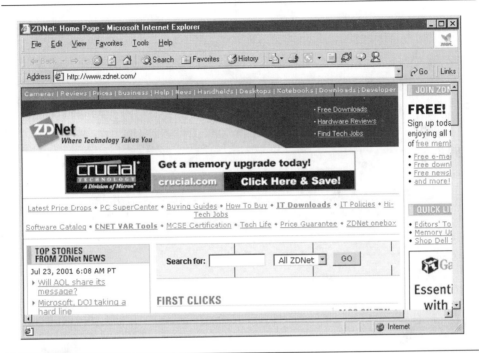

FIGURE C-4   ZDNet

PDABuzz

PDABuzz, shown in Figure C-5, is a well-rounded PDA site that covers all kinds of news and information, and even includes discussion boards on PDAs. There is a specific RIM discussion board that you should check out. Also, this is a great site to review from time to time since it is specific to the PDA market.

The Gadgeteer

The Gadgeteer is just what the name suggests—an all-around site that explores and reviews gadgets of all kinds, including PDAs and related mobile communication devices. You can find a lot of quick and helpful information at this site (shown in Figure C-6), and this is a particularly good place to visit if you want to see what is new and upcoming in the PDA world.

C

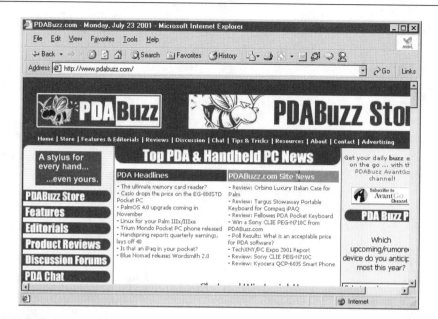

FIGURE C-5   PDABuzz

FIGURE C-6   The Gadgeteer

Geek.com

Geek.com, shown in Figure C-7, is a Web site devoted to techno-gadgets and computers. You'll find a general wireless section here as well as a PDA section. Some information may be specific to the BlackBerry, but most is more generalized. The site does have some interesting stuff—be sure to check out the PDA tips and tricks as well as the horror stories.

PCWorld.com

PCWorld.com, which is a division of *PC World* magazine, is an all-around site covering a variety of news, developments, and technology reviews of basically all electronic devices—from computers to handhelds. This site, shown in Figure C-8, is an excellent one to watch for general information about the computing industry, both in terms of news and developments. You can find information about the BlackBerry here, and basically any other topic you are interested in as well.

FIGURE C-7   Geek.com

C

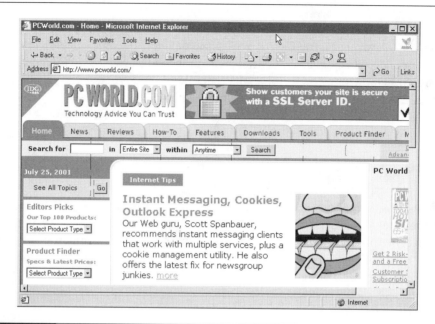

FIGURE C-8 PCWorld.com

Wireless.com

Of course, the BlackBerry's success comes from wireless technology and your ability to stay connected, no matter where you are. If you want to keep track of the wireless industry, Wireless.com, shown in Figure C-9, is a great site to check out. Some of it is a little heady, but if you really want to learn more about wireless connectivity, this is a great one to surf.

Mazumi Wireless

This infozine, shown in Figure C-10, is a great site to visit for all kinds of wireless information, reviews, and info on gadgetry. You'll find this site full of practical information, up-to-date news about mobility and mobile devices, and articles about connectivity and services.

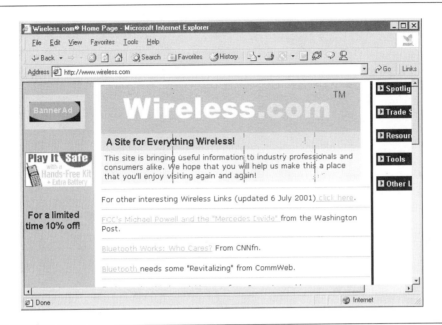

FIGURE C-9   Wireless.com

FIGURE C-10   Mazumi Wireless

C

Index

References to figures and illustrations are in italics.

10Best.com, 185, *186*

A

ABCNEWS.com, 180
About option, 54
address book, 25, 150–153
    composing messages, 160
    creating a new filter, 162–164
    creating entries, 154–156
    deleting addresses, 159
    editing addresses, 158–159
    editing options, 154
    filtering during synchronization with PIM applications, 160–164
    keyboard shortcuts, 362
    Notes field, 158
    options, 152–154
    searching, 159
    viewing addresses, 156–157
Afaria, 282
alarms, 26–27
    configuring, 218–221
    stopping, 220
alerts, in PocketGenie, 269, 275–278
ALT key, 37, 38
    changing clock settings, 221
ALT-SHIFT, 39

Application Loader, 21, 96–98
    running, 99, *100*
applications, 29–30
    Application Loader, 96–98, 99, *100*
    compressed, 285
    configuring PIM applications for Intellisync, 98–104
    crashing, 342
    Curt's top ten picks, 365–370
    downloading, 286–288
    installer, 291, *292*
    installing, 293, *294*
    troubleshooting problems, 348–351
    unzipping, 288–290
    zipped, 285
Ask@OracleMobile, 253–260
    customizing, 258, *259*
    dictionary, 256
    dining reservations, 256
    driving directions, 255
    flight information, 255
    horoscopes, 256
    lottery information, 256
    movie information, 256
    registering with, 257
    stock quotes, 255
    traffic information, 256
    translations, 256
    using, 257–260
    weather information, 256
AstrologyIS.com, 187
Attachmate, 306–307, 370

381

INTERNATIONAL CONTACT INFORMATION

AUSTRALIA
McGraw-Hill Book Company Australia Pty. Ltd.
TEL +61-2-9417-9899
FAX +61-2-9417-5687
http://www.mcgraw-hill.com.au
books-it_sydney@mcgraw-hill.com

CANADA
McGraw-Hill Ryerson Ltd.
TEL +905-430-5000
FAX +905-430-5020
http://www.mcgrawhill.ca

**GREECE, MIDDLE EAST,
NORTHERN AFRICA**
McGraw-Hill Hellas
TEL +30-1-656-0990-3-4
FAX +30-1-654-5525

MEXICO (Also serving Latin America)
McGraw-Hill Interamericana Editores S.A. de C.V.
TEL +525-117-1583
FAX +525-117-1589
http://www.mcgraw-hill.com.mx
fernando_castellanos@mcgraw-hill.com

SINGAPORE (Serving Asia)
McGraw-Hill Book Company
TEL +65-863-1580
FAX +65-862-3354
http://www.mcgraw-hill.com.sg
mghasia@mcgraw-hill.com

SOUTH AFRICA
McGraw-Hill South Africa
TEL +27-11-622-7512
FAX +27-11-622-9045
robyn_swanepoel@mcgraw-hill.com

**UNITED KINGDOM & EUROPE
(Excluding Southern Europe)**
McGraw-Hill Education Europe
TEL +44-1-628-502500
FAX +44-1-628-770224
http://www.mcgraw-hill.co.uk
computing_neurope@mcgraw-hill.com

ALL OTHER INQUIRIES Contact:
Osborne/McGraw-Hill
TEL +1-510-549-6600
FAX +1-510-883-7600
http://www.osborne.com
omg_international@mcgraw-hill.com